Woodworking

FOR

DUMMIES®

P9-AQV-381

Woodworking FOR DUMMIES®

by Jeff Strong

WILEY

Wiley Publishing, Inc.

Woodworking For Dummies®

Published by
Wiley Publishing, Inc.
111 River St.
Hoboken, NJ 07030
www.wiley.com

Copyright © 2004 by Wiley Publishing, Inc., Indianapolis, Indiana

Published simultaneously in Canada

No part of this publication may be reproduced, stored in a retrieval system, or transmitted in any form or by any means, electronic, mechanical, photocopying, recording, scanning, or otherwise, except as permitted under Sections 107 or 108 of the 1976 United States Copyright Act, without either the prior written permission of the Publisher, or authorization through payment of the appropriate per-copy fee to the Copyright Clearance Center, 222 Rosewood Drive, Danvers, MA 01923, 978-750-8400, fax 978-646-8600. Requests to the Publisher for permission should be addressed to the Legal Department, Wiley Publishing, Inc., 10475 Crosspoint Blvd., Indianapolis, IN 46256, 317-572-3447, fax 317-572-4447.

Trademarks: Wiley, the Wiley Publishing logo, For Dummies, the Dummies Man logo, A Reference for the Rest of Us!, The Dummies Way, Dummies Daily, The Fun and Easy Way, Dummies.com, and related trade dress are trademarks or registered trademarks of John Wiley & Sons, Inc. and/or its affiliates in the United States and other countries and may not be used without written permission. All other trademarks are the property of their respective owners. Wiley Publishing, Inc., is not associated with any product or vendor mentioned in this book.

LIMIT OF LIABILITY/DISCLAIMER OF WARRANTY: WHILE THE PUBLISHER AND AUTHOR HAVE USED THEIR BEST EFFORTS IN PREPARING THIS BOOK, THEY MAKE NO REPRESENTATIONS OR WARRANTIES WITH RESPECT TO THE ACCURACY OR COMPLETENESS OF THE CONTENTS OF THIS BOOK AND SPECIFICALLY DISCLAIM ANY IMPLIED WARRANTIES OF MERCHANTABILITY OR FITNESS FOR A PARTICULAR PURPOSE. NO WARRANTY MAY BE CREATED OR EXTENDED BY SALES REPRESENTATIVES OR WRITTEN SALES MATERIALS. THE ADVICE AND STRATEGIES CONTAINED HEREIN MAY NOT BE SUITABLE FOR YOUR SITUATION. YOU SHOULD CONSULT WITH A PROFESSIONAL WHERE APPROPRIATE. NEITHER THE PUBLISHER NOR AUTHOR SHALL BE LIABLE FOR ANY LOSS OF PROFIT OR ANY OTHER COMMERCIAL DAMAGES, INCLUDING BUT NOT LIMITED TO SPECIAL, INCIDENTAL, CONSEQUENTIAL, OR OTHER DAMAGES.

For general information on our other products and services or to obtain technical support, please contact our Customer Care Department within the U.S. at 800-762-2974, outside the U.S. at 317-572-3993, or fax 317-572-4002.

Wiley also publishes its books in a variety of electronic formats. Some content that appears in print may not be available in electronic books.

Library of Congress Control Number: 2003112654

ISBN: 0-7645-3977-9

Manufactured in the United States of America

10 9 8 7 6 5 4 3 2

1B/SV/QS/QU/IN

 is a trademark of Wiley Publishing, Inc.

About the Author

Jeff Strong began creating sawdust at a very young age while helping his father, a master craftsman, build fine furniture. An accomplished woodworker, Jeff has designed and built countless pieces of furniture and currently accepts commissions to build his creations. His woodworking style marries Arts and Crafts, Southwestern, and Asian influences. This is his third book.

Dedication

This book is dedicated to my dad who shared with me both the skills and love of woodworking.

Author's Acknowledgments

First, I want to thank my wife, Beth, for encouraging my woodworking despite seeing less and less of me, and my daughter Tovah for inspiring me to create unusual designs.

I'm also grateful for the persistence of my agent, Carol Susan Roth, and the vision of my acquisitions editor, Tracy Boggier, both of whom were essential in getting this book off the ground. Thanks also go to my project editor, Allyson Grove, whose skill and easy-going nature made this project all the more enjoyable.

I'd like to acknowledge the skills and expertise of the technical editor, Robert Lasso and copy editor, Jennifer Bingham: You both made me look like I know what I'm doing.

Publisher's Acknowledgments

We're proud of this book; please send us your comments through our Dummies online registration form located at www.dummies.com/register/.

Some of the people who helped bring this book to market include the following:

Acquisitions, Editorial, and Media Development

Project Editor: Allyson Grove

Acquisitions Editor: Tracy Boggier

Copy Editor: Jennifer Bingham

Editorial Program Assistant: Holly Gastineau-Grimes

Technical Editor: Robert Lasso

Editorial Manager: Michelle Hacker

Editorial Assistant: Elizabeth Rea

Cover Photos: ©Jim Craigmyle/CORBIS

Cartoons: Rich Tennant, www.the5thwave.com

Production

Project Coordinator: Maridee Ennis

Layout and Graphics: Seth Conley, Heather Ryan, Jacque Schneider

Special Art: Precision Graphics

Proofreaders: TECHBOOKS Production Services, Susan Moritz, Carl William Pierce, Brian H. Walls

Indexer: TECHBOOKS Production Services,

Special Help
Kristin DeMint

Publishing and Editorial for Consumer Dummies

Diane Graves Steele, Vice President and Publisher, Consumer Dummies

Joyce Pepple, Acquisitions Director, Consumer Dummies

Kristin A. Cocks, Product Development Director, Consumer Dummies

Michael Spring, Vice President and Publisher, Travel

Brice Gosnell, Associate Publisher, Travel

Suzanne Jannetta, Editorial Director, Travel

Publishing for Technology Dummies

Andy Cummings, Vice President and Publisher, Dummies Technology/General User

Composition Services

Gerry Fahey, Vice President of Production Services

Debbie Stailey, Director of Composition Services

Contents at a Glance

Table of Contents

Introduction

So, you want to work with wood? Well, I can't think of a better way to spend your free time than building a tangible project that will last for a lifetime or longer.

Woodworking For Dummies is a great place for you to start developing the skills of a craftsperson and gaining the satisfaction of creating a work of art (or at least a decent table or bookcase). This book gives you the essential information to help you do just that.

About This Book

Woodworking For Dummies introduces you to the wonderful world of woodworking (how's that for alliteration?). Whether you have very little knowledge of the hobby or some experience but with a few gaps in your knowledge base, this book is for you.

I tried to write a book that contains all the essential information for the novice woodworker as well as some more advanced tips and tricks to jumpstart your existing woodworking skills. You won't find any useless theories or unnecessary technical jargon to bog you down. What you will find is practical, hands-on information and advice that will save you hours of frustration (pretty good deal, huh?).

Here's some of what I cover in this book:

- ✔ Choosing the right wood for your projects
- ✔ Getting the best tools for you and your goals
- ✔ Setting up your workshop
- ✔ Making wood joints and knowing the best joint for the job
- ✔ Building projects that you'll be proud of
- ✔ Sanding and finishing

If that's not enough, I also try to make this book as fun as possible to read. After all, there's no sense in suffering through a book, is there?

How to Use This Book

This book is organized modularly, which means that you can read it from cover to cover and progressively build your woodworking knowledge. Or you can skip around and choose a subject that interests you from the table of contents or index, and start reading it immediately without feeling lost. Throughout the book I also include cross-references to where you can find more information about a subject.

Conventions Used in This Book

Woodworking is a fairly technical subject with its own rules and language. Because of this, I include a lot of terms you may not be familiar with. Rather than include a glossary of terms, I've chosen to provide definitions or cross-references for terms that are part of the woodworking vocabulary. These terms are in italics to help you identify them.

Not So Foolish Assumptions

When I wrote this book, I made some assumptions about you, the reader.

First, I assumed that you want to build furniture projects and not a house or some other large-scale construction project. For that, you're probably better off with a book on carpentry, because if you apply all the little details that go into a good piece of furniture to framing a house, for example, it'll take you too long to get the job done. (Of course, it will look awesome and be a work of art when you're through.)

Second, I assumed that you want to do things the fast and easy way and not necessarily the old-fashioned way. As you'll likely find out by talking to other woodworkers, you can find almost as many ways to perform a task as you can find woodworkers. Everyone has his own unique way to do things and mine involves taking advantage of modern tools and shortcuts, rather than using old-fashioned, time-consuming, and often frustrating approaches that can be done better with modern tools and approaches (do you sense a little bias here?). For example, if you want to find out how to craft dovetails by hand with a chisel and backsaw, buy another book. But if you want to make joints that are just as strong and beautiful in a fraction of the time with a router and a jig, then this book is for you. (Don't worry, in this book, you will still get to see many of the traditional ways things are done, if for no other reason than to help you decide for yourself how you want to approach a task.)

Aside from these two things, I don't assume that you want to make a certain type of furniture or whether your goals include wanting to make a few things for your house or getting really serious and entering your work in juried shows.

How This Book Is Organized

Woodworking For Dummies is organized into six parts so that you can find the information you're looking for quickly and easily. What follows is a closer look at each part and what it covers.

Part I: What's All the Buzz about Woodworking?

Part I is your introduction to woodworking, wood, and woodworking shops. Chapter 1 gives you an overview of the woodworking process and gets absolute beginners up to speed on this fascinating hobby. Chapter 2 helps you to understand the unique qualities of wood. You discover the various types of wood used in furniture and how to find and buy the right boards for your projects. Because woodworking is an inherently dangerous activity, Chapter 3 shows you how to create a safe working environment and gives you some guidelines for working as safely as possible.

Part II: Tool Time: Selecting and Setting Up Your Equipment

Part II is the section for anyone who loves tools. Chapter 4 helps you determine the best tools for your goals. It opens your eyes to the type of woodworking you intend to do and what tools will help you accomplish your goals. Chapter 5 introduces you to the tried-and-true hand tools and provides tips on how to choose and use them. Chapter 6 explores portable power tools. It gets you up to speed on what to use for what purpose. Chapter 7 is all about the big machines. This chapter gives you the lowdown on the machines that most woodworkers drool over (and that make woodworking easier, faster, and more fun). Chapter 8 helps you set up your tools and lets you get started using them by providing some projects to make some tool helpers called *jigs*.

Part III: Together Forever: Basic Wood Joinery

Part III gets into the nuts and bolts of joining wood together (you don't use actual nuts and bolts, though). Chapter 9 is all about adhesives (glues). This chapter demystifies all the different glue choices you have to contend with. After reading this chapter, you'll be able to walk into a woodworking store and get the right glue for you. Chapter 10 shows you how to make all the wood joints you'll encounter in this book. Wood joints are the basis for almost all woodworking, and making them well is the difference between a project that lasts for a few years (at most) and one than is still solid after generations. Chapter 11 offers your wood joints some assistance with mechanical fasteners such as screws and nails. This chapter shows you when adding a nail or screw to your project can help and when it's a waste of effort.

Part IV: Getting Your Hands (And Shop) Dirty: Turning Raw Wood into Furniture

Part IV is filled with really cool projects. The purpose of this section is to give you some woodworking experience and to progressively build your skills. Chapter 12 leads you through the process of making a project so that you know what you're getting into before you begin cutting wood. Chapter 13 gets you started woodworking with the easiest project to build — a bookcase. Not just one bookcase, but several, so you're sure to find one that fits your design ideals. Chapter 14 builds on the skills you developed in Chapter 13 by helping you build tables. Like Chapter 13, you have several table designs to choose from (heck, build 'em all; you can never have too many tables!). Chapter 15 ups the ante by providing projects for making cabinets with either drawers or doors. Again, you get to choose among several really good designs (if I do say so myself).

Part V: The Grand Finale: Sanding and Finishing Your Masterpiece

A woodworking project wouldn't be complete without the finish. Part V helps you make this often hated (trust me, I'm being nice here) process of sanding and finishing into a chore that you'll love (okay, maybe just *tolerate*). Chapter 16 explores the often short-shrifted process of filling and sanding the wood smooth. Chapter 17 shows you how to add color to the wood. Chapter 18 demystifies the topcoat process. In this chapter, you discover the best type of finish for your project and go through the steps of applying it for best results.

Part VI: The Part of Tens

A staple of every _For Dummies_ book, Part IV presents the Part of Tens. Chapter 19 includes ten good habits to get into to make your woodworking experience safer. Chapter 20 offers ten woodworking pitfalls that almost everyone encounters at one time or another. (Oh, and ways to avoid or fix them, too.) Chapter 21 gives you some woodworking resources so that you can keep expanding your woodworking knowledge.

Icons Used in This Book

As in all _For Dummies_ books, I include a few icons to help you along your way. They include:

Certain techniques and information bear repeating. This icon gives you those gentle nudges to keep you on track.

This icon highlights expert advice and ideas that can help you to make better projects.

Woodworking is an inherently dangerous hobby. This icon alerts you to those times when you need to take extra care so as not to injure yourself or damage your workpiece or tools.

This icon contains some background information about the material you're working with to help you better understand the reason for doing a task a certain way.

Sometimes I know of tools that I find really make a difference in performing a task. This icon lets you know when I think a tool is, well, terrific.

Throughout the book, I provide some less inspiring technical background on a subject. This icon shows up in those instances so that you can brace yourself for some more dense information.

Where to Go from Here

If you're an absolute beginner I recommend that you start with Chapter 1 to get an overview of the woodworking process. If you've had a chance to watch someone woodwork or have done some basic building yourself and you're ready to set up a workshop of your own, check out Part II.

If you have a shop and all the tools you want and you're looking to dig into building some furniture, you can go to either Part III where I describe glues, joints, and mechanical fasteners or you can just dive right in and start building some projects in Part IV.

No matter where you start, remember that you can always backtrack if you find that you're missing some information. In this case, you'll find the table of contents invaluable because it lists every topic that I cover.

Part I
What's All the Buzz about Woodworking?

The 5th Wave   By Rich Tennant

"These are no ordinary beavers, Vern."

In this part . . .

You've seen a few shows on TV and working with wood looks pretty fun. After all, you get to use your hands and create something that you can proudly display to your friends and family. But where do you begin to learn to do woodworking? This part provides you with the basic vocabulary from which to build your woodworking skills. Chapter 1 shows you all the steps involved with making a woodworking project, Chapter 2 introduces you to the various qualities of wood, and Chapter 3 helps you get up to speed with your woodworking space and workshop safety.

Chapter 1

Discovering the Basics of Woodworking

*I*f you're like me (and all the other woodworkers I know), you became interested in woodworking because you wanted to use your hands to build something of lasting value. Maybe the motivation was partly economic — why pay a fortune for poorly made, ugly furniture, right? — and partly a need to create something of your own.

Regardless of why you got interested in woodworking, you want to know how this whole craft works. Well, this chapter leads you through the basics of the woodworking process and shows you where to go in this book for answers to your questions.

Getting the Lowdown on Wood

One of the most important aspects of woodworking is understanding the properties of wood. I know this seems obvious, but you'd be surprised about how many woodworkers I talk to who don't know why wood acts the way it does. Wood changes with the weather and the stresses put upon it (such as when it's stacked in a pile under a bunch of other wood). It expands and contracts and can twist, warp, or cup depending on the stresses that exist within it (from the direction of the grain in the board). Being able to look at a board and determine where those stresses are and how they may impact the board as it experiences changes in humidity requires some basic understanding of wood and how it's made.

Many species of wood fall into two general categories: hardwoods and softwoods. Knowing which type of wood is which and being able to choose the right wood for your goals can help reduce the negative impact of the inherent instability that is a part of solid wood. As you discover the variability of wood, you'll undoubtedly come to appreciate that some wood products allow you the same level of beauty without having to worry about the wood changing shape on you. These include veneers and manufactured wood products such as plywood and Medium Density Fiberboard (MDF). All this talk of wood is covered in more detail in Chapter 2.

Setting Up Shop

You need tools to work with wood. And most woodworkers think tools are great. I know I love buying and using tools. Heck, I'm the first to admit I have a problem. (Does anyone know of a 12-step program for tool addicts?) I buy tools like candy (well, more than I buy candy, actually). I have special tools for almost any imaginable task and I can't ever seem to get enough. Such is the life of a woodworker.

You don't need to get addicted to buying tools, but you will become dependent on using them. That's okay because by knowing how to use your tools you can build just about anything that you can imagine.

Tooling up

I dedicate several chapters in this book to exploring the exciting world of tools. From age-old hand tools to the most modern machine for milling wood, Chapters 5, 6, and 7 cover them all (well, not *all* of them, that would be insane, not to mention take up the entire book). Not only do you get to see what tools are what, you also get a glimpse into how to use each of them safely and effectively.

Working safely

Speaking of safety, woodworking is one of the most dangerous hobbies that you can get into. Wood is harder than skin and bone, and the tools that you use to cut and shape wood can do real damage real fast if you happen to slip or make a mistake. Not to worry, though. Chapter 3 gives you the heads up on creating a safe shop in which to work and on keeping safe while working. As an added bonus, Chapter 19 offers ten habits to get into that can make your woodworking time accident free.

Getting organized

With all this tool talk, you'll probably be tempted to buy every one that I describe in this book. Well, to keep you from going broke, I offer some advice on which tools to buy when, so that you can slowly and sanely build your workshop as you build your woodworking skills. See Chapter 4 for more on this topic. Chapter 8 helps you set up your shop so that you can get to all of your tools without hassle. You can also explore shop essentials, such as lighting and electrical requirements, to ensure that you can see what you're doing and can run all the tools you want to use.

Working with Woods

Woodworking is not all about tools and wood. Okay, it largely is (especially if you're a gear junkie like me). But even more important are the skills required to use the tools to craft the wood into the projects you want to create.

Putting the wood together

The first step in developing woodworking skills is to be able to discern the best glues, joints (ways of connecting two pieces of wood), and fasteners to use. Whether you need a dovetail joint for a drawer front or a mortise-and-tenon joint for a table leg, Chapter 10 introduces you to the wonderful world of wood joints. With an understanding of the joints in Chapter 10, you can build any furniture project and make it strong and durable.

Of course, these wood joints would be almost useless without some sort of adhesive to go with them. Chapter 9 walks you through the most common types of adhesives available for woodworkers and shows you the best one for each job. In Chapter 11, I go over the ins and outs of screws and nails and show you when and where to use them to improve the strength of your joints.

Following plans

The key to making furniture is having a plan. (Or is that the key to life? I always forget.) The good news for beginning woodworkers is that you don't need to develop the plan; you need only to follow it. Project plans are abundant and easily found (check out Chapter 21 for some project-plan resources). After you get familiar with the way plans are written, you can build just about anything (depending on your skills, of course).

After you review the plans that you've chosen, you can pick out the wood and other materials and get to work. (Check out the Cheat Sheet and Chapter 2 for information on buying wood.)

But, before you start cutting, spend some time figuring out which board to cut the part from. Tabletops, for example, look best if you choose boards that have similar grain patterns and overall color. Likewise, drawers and doors look great if you can use one board for pieces that are next to each other. Chapter 12 helps you figure all this out.

Building projects (and skills)

As far as I'm concerned, you can never have too many project plans to choose from. For example, I may like a Craftsman-style table, but you may think that the style is too clunky looking and prefer the elegant lines of a Shaker design. With this in mind, I provide three chapters of project plans, each with several variations on basic projects that not only give you some great furniture but also help you progressively build your woodworking skills.

Chapter 13 details making bookcases — the basic part of a carcass. Chapter 14 digs into tables where you get a chance to practice your edge-to-edge joints for building tabletops and use the most common and durable joint that exists — the mortise and tenon. Chapter 15 goes a little farther by providing plans to make a dresser and an armoire. By the time you finish with these chapters, you'll be well on your way to feeling comfortable making furniture and will be ready to tackle more ambitious projects.

Finishing up

When the project is together, you're only halfway done. The next step involves getting a smooth, blemish-free surface and preparing the wood for a stain or topcoat. Chapter 16 helps you explore the varied world of sandpapers and wood fillers.

After you have smoothed the wood, you can then decide whether you want to add any color and, if so, what type. You can choose from stain or paint and from water-based, oil-based, or lacquer-based products. You have many options and I'm sure you can find one that works for you. Chapter 17 helps you make sense out of all the choices and shows you how to apply these products.

The final step in any woodworking project is protecting the wood from moisture and damage. Chapter 18 includes lots of information about the most common types of topcoats. Because not all of them provide the same degree of beauty and protection, you get a chance to compare the pros and cons of each topcoat so that you can choose the best option for you and your project.

Moving on

As much as I'd like to provide a book with everything you'll ever need to know about woodworking (as if I even know all that!), it's just not possible. Chapter 21 is my way of helping you to keep exploring this immense craft by providing you with a bunch of resources. This chapter contains contact info for woodworking magazines, addresses for helpful Web sites, and ideas to help you keep expanding your knowledge and skills.

Chapter 2

Wood You Be Mine? Appreciating Wood for All It's Worth

....

In This Chapter

▶ Understanding the characteristics of wood

▶ Looking into the different kinds of solid wood

▶ Discovering everything you want to know about veneers

▶ Understanding plywoods and manufactured boards

▶ Figuring out where to find wood

▶ Knowing the basics on buying

....

*T*his chapter is all about wood. Hardwood, softwood, plywood, veneer wood. Plain-sawn wood, rift-cut wood, quarter-sawn wood. Solid wood, man-made wood. Wood, wood, wood. Did I mention this chapter is about wood?

The number one thing to know is that wood isn't a static thing. It's a natural product that's constantly in movement. As a woodworker, your job is to understand how wood moves and how to use that movement to your best advantage (or at least how to keep it from ruining your masterpiece). This chapter helps you to understand how boards are made out of trees and to discover that the way the log is cut determines its ultimate strength and stability (and its beauty). Additionally, you explore the characteristics of a variety of species of hardwoods and softwoods.

But that's not all. In this chapter I talk about one of modern times' greatest gifts to the woodworker: manufactured boards (also called sheet goods) and veneers. Yep, wood technology can help you keep your sanity while also speeding up the process of making furniture. Oh, and it can also save you some bucks in the process. What's not to like about that?

Board Basics: Knowing What to Look For

If you've ever been to a lumberyard and seen the huge stacks of varying lengths, thicknesses, grain patterns, and colors of wood, you understand what a daunting task it is just to find a couple of boards that match. Luckily, with just a few pieces of information and a little patience (and a decent lumber-yard) you can find some great wood.

Making the grade

Every board at the lumberyard has a grade assigned to it. A *grade* is a code that tells you about the board you're looking at. Grades refer to the quality of the *grain* (the way growth rings appear in the board) and the number of *defects* (knots, holes, cracks, and so on) in the board.

Sure, you can look a board over carefully and grade it yourself (which you should do anyway), but an official grade can speed up the process by weeding out the boards which are simply too full of defects. The National Hardwood Lumber Association (NHLA) lists seven grades of wood:

- ✔ Firsts
- ✔ Seconds
- ✔ Selects
- ✔ No. 1 Common
- ✔ No. 2 Common
- ✔ No. 3A Common
- ✔ No. 3B Common

Because the rules for determining the grade of a board are very complicated and species-dependent, I can't go into too much detail about them in this book. (If you have an inquiring mind and want to know the details, however, see the NHLA Web site www.natlhardwood.org.)

For woodworking, you want wood with few defects and as good a grain pattern as possible. For the most part, you want the top two grades of wood: Firsts and Seconds. These two are often grouped together and referred to as *FAS* (Firsts and Seconds). Most decent lumberyards are well stocked with FAS boards and some Selects. The "common" classes aren't used in furniture-making because they contain far too many defects.

Drying and storing cut boards

After the wood is cut it needs to dry before it can be used, and drying the wood causes shrinkage in the board. So it's important that the board be allowed to dry evenly or it twists, bows, or warps. If you buy wood from a lumberyard, it's already been dried, but you want to acclimate it to your shop before you work with it. This way the wood will make any changes it needs to make with the different humidity level in your shop, and you don't get any nasty surprises like a table leg that twists after you've glued your project together.

The best way to acclimate your wood to the humidity of your shop is to create horizontal racks and lay the boards flat on them (more about this process in Chapter 7). Leave them for a few days, and they're ready to go.

Resist the temptation to buy "common" grades of wood for furniture even when the price seems great. Cutting all the defects out takes a ton of time. Besides, by the time you make the lesser quality wood usable, you don't have much wood left over. When you buy a cheap board and cut it up to find usable parts, you spend more money than it costs you to buy the better quality stuff to begin with.

Understanding how wood is cut

To get a flat board, you have to cut a round log in a particular way so you can get the grain to run how you want it to. The orientation of the blade in relation to the log and its growth rings determines the type of cut the board ends up with. You can cut a log in three main ways:

- **Through and through:** This type of milling involves progressively cutting the log from one side to the other (see Figure 2-1).

  Through and through milling is the simplest and most efficient way to cut a log. Milling through and through results in plain-sawn, rift-sawn, and quarter-sawn boards because the orientation of the growth rings changes as the boards are sliced off the log (see the "Choosing the right wood cut for you" section later in this chapter for more information).

- **Plain-sawn:** Plain-sawn milling involves cutting the log from the outside to the center on all four sides. The very center of the log (the pith) is left alone. Check out Figure 2-2 to see how plain-sawing is done. This type of milling produces plain-sawn and rift-sawn boards.

✓ **Quarter-sawn:** Quarter-sawn milling is the least efficient way to cut a log, but it produces some of the best boards. You can mill a quarter-sawn board in two ways: the preferred way (Figure 2-3 left) and the practical way (Figure 2-3 right). Unless you have a mill of your own or you own the log and have it milled to your specifications, you're going to have to live with the practical method of quarter-sawing wood. Don't worry, this is still a great way to mill a log and, because it's more efficient than the "preferred" method, it doesn't cost you an arm and a leg to buy (maybe just the arm).

Quarter-sawn boards (see next section) are more stable and attractive (to me, anyway) than the other types of boards, but they are much more expensive. They're also unavailable for some types of wood.

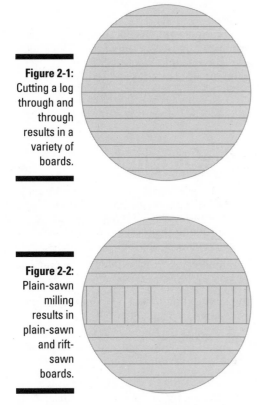

Figure 2-1:
Cutting a log through and through results in a variety of boards.

Figure 2-2:
Plain-sawn milling results in plain-sawn and rift-sawn boards.

Figure 2-3: Quarter-sawing a log can be performed two ways: the pre-ferred method (left) and the prac-tical method (right).

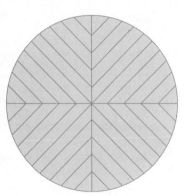
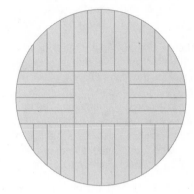

Choosing the right wood cut for you

When you get to the lumberyard (or when you order over the phone) you have three choices of wood cuts: plain-sawn, rift-sawn, and quarter-sawn. The differ-ence between each of the types of cuts is in how the growth rings relate to the *face* (wide side) of the board.

The relationship between the growth rings and the face of the board deter-mines its overall stability (the amount of movement that occurs with changes in humidity). For example, plain-sawn boards have growth rings at a low angle to their faces so these boards will have as much as ¼-inch movement across a 12-inch-wide board as the climate gets drier or wetter. Rift-sawn boards, because the growth rings are at a steeper angle to the face, move less (maybe as much as ⅛-inch for a 12-inch board). Quarter-sawn boards have the least amount of movement with changes in humidity because the growth rings are at an almost 90 degree angle (almost no discernible change in width with changes in humidity). This makes the quarter-sawn board the most stable type of cut available. Regardless of the cut type, the length and thickness of the board changes very little as the humidity changes.

Plain-sawn

Plain-sawn boards are the most common boards at your lumberyard (check out Figure 2-4 for a look at a plain-sawn board). When you choose or order wood without designating the type of cut, you get plain-sawn boards. Plain-sawn boards have growth rings that run less than 30 degrees against the face of the board.

Anatomy of a tree

Without the tree, woodworkers wouldn't have anything to build from. It's a shame, however, that so little of the tree can be used for furniture. (At least the rest can be used for other stuff like the paper that this book is printed on.) The trunk of the tree is where woodworkers get wood for projects. The branches, on the other hand, don't make good wood for furniture because they contain too many defects and aren't as strong.

A tree consists of several layers. From inner-most to outermost they are

- **Pith.** The pith is the core of the tree. It's unusable for woodworking because it's weak and often contains fungus.

- **Heartwood.** The heartwood is the "heart" of the tree, providing its strength. This wood is one of two sections used for lumber (the second is the sapwood, listed next) and the best wood for furniture-making. You can tell the heartwood from the sapwood because it has a darker color.

- **Sapwood.** The sapwood is newer growth that allows nutrients to travel through the tree. The sapwood isn't as desirable as the heartwood for woodworking because of its color (it's lighter, almost white in many cases) and the fact that it's less stable than the heartwood (sapwood expands and contracts more with changes in humidity). It can be used for woodworking but it needs to be stained separately.

- **Cambium layer.** The cambium layer is the outer layer of living wood that forms new wood and bark. This layer is stripped off the log and not used in the final board.

- **Phloem or blast.** Phloem or blast refers to the living inner tissue located directly under the bark. This layer can also be included in the bark.

- **Bark.** The protective outer layer of the tree.

Plain-sawn boards are the most economical of the solid wood boards, but because the grain runs at an angle close to the face of the board, they tend to cup or warp more easily so they're less stable than rift-sawn or quarter-sawn boards.

When using plain-sawn board, carefully consider the way the grain runs in relation to the face of the board and plan your projects accordingly. You may have to cut out sections in order to get the most stable end product. Check out Chapter 12 for ways to minimize the problems with plain-sawn boards.

Rift-sawn

Rift-sawn refers to boards where the growth rings meet the face between 30 and 60 degrees (see Figure 2-5). Rift-sawn boards have a straight grain pattern as opposed to the circular pattern of the plain-sawn boards. They are also more stable and more expensive than plain-sawn wood (costing as much as 50 percent more).

Quarter-sawn

Quarter-sawn boards are the most stable and most expensive of the three options. Quarter-sawn boards have growth rings not less than 60 degrees from the face (see Figure 2-6). Quarter-sawn boards have a straight grain pattern with a "flake" or "ribbon-like" figure in the wood. This is beautiful wood, but you pay for it — often costing almost twice as much as the same species of plain-sawn board. Quarter-sawn oak is a popular wood to use with Arts and Crafts and Mission style furniture.

Which cut you choose depends on your budget, the availability of the species you want, and your design aesthetic. Each of these three choices can produce some great woodworking projects as long as you plan ahead when you cut (you can find out more about choosing the best part of the board to cut in Chapter 12).

Figure 2-4:
A plain-sawn board has a circular grain pattern and growth rings less than 30 degrees from the face.

Figure 2-5:
Rift-sawn boards have a straight grain and growth rings between 30 and 60 degrees of the face.

Figure 2-6:
Quarter-sawn boards have growth rings at greater than 60 degrees from the face and straight grain with a "flake" pattern.

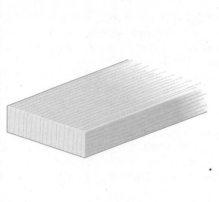

Dealing with defects

No matter how much you wish otherwise, no board is perfect. All wood has cracks or dents, checks or splits, cups or twists, shakes or warps, or any combination of these. Being able to understand and deal with the various defects allows you to use the board to its best use. Defects essentially come in two varieties: Those that are easy to deal with and those that aren't.

✔ **Defects that are easy to deal with:** Include knots, splits, cracks, and checks (see Figure 2-7). These defects affect only a small area of the board (if they exist over the majority of the board, don't buy it). Just plan the way you cut the board for your projects with these defects in mind. Chapter 12 details how to do this.

✔ **Defects that aren't easy to deal with:** Include warps, twists, or bows (check out Figure 2-8). For the most part, these types of defects are the result of uneven drying and working with them is time-consuming and often frustrating. If you see wood at the lumberyard that is warped, twisted, or bowed, set it aside and choose other boards.

If you get home and find some boards with these defects or if these problems develop as the wood sits in your shop, don't throw it away. It will take some work, but you can fix the defects by methodically using a table saw, planer, and jointer. This process (called *pre-milling*) is explained in Chapter 12.

Figure 2-7:
Common
wood
defects
that you
can easily
deal with.

Figure 2-8:
Common
wood
defects
that are
hard to
deal with.

When choosing wood at the lumberyard, place one end of the board on the floor and hold the other end to your eye. Look down the board to locate any irregularities such as a bow, twist, or cup. Avoid the boards that aren't straight and true. You may end up rejecting a lot of boards before you find the ones that work for you. Also, as you examine each board look for other defects such as splits and cracks and examine the grain pattern and overall color of the board (the color can vary widely from tree to tree). Try to choose boards that match (again, this may weed out quite a few boards).

Sorting Through the Types of Solid Wood

Solid wood — that is, wood cut into boards from the trunk of the tree — makes up most of the wood in a piece of furniture. The type of wood you choose determines the beauty and strength of the piece. Many varieties of wood are available and each has its own properties. In the following two sections I introduce you to the most common types of soft- and hardwoods.

Sampling some softwoods

Softwoods aren't weaker than hardwoods. Softwoods come from coniferous trees such as cedar, fir, and pine and tend to be somewhat yellow or reddish in appearance. Because most coniferous trees grow fast and straight, softwoods are generally less expensive than hardwoods. It's also relatively easy to find *sustainably grown* softwoods (woods grown on tree farms to ensure a endless supply of wood); this means you're not contributing to the deforestation of the world and will always have a supply of wood for your projects.

Following is a list of common softwood varieties and their characteristics. See the color section to get a look at these woods.

Cedar

The most common type of cedar is the western red variety. Western red cedar, as its name implies, has a reddish color to it. This type of wood is relatively soft (1 on a scale of 1 to 4), has a straight grain, and has a slightly aromatic smell. Western Red cedar is mostly used for outdoor projects such as furniture, decks, and building exteriors because it can handle moist environments without rotting. Western red cedar is moderately priced and can be found at most home centers.

Fir

Often referred to as Douglas Fir, this wood is very soft, has a straight, pronounced grain, and has a reddish brown tint to it. Fir is most often used for building; however, it's inexpensive and can be used for some furniture-making as well. It doesn't have the most interesting grain pattern and doesn't take stain very well, so I'd recommend using it when you intend to paint the finished product. Douglas fir is pretty hard, rating 4 on a scale of 1 to 4.

I mention this wood because it is very common at your local home center and it's so inexpensive you'll probably be tempted to make something with it.

Pine

Pine comes in several varieties, including Ponderosa, Sugar, White, and Yellow, and all of them make great furniture. In my neck of the woods (southwest United States), pine is the wood to use (although I prefer oak and cherry, go figure). Pine is very easy to work with and, because most varieties are relatively soft, it lends itself to carving.

Pine generally takes stain very well (as long as you seal the wood first; see Chapter 17), although Ponderosa pine tends to ooze sap, so be careful when using this stuff. Pine is available from most home centers, but it's often of a lesser grade than what you can find at a decent lumberyard.

Redwood

Like cedar, redwood is used mostly for outdoor projects because of its resistance to moisture. Redwood (California redwood) is fairly soft and has a straight grain. As its name suggests, it has a reddish tint to it. Redwood is easy to work with, is relatively soft (2 on a scale of 1 to 4), and is moderately priced. You can find redwood at your local home center.

Honing in on hardwoods

Most woodworkers love to work with hardwoods. The variety of colors, textures, and grain patterns makes for some beautiful and interesting-looking furniture. The downside to hardwoods is their price. Some of the more exotic species can be too expensive to use for anything more than an accent.

Some hardwoods are becoming very hard to find and are being harvested without concern to their eventual extinction (Brazilian rosewood comes to mind). Not only is this hard on the environment, it drives the price of the wood so high that making furniture out of it is out of the question for most woodworkers. If you can, try to buy wood from a sustainable forest (commercial tree farms that ensure the supply of the wood). Check out the National Hardwood Lumber Association (www.natlhardwood.org) or www.smartwood.com for ways to support sustainable forestry.

Following is a list of common hardwoods and their characteristics. See the color section to get a look at these woods.

Ash

Ash is a white-to-pale-brown colored wood with a straight grain. It's pretty easy to work with (hardness of 4 on a scale of 1 to 5) and takes stain quite nicely, but ash is getting harder and harder to find. You won't find ash at your local home center — it's only available from larger lumberyards. Ash is a good substitute for white oak.

Birch

Birch comes in two varieties: yellow and white. Yellow birch is a pale yellow-to-white wood with reddish-brown heartwood, whereas white birch has a whiter color that resembles maple. Both types of birch have a hardness of 4 on a scale of 1 to 5. Birch is readily available and less expensive than many other hardwoods. You can find birch at many home centers, although the selection is better at a lumberyard.

Birch is stable and easy to work with. However, it's hard to stain because it can get blotchy, so I prefer to paint anything that I make with birch. If you must stain it, check out Chapter 16 for some tips on dealing with this difficult wood.

Cherry

Cherry is one of my all-time favorite woods; easy to work with, stains and finishes well with just oil, and ages beautifully. Cherry's heartwood has a reddish-brown color to it and the sapwood is almost white. Cherry has a hardness of 2 on a scale of 1 to 5. This is a very common wood for furniture-making and is available from sustainably-grown forests. You won't find cherry at your local home center, so a trip to the lumberyard is necessary if you want to use it. Because it's in demand, cherry is getting somewhat expensive compared to other domestic hardwoods, such as oak and maple.

Mahogany

One of the great furniture woods, mahogany (also called Honduran mahogany), has a reddish-brown to deep-red tint, a straight grain, medium texture, and a hardness of around 2 on a scale of 1 to 5. It takes stain very well and looks great with just a coat (or 10) of oil (for more on oil finishes, see Chapter 18).

The only drawback is that mahogany isn't being grown in sustainable forests (not a big deal unless you want to ensure that it'll be around forever. This isn't enough of a drawback to stop me from using mahogany, but I'd love for it to be made sustainably.) Forget going to your home center to get some — the only place to find mahogany is a decent lumberyard (and it'll cost you).

Maple

Maple comes in two varieties: hard and soft. Both varieties are harder than many other woods; hard maple is so hard (a 5 on a scale of 1 to 5) that it's difficult to work with. Soft maple, on the other hand, is relatively easy to work with. Because of their fine, straight grain, both varieties are more stable than many other woods. They also tend to be less expensive than other hardwoods. You won't find maple at your local home center, but most lumberyards have a good selection of it.

Oak

Oak is one of the most used woods for furniture. Available in two varieties — red and white — oak is strong (hardness of about 4 on a scale of 1 to 5) and easy to work with. White oak is preferred for furniture-making because it has a more attractive figure than red oak (white oak is also resistant to moisture and can be used on outdoor furniture).

This is one wood that can be found quarter-sawn (see the "Choosing the right wood cut for you" section earlier in the chapter for more on quarter-sawn wood). In fact, quarter-sawn white oak is less expensive than some other hardwoods like cherry, for instance. The grain has a beautiful "ray flake" pattern to it. Red oak can be found at most home centers, but if you want white oak, make a trip to the lumberyard.

Poplar

Poplar is one of the less expensive hardwoods. It's also fairly soft (1 in hardness on a scale of 1 to 5), which makes it easy to work with. Poplar has a white color with some green or brown streaks in the heartwood. Because poplar is not the most beautiful wood, it's rarely used in fine furniture and if it is, it's almost always painted. I like to use poplar for drawers (where it won't be seen) because it is stable and inexpensive. You can find poplar at larger home centers, but a lumberyard will have a better selection.

Teak

Teak is becoming rarer as the days go on, but it is the staple for fine outdoor furniture. Teak is highly weather-resistant and beautiful (not to mention expensive — can you believe almost $24 a board foot?). Teak has an oily feel and a golden-brown color. It rates a 3 on a scale of 1 to 5 for hardness and is only available from larger lumberyards and specialty suppliers.

Walnut

With a hardness of about 4 on a 1 to 5 scale, walnut is a rich brown wood that's easy to work with. Unfortunately, walnut is somewhat expensive (usually around $8 a board foot) and finding large boards for big projects is getting difficult. In spite of this, walnut is still a great wood to work with and lends itself nicely for use as accents and inlays to dress up a project. You won't find walnut at your local home center and you may need to special order it from a lumber-yard if you want a large quantity.

Looking Beneath the Surface of Veneers

Veneer is very thin wood, generally around $\frac{1}{32}$ inch. Veneer can be created two ways: by cutting and by slicing. Each way has its own advantages.

✔ **Rotary cutting:** Rotary cutting involves putting the log on a giant lathe (a tools the rotates the wood) and spinning the log while a knife cuts away the outer layer of the log. Rotary cutting produces the most amount of wood from a log, but the grain pattern ends up looking "watery." Rotary cut veneers are used mainly for construction-grade plywoods, not for furniture.

✔ **Slicing:** Slicing involves cutting the log in half lengthwise and slicing off sheets of the log from that cut. Each slice is kept in its original order so that the entire log of sheets (called a *flitch*) can be arranged to have a consistent look.

Depending on how the log's growth rings are oriented to the blade, a variety of grain patterns can be made by slicing veneers. Just like solid wood, sliced veneers can be produced with plain-, rift-, and quarter-sliced (sawn) grain patterns. See the "Choosing the right wood cut for you" section earlier in the chapter for more details on plain-, rift-, and quarter-sawn cuts.

Because veneering a log creates so much usable wood, even the rarest woods can be made affordable and available for the average woodworker. Veneers are sold in sheets and priced by the square foot. Most good lumberyards have a decent selection of veneers, but if you want some of the more exotic types of wood you may need to find a mail-order supplier. Look for these in the classified section of woodworking magazines (check out Chapter 20 for a list of the most popular magazines).

Large pieces of veneer are often shipped rolled up. You need to flatten them before you can use them. Be very careful! Gently roll open the veneer and lay it flat. If it doesn't want to lay flat, spray some steam on it (a steam iron held an inch or two off the wood does the trick) then gently press it down. Place it between two pieces of plywood or MDF for a few hours (see the "Playing with Plywood [and Other Manufactured Boards]" section for definitions of plywood and MDF).

Playing with Plywood (and Other Manufactured Boards)

My dad was a firm believer in plywood and other manufactured boards (collectively called *sheet goods*). In fact, he preferred sheet goods to solid wood. Sure, he used solid wood for some things — table legs and tops (sometimes), rails and stiles for doors, edging details — but he avoided it if he could. For a long time I looked down on this practice, because I thought using sheet goods was "unnatural." (I mean, it is called a "manufactured material.") I hate to admit this, but it took me a long time and many frustrations dealing with the inherent movement of solid wood before I understood his way of thinking. Now I can say (without hanging my head in shame) that I use plywoods too.

Why have I come to change my mind about sheet goods? Well, these manufactured products are much more stable and predictable than solid wood. Solid wood is constantly moving — expanding and contracting — and it's prone to twisting and warping, whereas sheet goods are not. Why? Plywoods are constructed by layering several sheets of thinly cut panels with the grain pattern alternating from one layer to the next, and other sheet goods use various methods to improve stability.

Grading: Knowing what you're buying

Plywood is graded according to the quality of its face (the large surface of the sheet). For woodworking, you want one side with an "A" grade if you want the piece to be seen. If it's not going to show, then you can use whatever you want (personally, I stick with "A" or "B" grades, because they don't cost that much more than the others). They all have the same structural integrity. Most plywood has one side that looks better than the other, so it's graded on both sides and says something like "A-B." This means that one side gets an "A" grade and the other gets a "B."

Here's a basic rundown of the plywood grades and what they mean:

- **A:** As you might expect, this is the finest grade; the surface is smooth with no holes or defects.
- **B:** May have some minor defects such as minor cracks or splits.
- **C:** More defects, enough to make this unusable for any exposed part.
- **C-plugged:** May be areas where some chunks of the facing veneer were missing and "plugged" (filled) with scrap wood. Again, if you hide it you may be able to use it.
- **D:** A surface with many defects and holes in the outer layer.

It's what's inside that counts: Considering cores

Plywoods come with several different types of *cores* (the material between the outer layers), which I explain in the following sections.

Veneer-core

Veneer-core has alternating layers of wood plies. This type of plywood is very common, but if you use it, be aware that your piece may have holes (called *voids*) in the inner layers that you can't see. Voids pose a problem when you cut the panel into smaller pieces, because you may cut into one and end up with a hole in the edge of the board.

Veneer-core plywood comes with a varying number of plies, from three up to eleven. For the most part, the number of plies relates to the thickness of the board (the more plies, the thicker the board). This isn't always the case, however. For example, you can buy plywood designed to be used for drawer sides; often called *drawer-side* plywood or *Baltic birch.* This type of plywood has more and thinner plies with fewer voids than regular veneer-core plywood. This is what I often use for drawer sides. It's more expensive than regular veneer-core plywood and can't be found at your local home center (good hardwood suppliers will have it), but I often like it a lot better than using solid wood for drawer sides, and the plies look good enough to just finish over with some oil or polyurethane.

Lumber-core

Lumber-core plywood consists of narrow strips of wood that run parallel to one another. These strips are sandwiched between two outer layers, which like the veneer-core plywood, have their grains running perpendicular to one another. This makes for both a stable and strong core.

Lumber-core plywood is not often carried by home centers, so you have to go to a good lumberyard to find it. It is definitely worth it if you want to build bookshelves or something that will carry a lot of weight, because it is stronger than veneer-core plywood.

Medium density fiberboard (MDF)

MDF has no layer so it isn't technically a plywood — MDF is made from sawdust and resins, but I include it in this section because MDF is often used like plywood and can be found at the core of some of the hardwood veneer products listed in the "Dressing up the core" section that follows.

Like plywood, MDF is very stable. But unfortunately it's not very strong, it's very heavy, and it can be hard to work with. In spite of all this, MDF is often used in cabinet making, but only where it won't be seen. Sometimes MDF is used in an area where it will be seen, but then it's painted. It paints very well, and after a couple of coats it looks pretty good. You can buy MDF from your local home center plain or with a veneer (such as oak or birch) or laminate over one or both faces.

MDF produces a ton of dust when you cut or sand it, so wear a dust mask when working with it.

Flake board

If the dust and mess from MDF are a deterrent to you, you might like flake board instead. Flake board, like MDF, is constructed from small pieces of wood and resins, and therefore it doesn't have the voids that may be present in regular plywood. However, it's stronger than MDF because it uses "flakes" of wood rather than sawdust, so the fibers are longer, which creates strength. It also produces a lot less dust. Flake board can be found at either a lumberyard or most home centers. Look for a product called OSB (oriented strand board).

Dressing up the core

Aside from having a variety of inner cores, plywood and sheet goods also come with a variety of outer skins (veneers). These include hardwoods and plastic laminates, the most popular styles.

Hardwoods

For the furniture-maker, hardwood-veneered plywoods are a dream come true. You get the benefits of plywood's stability and veneer's economy. Many varieties of hardwood-veneered plywoods are available. These include

- ✔ Oak
- ✔ Cherry
- ✔ Birch
- ✔ Maple
- ✔ Mahogany

These hardwood-veneered plywoods are great for building cabinets, shelves, and other project pieces that require a large piece of wood. The only disadvantage to hardwood veneer plywoods is that you have to dress up the edges of the board, because the hardwood veneer is only on the two faces of the board. Look in Part IV for more on how to do this.

Plastic laminates

Plastic laminates are plywoods (or most commonly MDF boards) with a thin outer layer of hard plastic on one or both sides. The trade name is melamine. I'm currently remodeling my kitchen and I'm using melamine to build the basic carcass of the cabinets. Any sides that show are covered with cherry veneer and the face frames, doors, and drawer fronts of the cabinets are all solid cherry. This gives me the beauty of cherry on the outside and the durability and easy clean-up of melamine on the inside.

I also built a worktable for my shop that has a melamine top. I use this table as my glue-up table because any spilled glue can easily be wiped off the melamine. If this were a wood top, glue clean-up would be much more difficult.

Doing it yourself

Creating your own unique plywood is as simple as gluing a piece of veneer onto the core of your choice (check out Chapter 8 for suggestions on which adhesives to use for this purpose). The most common cores for this procedure are MDF and flake board, because they don't have any voids in their surfaces and are very inexpensive. Some woodworkers use Baltic birch instead, but it does cost more.

Considering the stability of plywoods and manufactured boards and the almost-unlimited variety of veneer stock available, you're limited only by your imagination in creating some truly unique and beautiful projects.

Searching for Wood in All the Right Places

Before you can do any woodworking, you need some wood (how's that for logic?). Well, this section can help you find the best places to get wood, whether it's from your local home center, a lumberyard, or by mail order.

Checking out your local home center

For many newbie woodworkers the home center superstore is the first stop for wood. These stores are handy for finding construction-grade wood and some common woods such as pine, red oak, birch, poplar, redwood and cedar. The advantage of getting wood from a home center is that it's very likely that you have one near your home. The disadvantage is that the wood selection is not as good as a lumberyard, and the prices are generally higher. Finding a home center is easy: you'll find them listed under "home improvement," "hardware stores," "building materials," or "lumber" in the Yellow Pages.

Finding a lumberyard

Chances are you haven't been to a real lumberyard, so you don't have any idea of all the wood that's out there. If you want the best selection of the largest variety of woods (not to mention the best prices in most cases), your best bet is to find a lumberyard in your area. Look in your Yellow Pages under "lumber," "hardwoods," or "woodworking." Both regular builder suppliers (like your local home center) and specialty wood suppliers are listed there, so you may have to do some calling around to see who carries the type of wood you want. Most large lumberyards that carry furniture-grade wood list hardwoods in their ads.

Finding mail/phone order suppliers

If you can't find a lumberyard in your area and your local home center doesn't carry the type of wood you want, check out the back of one of the woodworking magazines I list in Chapter 21. In some cases, these suppliers offer some of the best prices and can get you types of wood, such as reclaimed/recycled (a nice way of saying "used") pine that can add character to your projects.

The only downside to mail order suppliers is that you can't pick out the wood you want and you have to pay shipping charges (check out the "Let your fingers do the walking: Ordering wood by phone" section later in this chapter for tips on ordering your wood this way). The upside is that you don't have to waste your time searching for wood in the lumberyard.

Buying Wood

The process of buying wood involves understanding the various ways wood is sold and being able to determine just how much wood you're buying. This section lays it all out for you.

From a home center

When you buy wood from a home center it's sold as *dimensional* lumber. This means that it's smooth on all four sides, cut to a precise width and thickness, and sold by the linear foot.

Dimensional lumber is available in sizes from 1 x 4 to 2 x 12. These numbers refer to the thickness and the width. Keep in mind that these measurements are not accurate. The board is actually ¼ inch (for "1x" boards) or ½ inch (for "2x" boards) thinner and ½ inch narrower. For example, a 1 x 4 is actually ¾ inch thick by 3½ inches wide, and a 2 x 12 board is actually 1½ inches thick by 11½ inches wide.

From a lumberyard

When you buy wood from a lumberyard, you buy it based upon the board foot. The wood will be either rough-milled or surfaced. The next couple sections explain these three terms (board foot, rough-milled, and surfaced) in more detail.

Calculating board feet

A *board foot* is a board that is 1 inch thick by 12 inches wide by 1 foot long. To make matters more complicated, 1-inch-thick wood is called 4/4 (this type of measurement refers to the number of ¼ inches the wood is thick) and not 1. For the most part, you can find wood that is 2/4 (½ inch) to 8/4 (2 inches) thick, with 4/4 being most common.

Calculating board feet can take some getting used to. For example, say you have an 8/4 board that is 6 inches wide and 1 foot long. This is one board foot.

To figure out how many board feet are in a piece of wood, multiply its length (measured in feet), width, and thickness (measured in inches), and divide this number by 12. This is often easier said than done, because boards are often different widths at different ends. In this case what I do is measure the width at each end, add those numbers together, and then divide in half. This gives me the average width. Then use the averaged number in your board-foot calculation. Always round your numbers to the nearest inch (thickness and width) or foot (length) when calculating board feet.

Take a pencil, measuring tape, scrap paper, and a calculator to the lumberyard with you and write down all the dimensions and total board feet for each board. This way you can double-check the salesperson's calculations and make sure you aren't being overcharged (which, unfortunately, happens a lot).

Rough-milled wood

Rough-milled wood is exactly that: rough. It has one straight edge, and both the top and bottom have deep saw marks on them. You have to plane them in order to smooth the surfaces and you need to *joint* them in order to get clean and straight edges (this is called pre-milling and I cover this process in detail in Chapter 12). These two processes can take a lot of time. I only recommend buying rough-milled wood if you have no other alternative and you have the tools (surface/thickness planer and jointer) to clean up the wood.

If you want to buy rough-milled boards, take a plane to the lumberyard and clean up an edge of the board so that you can see the board's color and grain pattern. It's obscured by the rough saw marks.

Surfaced boards

Surfaced wood is already planed on one face (called *S1S*) or both faces (called *S2S*) of the board. One edge is jointed, but the other edge is rough. Unlike dimensional lumber, surfaced boards aren't the same width all the way along their length. They may be 6 inches on one end and 8 inches on the other, for example.

I prefer to buy surfaced wood because it allows me to see the color and grain pattern of the entire board and I can get right to working on the project when I get the wood home instead of spending my time planing and jointing the board. Most lumberyards sell surfaced wood.

Surfaced wood is slightly thinner than the rough-milled board because it went through the planer. You're paying for the thickness it was before surfacing, so a 4/4 S2S board is actually about $\frac{3}{16}$ inch thinner. If you need a board to be exactly 1 inch thick, you need to buy a 5/4 board and plane it down a bit.

Buying wood can take a lot of time. You have to inspect each board for trueness (no warps, cups, or bows), color and grain compatibility, and calculate its size (in board feet). Then you have to wait as the salesperson does his calculating. Expect to spend several hours at the lumberyard in order to get enough wood for your next project.

Let your fingers do the walking: Ordering wood by phone

Don't laugh. I buy a lot of my wood over the phone. In fact, I can't remember the last time I actually went to a lumberyard to pick out my wood (the closest decent lumberyard is about 100 miles from my shop). I just call my supplier, and they deliver it within a couple of days. The best part for me is that I don't have to spend half the day driving to the lumberyard, sorting through stacks and stacks of wood, and loading and unloading my truck. The downside is that I sometimes get some wood that I have to get creative to use.

If you choose to order over the phone, keep these tips in mind:

✔ Specify that you want boards from the same tree (if possible) and tell the person taking your order what types of boards you want (very little sapwood, similar color/grain pattern, for example). Most suppliers who deliver will try their best to get you what you want.

✔ Always order about 20 percent more wood than you think you need for your project. I guarantee that you'll use more wood than you initially plan on and that you'll get some boards that you wouldn't have picked out yourself (you can always use them for a less important part of the project, though). Besides, if you don't have enough wood you have to make another order, and the delivery costs for a small amount can really add up.

✔ Check each board before you accept the shipment and send back any that are unacceptable to you.

Chapter 3

Putting Safety First in Your Workshop

Woodworking is an inherently dangerous pastime. Wood is stronger than skin and bone. All the tools you're using are designed to separate wood fibers, so imagine what these tools can do to your fingers, hands, arms, and so on. I don't write this to scare you, rather to instill in you a healthy respect for the power of the tools of the woodworking trade.

The good news is that you can minimize the dangers of woodworking by taking a few simple steps. All you need is attentiveness to the task, proper preparation, and a shop that is set up with safety in mind. This chapter helps you achieve all these goals.

Protecting Yourself from Injury

The most common injuries in the wood shop don't result from the serious accidents where a tool gets out of control, but rather the little things that can build up over time such as eye, hearing, and breathing problems. In many cases, you won't know you've been hurt until years later when you find that you can't hear as well as you used to or your breathing gets more difficult. This section provides you with the information you need to keep your eyes, ears, and lungs in tip-top shape for the long term.

Eye protection

Nothing is more important than protecting your eyes when you work with wood. Dust and wood chips constantly fly around, and without eye protection some of that stuff gets in your eyes. (I talk about ways to cut down on dust in your shop in the section, "Where's Mr. Clean When You Need Him? Keeping Your Shop in Ship-Shape" later in the chapter.)

Check out these different types of eye protection:

✔ **Safety glasses:** Safety glasses often have open sides but protect your eyes from things flying directly at them (you can find some safety glasses with side protection). They are lightweight and generally comfortable to wear.

✔ **Safety goggles:** These offer slightly more protection than safety glasses because they have shields on the sides of the eyes. They can be more cumbersome to wear and sometimes fog up in very humid weather.

✔ **Face shields:** Face shields aren't necessary for most woodworking tasks (although glasses and goggles are), but are essential if you end up using a lathe (see Chapter 4). Chips and large chunks of wood often fly through the air when turning wood, and a face shield keeps you from getting bruises and cuts all over your face.

Hearing protection

Power tools (see Chapters 6 and 7) can get very loud. In fact, a router can produce more than 110 decibels when cutting hard wood. This is as loud as a rock concert. If you want to be able to hear clearly after a few years of woodworking you need some ear protection.

Check out the following list for some ear protection options:

✔ **Earplugs:** Earplugs fit right into your ear canal and are often made of foam or plastic. Though inexpensive and effective at reducing sounds by about 20 decibels, they can be difficult to fit properly. Make sure they fit tightly in your ear canal. Unless they completely block out air they don't work.

✔ **Earmuffs:** Earmuffs look like large headphones (in fact, some *are* headphones). They cover your ears and often reduce sound more than earplugs can. The disadvantage is that, in order to work effectively, they must press pretty hard against your head. This can be somewhat uncomfortable after a while.

One great advantage to earmuffs is that you can buy them with AM/FM radios and listen to your favorite radio station while you work (don't turn them up too loud or you defeat the purpose of wearing them!).

> ✔ **Noise cancellation headsets:** The sound outside the headset is sampled and cancelled out via a computer-controlled process. What you end up hearing is almost total silence. This luxury comes at a price, though; they are expensive (around $200).

You can buy integrated ear muffs-safety glasses that keep you from having to put on two pieces of gear when you work. You can find these through most woodworking stores or suppliers.

Breathing protection

With all the dust and fumes present in a woodworking shop, it's really a good idea to invest in some lung protection. There are essentially two types:

> ✔ **Dust masks:** Dust masks filter the dust created when you cut or sand wood. Dust masks are inexpensive (a couple of bucks) and can be found at hardware stores, home centers, woodworking stores, and even some supermarkets.

> ✔ **Respirators:** Respirators not only filter out dust, but also trap fumes that are released when you work with finishes that have volatile organic compounds (VOCs). The level of protection from VOCs varies depending on the particular model of respirator. Check out the specifications before you buy. Respirators cost between about $20 and $50 and can be found at both home centers and woodworking suppliers.

Where's Mr. Clean When You Need Him? Keeping Your Shop in Ship-Shape

The cleanliness of your shop is as important as how you work within it. Knowing how to deal with potential problems such as dust and fumes makes you a safer woodworker and allows you to spend more time and energy actually working with wood rather than working on cleaning your shop.

Taming dust

One of the biggest disadvantages of working with wood is the enormous amount of dust that you produce. You can't avoid creating it, but you can contain it. In fact, one of the best investments you can make in your shop is a good dust collection system. There are three machines to consider, and I detail them here.

Wet/dry vacuum

A wet/dry vacuum is great for sucking dust off portable tools like sanders, routers, and plate jointers and for cleaning the floors when you're done working. For general cleaning, such as the floors, any old wet/dry vac will do, but if you want to catch the dust off the portable tools in your shop you need to get a vacuum that has a fine filter. Unfortunately, wet/dry vacuums with decent filtering cost a lot more then basic ones do. In fact, the least expensive one with decent filtering that I've found is around $130.

If you already own a wet/dry vac but it doesn't have a fine particle filter, you can buy an after-market filter that attaches to most wet/dry vacs. Check out a woodworker supply company to see if it has one that fits on your brand of wet/dry vac. They cost around $30.

Dust collector

A dust collector is one of the most important tools in your shop because it can reduce the mess of woodworking and make your shop a much safer place to work. A dust collector (see Figure 3-1) collects dust created by the large machines in your shop. Dust collectors are essentially large vacuums that connect to your power tools with a hose. A properly sized collector can be used to suck up the dust from several machines at once.

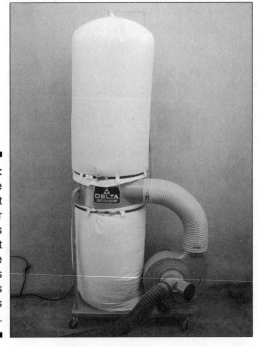

Figure 3-1:
A single stage dust collector captures the dust from large machines such as table saws and jointers.

There are two basic kinds of dust collectors:

  ✔ A single stage dust collector draws both dust and wood chips into the same bag

  ✔ A two-stage collector separates the larger chips of wood from the dust

Single stage models are the most popular and run from around $150 up to around $400. Because two-stage collectors are used for central dust collection (all the machines in the shop are attached to it), they cost a bit more, usually around $500 and up. For most amateur woodworkers, though, a single stage dust collector is more than adequate.

You can get a "separator" that attaches to a metal garbage can and is positioned inline between your tool and your single stage dust collector. This allows the large pieces of sawdust to drop into the garbage can while the finer dust particles continue on to the dust collector. The advantage to this is that you don't need to empty the dust collector's bag as often, and it reduces the wear on the motor by keeping the large pieces out of the dust collector. This is an inexpensive (around $30) way to turn your single stage collector into a two-stage collector. Most woodworking supply companies offer inline separators.

Single stage collectors come in three sizes: 1, 1½, and 2 horsepower. Each size collects different amounts of dust based on the amount of air that they draw, which is calculated in cubic feet per minute (CFM). The higher the CFM rating, the more power the system has. As a general rule, if you want to collect dust from a table saw, you need about 350 CFM. Figure 3-2 shows the CFM requirements of common woodworking machines.

Figure 3-2: CFM requirements for common woodworking machines.

Tool	CFM Requirement
Bandsaw	300
Drill Press	200
Jointer	350
12 inch Planer	400
Table Saw	350

Air cleaner

An air cleaner (see Figure 3-3) is a must. Dust collectors and wet/dry vacs contain the larger dust particles, but an air cleaner filters your shop's air (down to 1 micron in many cases) so that you can breathe after you're done cutting.

Figure 3-3:
An air
cleaner
helps you
breathe
easier in
the shop.

An air cleaner should be used in conjunction with either a wet/dry vac or dust collector because the air cleaner catches only the fine airborne particles and not the larger sawdust.

Dealing with fumes and ventilation

If you're going to do any finishing (see Chapters 17 and 18) in your shop, then you need to plan how you're going to get the fumes out of your space. The accumulation of volatile organic compounds (VOCs) from oil-based finishes is a health- and safety-hazard that must be dealt with. The easiest solution is to open a window or door and let the fresh air in. However, the potential disadvantage to this approach with slow drying finishes is that dust particles can collect on the tacky finish and become nearly impossible to remove, giving your finish a rough texture.

The solutions to this problem are:

- Use a fast-drying finish (see Chapter 18 for details)
- Use water-based instead of oil-based finishes

✔ Create a finishing room with proper ventilation

This room should include fans and air exchangers to remove the bad air and replace it with clean air. Remember that you need to remove more than dust particles; you also need to remove fumes, and the only way to do that is to bring fresh air into the room.

As an added precaution against VOCs, always wear an appropriate respirator when you work (see the section, "Breathing protection," earlier in the chapter for details).

What? No maid?: Tips for keeping your shop tidy

Yeah, it's a bummer that you don't have someone to clean up after you (if you do, could you send him over here when he's done? I have a huge mess to deal with).

After a long, tiring day of woodworking, you'll be tempted to just leave your shop without taking the time to straighten things up a bit. I strongly advise against this strategy for two reasons:

✔ It's not safe.

✔ Nothing is more depressing than walking into a dirty shop in the morning and having to clean up before you can actually get any work done.

Before you leave your shop for the day, take a few minutes and sweep the floors, put away your tools, and generally straighten everything up. You'll be glad you did the next time you want to work in your shop. Better yet, keep your shop clean throughout the day. Here are some tips:

✔ **Put away your tools when you're done using them.** This is especially important if you have a small shop, because clutter can get in the way and cause you to use a tool incorrectly, increasing the likelihood of having an accident.

✔ **Sweep the floors when you're done using a tool.** By sweeping up the dust and wood chips as you create them (well, not right then. Wait until you turn off the saw), you'll take a lot less time at the end of the day to straighten up.

✔ **Close up items that give off VOCs tightly when you're done using them, and place solvent soaked rags in airtight metal containers.** Taking care of things right away prevents you from forgetting at the end of the day. Besides, you don't want to breathe those fumes all day long!

Taking Care with Bits and Blades: Basic Tool Safety

Dust and fumes aren't the only things you have to watch out for in your shop. Your tools themselves present unique safety hazards and require specific precautions. I won't go into detail in this section on every tool's safety specifications (check your owner's manual for that information), but I give you the safety lowdown on two of the most popular and powerful tools: the table saw and the router.

Table saw

This is the tool you're likely to use the most in your shop (check out Chapter 7 for more on the table saw). The table saw is designed with a stationary blade into which you feed wood. This setup can pose several problems, but if you follow the advice in the following list you can minimize any headaches:

- **Always use a push stick and feed the wood into the blade gently.** As you push the wood into the spinning blade, your hand can slip off the wood and toward (if not into) the blade. For plans to make a push stick check out Chapter 8.

- **Don't make any sudden changes in feed rate; otherwise, you open the door for kickback.** Kickback occurs when the blade grabs the wood and sends it flying back at you. This is how most injuries associated with table saws occur. Kickback happens so suddenly that you have no time to react. I once had a board fly up off the saw and hit me in the shoulder. I was black and blue for weeks. The best way to avoid kickback is to feed the wood gently and stand slightly off to the side as you feed the wood into the blade.

- **Always use a clean, sharp blade when you cut.** A dull or dirty blade forces you to feed the wood with more pressure, which increases the likelihood that your hand will slip from the board and into the blade. It also increases the possibility of kickback.

- **Make sure the saw's fence is parallel to the blade.** If it's not parallel then the wood could get bound up as you feed it, increasing the likelihood of kickback.

- **Use a featherboard when cutting small or thin wood, because these types of wood are more likely to kick back at you.** A featherboard is simply a piece of wood or plastic with long flexible fingers that are positioned to hold the wood against the fence or table. (Check out Chapter 8 for plans for making a featherboard.)

✔ **Never remove the blade guards from your saw.** Guards are an essential part of the saw and increase its safety considerably.

✔ **Always attach a gauge block to the fence when you cut using the miter gauge (see Chapter 7).** A *gauge block* is simply a board attached to the saw's fence that you use to set the length of the board when you crosscut. This keeps the wood you feed into the saw from binding between the blade and fence.

Router

The router (for more about the router, see Chapter 6) has a bit that spins anywhere from 15,000 to 25,000 rpm. If you accidentally touch the bit on something it can do some real damage. Here are some safety tips to keep in mind:

✔ **Don't lift the router base from the wood until the bit has completely stopped.** This keeps you from accidentally bumping the bit on something.

✔ **Keep the bit away from the wood when you turn it on.** The force of the spinning bit may cause you to lose control of the router and gouge your work.

✔ **Make sure the bit is secure.** When you load the bit into the router, leave a small gap ($\frac{1}{16}$ of an inch or so) between the end of the bit's shaft and the bottom of the *collet chuck* (the place where you put the bit in the router). This allows the bit to be held straight and securely and facilitates the release of the bit. Tighten the collet so the bit is firmly set.

✔ **Move the router in the correct direction.** The bit spins clockwise (when seen from above the router). In order to keep the bit from "climbing" out of the wood, you need to move with the bit rotating into the wood (more in this in Chapter 6). In other words, when making a cut on the edge of a board, cut on the right side of the board and push the router away from you or face the board and move the router to the right as you cut.

✔ **Periodically retighten the bit in the collet if you make a lot of cuts.** Sometimes the bit loosens, so it's important to check that it hasn't done so and correct it if it has.

✔ **Be especially careful when using large bits.** It's harder to control the router with a large bit.

✔ **When routering out a lot of material, make several smaller passes rather than one large one.** It takes more time, but you get a better cut and it's much safer.

Part II
Tool Time: Selecting and Setting Up Your Equipment

The 5th Wave   By Rich Tennant

"I'll tell you where your tape measure is if you promise to be more careful where you put your wood glue."

In this part . . .

Without tools, you can't work with wood. It doesn't matter if you end up using hand tools or power tools, small tools or large machines, all that really matters is that you use the best tools for the job and know how to use them safely. To get you started on the right foot, Chapter 4 helps you determine your goals and tool needs. Chapter 5 introduces you to hand tools, and Chapter 6 gives you the lowdown on portable power tools. Chapter 7 digs into large stationary power tools. And, finally, Chapter 8 takes a look at the various workshop setups you may have.

Chapter 4

Gearing Up: Choosing Tools That Are Right for You

If you want to work with wood, you need some tools. The number and type of tools that you need depends on your working style, budget, and the particular kind of woodworking you want to do. In this chapter you determine what your work style is and figure out what tools you need to start out — and eventually move forward — in this hobby.

Figuring Out Your Work Style

The question of work style has a lot to do with the type and number of tools that you end up needing (and wanting). For example, if you have very little space to work in and/or noise is an issue (if you live in an apartment in the city, for example), then you may want to use hand tools almost exclusively. You won't be the fastest woodworker around, but you'll have the pleasure of creating something entirely by hand.

If you're like most woodworkers, you'll end up with a few large machines, some smaller power tools, and some hand tools, especially if you have access to a decent space — a basement or garage, for example (Chapter 8 goes into detail about different types of workshop spaces and can help you figure out what tools will fit). Your budget (which I talk more about in the next section) and the style of furniture you plan on making influence which tools you buy.

For example, if you're making traditional Windsor chairs, your tool needs are different than if you intend to make Craftsman style bookcases. Your best bet is to find out what tools you need for your style before you start shopping. Take a look at some project plans that you might want to make and see what tools are recommended for that project (Chapter 21 has some resources for project plans).

Determining How Much to Spend

The variety of tools you buy is almost always limited by the amount of money that you can spend. So the bottom line is, "How much do you have?" (I'll wait here while you count your pennies.) Wait; maybe it's better to look at this from another angle. How about the question, "What does it cost to set up a basic woodworking shop?" This section tells you which tools are the most important to get right off the bat and what tools you can add as you go.

Woodworking is not all about the tools (as much as some longtime woodworkers prefer to think otherwise). Your skills and imagination make great woodworking projects; tools can only take you so far. Don't get swept up into the belief that you need a particular tool in order to do or make something. There are almost as many ways to do something (make a joint or glue up a tabletop, for instance), as there are woodworkers. Sometimes having limitations on your tools causes you to re-think the problem and come up with unique solutions.

Tooling up: Finding tools reviews

As you start looking around for tools for your shop, the sheer number of options may overwhelm you. There are tons of makers of each tool that you need for your shop, so choosing the right one may be difficult (especially because you can't take a bunch home to try out first). So read some tool reviews. Most major woodworking magazines have tool reviews (I list the magazines in Chapter 21). I highly recommend that you subscribe to these magazines before you start buying tools (or at least before you've fully outfitted your shop). The writers of the reviews have taken the time to try each machine that they review and often give you a rundown on the pros and cons.

If you can get on the Internet, you can check out a magazine's Web site, which often contains reviews. Or do a search on Google (the Internet search engine at www.google.com). Type in the tool you want to know about by using the keywords **tool review**. You'll likely get dozens of Web pages to check out.

Resist the temptation to go out and buy a tool just because it's shiny and new. Think long and hard about what that tool can do for you and whether you can do that same thing with a tool you already have. Some tools, such as those I list in the "Revealing really useful extras" section later in this chapter, aren't necessary but *can* speed up the process of woodworking and make a job easier. For some people, the benefits of ease and speed outweigh the monetary cost, whereas for others, money is scarcer than time and energy. Only you (oh, and probably your spouse) can decide what tool is "necessary" for you.

Starting out: Just the basics

So what does a basic woodworking tool setup look like? Well, it depends on many factors, but here's what I would buy if I were just starting out. (This list includes quite a few tools that you may already own if you've been doing any kind of home improvement projects.)

All the tools listed in the following three sections are covered in detail in Chapters 5, 6, and 7. I give only a short description of these tools in this chapter.

- **Backsaw:** Some people have a lot of handsaws, but the one that gets used most is the backsaw. A good backsaw gives you years (heck, decades) of service and makes detailed cuts quickly and easily. Pulling this guy out is often faster than setting up your table saw. Expect to pay between $30 and $60 for a good one — a cheap price to pay for such a useful tool.

- **Carpenter's framing square:** A carpenter's framing square is an inexpensive ($10 to $20) tool that helps make the process of squaring up cabinets and other right angle (90 degree) joints quick and easy.

- **Chisels:** Even if you don't think you'll be working without power, a set of four chisels will help you to clean up joints, and you'll find quite a few uses that you never thought of (no, please don't open your paint and stain cans with a chisel!). Expect to spend around $50 for a basic set.

- **Circular saw:** A circular saw is a must if you work in sheet stock (plywood, MDF, and so on — for more information on sheet stock, see Chapter 2). Throw your sheet on a couple of sawhorses (see later bullet about this) and cut it down before you drag it into your shop. (Heck, I do this before I even take the wood completely off my truck.) Your back will thank you. It's worth every penny of the $50 or so.

- **Clamps:** You can never have too many clamps, because without enough clamps, assembling your projects becomes much more difficult. Get a variety of sizes. Plan on spending a couple hundred dollars for your first round of clamps.

✔ **Hammer:** Chances are that you already have a good hammer, but if you don't, go get one. While you're at it, get a wooden mallet too. You'll use it all the time with your chisels (please don't use the metal hammer on the chisels). Expect to pay $25 to $50 for both.

✔ **Hand drill:** By "hand drill" I don't mean one of the "crank by hand" numbers; I mean a basic power drill. If you can afford it, get one with a ½-inch *chuck* (the part that holds the drill bit). A ½-inch drill costs between $50 and $75.

✔ **Jigsaw:** For curves on a budget, a jigsaw does quite a bit for you. Even if you do end up with a scroll saw or band saw down the line, you'll still find yourself reaching for a jigsaw for some things. Consider it $50 or so well spent.

✔ **Jointer:** I went a long time before I bought a decent jointer and all I can say is: Don't wait as long as I did. A good jointer is a necessity if you want to work with less-than-perfect wood (this covers all solid wood) or if you want to edge-glue boards (tabletops, for instance). A decent 6-inch jointer runs about $500.

✔ **Marking knife or gauge:** These are much more accurate than a pencil and they don't cost very much — usually between $10 and $20.

✔ **Plunge router:** As you begin woodworking, you'll find that a router is one of your more versatile tools, and a decent plunge router makes life a lot easier. A 1½ horsepower router is plenty powerful enough for most applications. Name brand routers run about $150 to $200.

✔ **Random orbit sander:** A random orbit sander can be used for a lot of things, and if you don't have any other sanders, this one will do the trick for a while. A good random orbit sander can be purchased for under $100.

✔ **Sawhorses:** Sawhorses are portable stands that have a ton of uses around the shop. You can use them to hold large sheet goods while you cut them with a circular saw. You can put a piece of plywood over them and use this setup as an assembly or finishing table. You can use sawhorses as in-feed and out-feed supports for your table saw (assuming they are at the same height as your table saw). I highly recommend that you get at least two.

✔ **Table saw:** If I could have only one large machine, the table saw would be my pick. This is the most versatile tool in the shop. You can *rip* (cut with the grain) or *crosscut* (cut across the grain) wood, make dados, rabbets, tenons and other joints (Chapter 10), and with a little imagination create non-linear shapes such as coved moldings and tapered legs. You can find many table saws on the market from simple tabletop saws ($300) to basic contractor models ($500 to $800) to full-blown cabinet saws (big bucks), so your budget dictates which category you're in. At the very least, look for a saw with a cast-iron table and wings (a basic contractor model will do).

✔ **Tape measure:** A regular metal tape measure ($10) is fine for most applications, but I also like to have a combination square ($15) and a carpenter's wooden ruler ($10) for more accurate measuring. (For more on measuring, check out Chapter 5.)

✔ **Thickness planer:** A 12-inch thickness planer is useful for dimensioning boards and cleaning up rough faces on boards. You have a lot of choices, because nearly every tool manufacturer makes a planer. Expect to pay around $300 for one.

✔ **Wet/dry vacuum:** In Chapter 3, I talk about the importance of dust collection for health and safety. Although I really believe that a good dust collector is necessary (especially if you have a table saw, thickness planer, or jointer), you can wait a little while to buy one if you get the right wet/dry vac. Good wet/dry vacs start at about $130.

✔ **Workbench:** You need a large flat surface to work on. You don't have to buy one of the expensive handmade workbenches, but you do need something solid and flat. Most people start with a homemade table with a large plywood top. If you do this, make sure the top is two layers thick and the base very solid. You can make your own workbench for around $150 in wood and a couple weekends of your time.

That's a pretty long list and, by my count, adds up to close to $2,500. Of course, you don't have to spend this all at once. In fact, if you buy used tools, you won't need to spend this much at all. I recommend that you go slowly in building your tools selection.

Advancing up: Adding more tools

As you get more involved in woodworking, the tools in the following list are nice to add to your collection:

✔ **Air cleaner:** The fine airborne dust created while woodworking is as much of a problem as the big chunks, so an air filter (cleaner) is a great complement to a dust collector. Air cleaners start around $200.

✔ **Band saw:** A band saw is a great addition to a shop when you want to do curved cuts (chair parts, for example), create thinner stock from thick boards (such as veneer), rip or crosscut wood, or make a variety of joints. A 14-inch band saw costs around $500.

✔ **Belt sander:** A belt sander is useful for sanding flat surfaces such as tabletops. The advantage of a belt sander over an orbital sander is that it takes off wood more quickly. This can also be a disadvantage, so you need to use one with care. Belt sanders cost around $100.

✔ **Clamps:** You can never have too many clamps. I recommend that, after you do a few projects, you re-assess your clamp situation because you'll have a better understanding of how many and what type of clamps you need. Choose the clamps you wished you had had when you assembled your projects.

✔ **Compound miter saw:** I really like miter saws. They make crosscuts quick, easy, and accurate. But honestly, this isn't an essential saw (that's why it's in this list instead of the "essentials" list). You can perform all the cuts that this saw can do on either a table saw or a band saw, only not as easily. Miter saws start at about $200 and go up from there.

✔ **Drill press:** A drill press is used to drill holes at precise angles and depths. This is a very useful tool for drilling holes for joints, hardware, and shelf supports. You can also get a mortising attachment for a drill press to make mortises much faster and negate the need for a dedicated benchtop mortiser (see next section). Drill presses run from about $200 for a tabletop model to $500 or more for a floor stand model.

✔ **Dust collector:** I debated whether to put this tool in the "essentials" section, but didn't because a wet/dry vacuum can get you by until you can afford a dust collector. A dust collector starts around $200 and goes up from there.

✔ **Router:** Get a 3 horsepower model with a router table; a powerful router fitted into a router table serves many uses. This is such a versatile item that you may just want to get one right away if you plan to create a lot of furniture with moldings or other decorative profiles. You can make a router table for around $150 in parts, and the 3 horsepower router costs between $200 and $300.

Going all out: When the sky's the limit

So you have tons of money and you just want to go for it? These are some things I'd add.

✔ **Air compressor and air nailer:** For cabinet-making (carcasses, check out Chapter 13), an air nailer is a luxury you may not want to live without. For just a few hundred dollars, you can get a pancake compressor and nailer combination set that really speeds things up.

✔ **Benchtop mortiser:** For me this is one of the more useful and most used tools in my shop, but then I make a lot of mortises. In fact, I can still feel the blisters on my hand from the 104 mortises I made by hand for an Arts and Crafts desk that I made for my wife (before I bought this machine). If you don't make a lot of mortise-and-tenon joints, this isn't a tool you need. A benchtop mortiser costs around $250.

✔ **Clamps:** Yes, even more clamps. Repeat after me: *You can never have too many clamps.* Remember, clamps help you put things together, and without enough, assembling a project is more difficult.

- ✔ **Lathe:** A lathe is a machine that spins a piece of wood so that you can make it round. Lathes run around $500. If you want to make early American chairs with turned legs or bowls, a lathe might be higher up on your list than this.

- ✔ **Oscillating spindle sander:** A spindle sander has a spindle of sandpaper that oscillates up and down as it spins. This keeps the sandpaper clear longer. These machines are great for sanding curved parts before you assemble them. If you make a lot of furniture with curves, this tool is indispensable. You can find decent oscillating spindle sanders for under $200.

- ✔ **Sanding station:** This unit has a belt and a disc sander. A sanding station is useful for sanding individual parts before they're assembled. This is almost a must-have if you make a lot of chairs. A sanding station can cost from several hundred dollars to well over a thousand, depending on the model and its features. For the most part, a $500 sander will work in a home shop.

The order in which you buy these tools depends largely on the type of work that you do. For example, because I make mostly Craftsman style furniture with mortise-and-tenon joinery (see Chapter 10 for more about mortise-and-tenon joints), a benchtop mortiser was very high on my list — even before a band saw, because I do very few radial cuts. On the other hand, if your taste runs more toward Early American furniture, you will find a lathe much more useful than a benchtop mortiser. Likewise, if you intend to make chairs or round tabletops, you definitely need to put a band saw high on your list. In fact, in this case, it would move onto the "essentials" list.

Revealing some really useful "extras"

After you have the basics covered, look for some tools and jigs (*jigs* are tool accessories; see Chapter 7 for some homemade jig plans) that can make life much easier and speed up the woodworking process.

You need to think very carefully about spending money on tools that you may not need, so in this section I help you weed through some of the "extras" that, in my opinion, are worth the expense. These are tools I find myself using almost every day.

- ✔ **Biscuit joiner:** A biscuit (plate) joiner is used to cut holes for *biscuits* (oval-shaped pieces of wood that fit into a slot to add strength to a joint) and makes life a lot easier when making tabletops. Expect to pay between $100 and $200 for a good biscuit joiner. This tool may be way higher up on the list for some woodworkers, especially if you want to do a lot of edge-to-edge (Chapter 10) gluing.

- ✔ **Panel cutter:** A panel cutter allows you to cut wide sheets on a table saw. This jig can be made in a couple hours, and I guarantee that you'll use it a lot if you end up making cabinets, dressers, bookcases, or anything with a large carcass. Check out Chapter 8 for plans for making the panel cutter.

✔ **Pocket hole jig:** A pocket hole jig is a great tool if you make a lot of *face frames* (structure added to the front of dressers and cabinets, for example). A good, sturdy pocket hole jig costs about $100.

✔ **Rolling tables:** I'm putting rolling tables on the "extras" list, but after you have a few around, you'll wonder why you waited so long to get them. Rolling tables should be set up to be the same height as your table saw so that moving around large stock is much easier. You don't need to buy a rolling table, because you can make a much better one in just a few hours. Check out Chapter 21 for some resources for rolling table plans.

✔ **Sliding crosscut table:** The sliding crosscut table is a more sophisticated version of the panel cutter, and it can cost a lot more. If you want to get the most out of your table saw and regularly need to cut long boards that are more than 12 inches wide (the maximum width that a sliding compound miter saw can cut), then a sliding crosscut table is a very handy thing. This table attaches to your table saw much like the panel cutter, only it slides smoothly and is designed to hold large pieces of wood. These tables cost around $300.

✔ **Tenoning jig:** If you end up making furniture that requires mortise-and-tenon joints (tables and chairs, for example), a tenoning jig is definitely an asset. You can make one out of plywood (check out Chapter 20 for some project plan resources), or you can buy a heavy-duty cast-iron one for around $100.

Chapter 5

Getting a Handle on Hand Tools

• •

• •

*W*oodworkers love power tools, but some projects require muscle and a well-made hand tool instead. In this chapter, I discuss familiar hand tools such as saws, clamps, and rulers. I also introduce some tools you may not yet be familiar with, such as marking gauges, chisels, and planes. You get a chance to see how these tools work and where they're best suited. With just a few well-chosen hand tools, you can do an almost unlimited number of woodworking tasks.

Measuring and Marking Your Wood

Accurately measuring the wood that you cut is essential to creating a piece of furniture that fits together properly. Unfortunately, it's incredibly easy to make mistakes when measuring. I can't even count the number of times I was in a hurry or just not paying attention and made simple measuring mistakes that I didn't notice until I tried to fit everything together. In this section, I try to save you the aggravation of having to re-cut wood by explaining step-by-step how to measure and mark your wood for optimal accuracy. Just don't try to shortcut this process (like I've been known to do) and you'll be fine.

Getting your measurements down pat with a measuring tape

A measuring tape is essential when marking long pieces of wood. Because most woodworking is done with boards 10 feet long or less, you really don't need a measuring tape any longer than that. I recommend 12-foot tapes because they're light and small.

When you first pulled a tape measure, you probably noticed that the hook on the end moved a little bit. This isn't a fault of the tape; rather, it allows you to get accurate measurements regardless of whether you measure the inside or outside of a board. Take a look at how this works in Figure 5-1. When you clip the hook over the board, the hook moves out its width so that the measurement is from the inside of the hook (where the edge of the board is — the photo on the left in Figure 5-1 shows this). When you measure from the inside of something (a drawer, for instance), the hook moves in its width, so that you are measuring from the outside of the hook (this is shown in the photo on the right in Figure 5-1).

When you measure on the inside (as shown in Figure 5-1), you also need to add in the width of the tape measure to get your measurement. Its size is written on the back of the tape measure.

Figure 5-1:
How to measure the outside of something (left); how to measure the inside of something (right).

Going the ruler route

Using a tape measure can be a hassle when you have only a short length to measure. In this case, a ruler is handy. Rulers come in many sizes — from 6 inches to several feet. I recommend using good metal (not brass, though, which is too soft) rulers in the shortest length necessary to make your mark. I find that I use my 12-inch and 24-inch rulers the most (see Figure 5-2). Some people swear by a 6-inch ruler, so try a few out and see what you like.

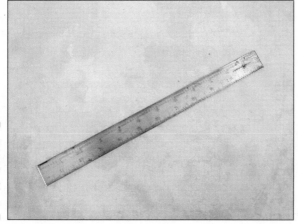

Figure 5-2:
Rulers come
in many
different
lengths.

When looking for a ruler, get one that has easy-to-read markings and $\frac{1}{16}$-inch markers on one side and $\frac{1}{32}$- or $\frac{1}{64}$-inch markers on the other. This way when you need to take measurements that are to the $\frac{1}{16}$ of an inch, you can easily see where you're marking. If your ruler has $\frac{1}{32}$- or $\frac{1}{64}$-inch markings on both sides, you sometimes have trouble discerning where your mark is.

If the markings are tough to read, apply a little black shoe polish to the ruler and the wipe it off. The shoe polish fills the marks and adds contrast so that the marks are easier to see. If the ruler is rusted or dirty, you can use a fine-grade steel wool to polish the surface.

Opting for a folding ruler

A folding ruler (see Figure 5-3) is one of my favorite marking tools, because it provides the stiffness of a ruler and the length and ease of use of a tape measure. The biggest advantage of a folding ruler is that you can have a stiff 6-foot ruler that fits in your back pocket. (The only problem I have with them is that my daughter loves to play with them and they often disappear from my shop.)

Marking it straight with a straightedge

Straightedges (straight firm pieces of metal, plastic, or wood) are incredibly useful in the wood shop. You can use them

 ✔ To mark a long cut

 ✔ As a guide for cutting or routing

 ✔ To check a board for flatness (see Figure 5-4)

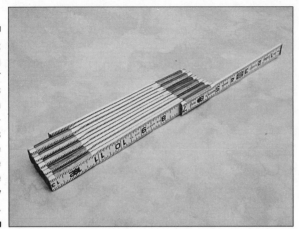

Figure 5-3:
A folding ruler combines the length and compactness of a tape measure with the stability of a ruler.

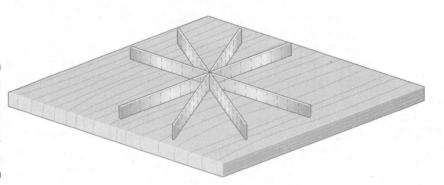

Figure 5-4:
Using a straightedge to check a board for flatness.

As with rulers, I suggest getting a couple straightedges in different lengths — a 24-inch and a 36-inch to start with. If you intend to use one as a guide for long cuts in plywood, a 96-inch (8-foot) straightedge is nice to have. If you don't want to buy a straightedge, you can make one yourself. Just use your table saw to rip a piece of hardwood or plywood to 4-inches wide or so, and then run the edges through your jointer to make them straight.

Measuring angles: Using squares

After you make the initial mark for length, you probably need to mark either a line across the board or one at another angle. This is where squares come in handy. You can choose from several types of squares:

✔ **Try square:** For a basic right angle mark, a try square (see Figure 5-5) is the way to go. A try square is a must if you crosscut boards by hand or if you want to check a corner for square (accurate 90-degree angle). Although squares with rosewood handles are beautiful, choose one with either metal or hard plastic if accuracy is important to you. You can get various length blades on them, but I've found that 12 inches is the most useful. Also, don't be afraid to return a square if it's not perfectly square (check out Figure 5-9 to see how to check a square for accuracy).

✔ **Miter square:** A miter square is set at an angle of 45 degrees on one side and 135 degrees on the other (see Figure 5-6). Miter squares are used to mark and check mitered (45 degree) corners. You won't necessarily need to buy a separate miter square because it will be part of a combination square (listed later in this section).

✔ **Sliding bevel square:** Also called the bevel gauge, this tool is useful for creating an infinite variety of angles (check out Figure 5-7). The bevel square is really handy if you have several cuts to make with the same angles (unless you're cutting 90-degree angles, in which case you only need your try square). If you need to set it at a precise angle, use a protractor to set that angle.

✔ **Combination square:** A combination square, as its name implies, is a square with more then one angle on it. With one of these, you can measure 90-, 45-, and 135-degree angles. Some hardcore square connoisseurs believe that a combination square is less than accurate, but I've never had a problem with one. So for me, a combination square serves double (and triple) duty as a try square and miter square. Heck, I also use it as a ruler. Check out Figure 5-8 and you can see that the combination square is designed to work for 90-degree, 45-degree, and 135-degree angles, but one of the best things a combination square can do is measure depth.

Combination squares come in several different sizes with a 12-inch being the most common. I find myself using this size the most with an 18-inch size second most.

If you're on a budget, you can get by with using a combination square instead of the try square and miter square. Keep in mind, however, that using a combination square in this manner may not be as accurate as using a try square or miter square.

✔ **Framing square:** For bigger projects, such as the carcass of a cabinet, an 18-inch square such as the combination square (see previous section) isn't long enough to mark a 90-degree angle. In this case, a framing square can do the trick. A framing square is a large L-shaped piece of metal used for construction work. The only drawback of a framing square is that it isn't as accurate as other squares because it's stamped out of sheet metal.

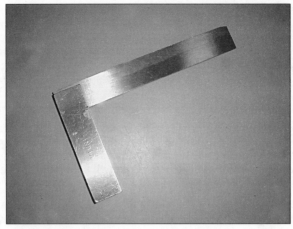

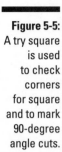

Figure 5-5:
A try square is used to check corners for square and to mark 90-degree angle cuts.

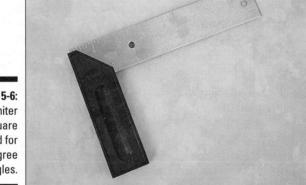

Figure 5-6:
The miter square is used for 45-degree angles.

Figure 5-7:
A bevel square (gauge) can be set at any angle.

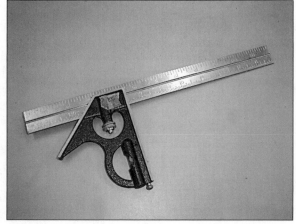

Figure 5-8:
A combi-
nation
square
is a great
all-around
square.

To test to see whether a square is, in fact, square, mark a line with it and turn the square over. If the line you marked matches the framing square, it's accurate. If not, you can see how far your square is off by measuring the distance of the gap at the top and dividing it in half. Check out Figure 5-9 to see how to do it.

Figure 5-9:
To check a
square for
accuracy,
mark a line
(left) and
turn the
square
around to
see whether
it lines up
(right).

Making the most out of marking tools

Measuring the board is only half the battle; you still have to mark it so that you can cut the wood. When you need to be within $\frac{1}{32}$ of an inch, using the wrong marking tool can throw off your measurement. Most people use a pen or pencil to mark the wood when they measure. This is handy, but you have another — better — way.

Pen or pencil: Handy, but less accurate

I'm sure you've seen the speedy woodworker on television pull a dull pencil from over his ear, mark a cut, and let the saw rip. I wonder whether you ever saw him try to put together all the pieces he cut this way? I doubt that everything fit just perfectly. The problem? The pencil lead (or pen ink) is wide enough so that you could be off as much as ⅟₃₂ or more of an inch without missing the mark.

If you insist on using a pencil or a pen to mark your measurements, make sure that that the writing implement has a very fine tip.

A case for accuracy: Marking knives and gauges

If you want to be truly accurate with your measurements then a marking knife or gauge is your best bet.

✔ A *marking knife* is simply a sharp knife. The advantage of a marking knife over a pencil or pen is that the blade is very thin and able to get right where you want it. Using a marking knife ensures that your mark is as close as possible to the spot that you measured.

✔ A *marking gauge* is designed to help you mark a set distance in from the edge of a board (see Figure 5-10). To use a marking gauge

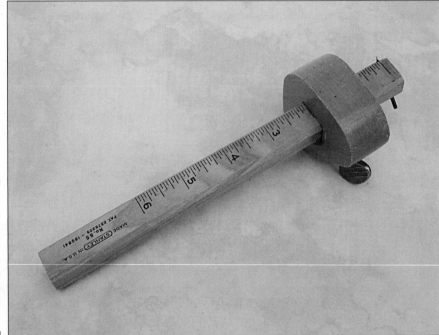

Figure 5-10:
Use a marking gauge to mark a distance from the edge of a board.

1. **Loosen the set screw and slide the stock (the piece of wood that slides) until the distance to the pin (the pointy thing) is the distance you want from the edge of the board.**

2. **Tighten the set screw.**

3. **Press the stock against the edge of the board, gently apply pressure to the pin, and slide it along the length of the board.**

   This gives you an accurate mark from which to cut your board.

Don't press too hard when you use a marking gauge; otherwise, you score a deep groove in the wood. If, for some reason (like marking a beveled edge), you don't cut the mark away, you're left with a groove in the wood that you need to sand out. A shallow mark is a lot easier in this regard than a deep one. Just mark the board deep enough so that you can see the cut and no deeper.

Using Saws: More Than One Way to Cut a Board

A saw is a saw, right? Wrong. As you look deeper into the issue, you can find quite a few options and, to the hardcore saw enthusiasts, very definite rules about what is used for what. With the hardcore saw people in mind, this section lays out the various handsaw options and lets you know the best one(s) to use for the type of cut you want to make.

Telling teeth patterns apart

The way the *teeth* (the part that does the cutting) of the saw are positioned directly affects how they cut through wood. You need to consider three things when thinking about saw teeth:

- ✔ **Set:** On most saws the teeth are bent out from the rest of the saw (the blade) so that the blade doesn't bind up as you saw. This is called the *set*. The overall width that is cut by the saw is called the *kerf*.

- ✔ **Shape:** *Rip* teeth are designed to cut the board along the grain, *crosscut* teeth are better suited for cutting against the grain, *fleam* (dual purpose) teeth can be used to cut with or against the grain cleanly, and *Japanese-style* teeth have a taller profile and steeper edges (deeper gullets).

- ✔ **Size:** Size covers both the number of teeth per inch (TPI) or points per inch (PPI) and the distance from the tip of the tooth to its base (which is called the *gullet*). As a general rule, ripsaws have fewer teeth per inch (as few as 5 TPI), whereas crosscut saws have more teeth per inch (as many as 12 TPI for a panel saw).

Distinguishing among saw designs

You base your decision about what saw to choose on the set, shape, and size of the tooth pattern (see the previous section for more on tooth patterns). Luckily, you don't have to think too much about this, because most saws are made with a specific purpose in mind. So instead of thinking "Well, I'm going to cut the board with the grain so I need a saw with rip teeth at 5 TPI," you can say "Get me the ripsaw." Now isn't that easier? This section gives an overview of some of the most common saw designs.

- **Backsaw:** A backsaw has fine teeth (from 12 to more than 20 TPI) and a stiffened back to keep the blade straight as you cut. The backsaw is used for fine-detailed cutting, such as making dovetails or tenons (see Chapter 9 for more about wood joints). Take a look at Figure 5-11 to see a backsaw.

- **Coping saw:** If you want to make curved cuts by hand, you need a coping saw. Coping saws (see Figure 5-12) have very thin blades with very fine teeth. A variation on the coping saw is the scroll saw, which has a deeper *reach* (space between the blade and the frame). Every shop should have either a coping or scroll saw.

- **Crosscut saw:** A crosscut saw's teeth are fine and sharp so that they can slice across the grain of the wood without tearing it up. The finely spaced teeth (around 8 TPI) have a sharp cutting edge on the front and a flat edge on the back.

- **Frame saw:** One of most ancient styles of handsaws, the framing saw is still unmatched in its versatility. What makes it so versatile is that you can change the blade quickly and easily and convert the saw from a ripsaw to a crosscut saw to a panel saw.

- **Japanese saw:** Japanese-style handsaws (see Figure 5-13) are the biggest new trend in woodworking saws. The blades on Japanese-style handsaws are shaped differently than those on Western-style saws. Japanese saws have more vertical teeth with deep gullets, and, unlike the Western ripsaws, crosscut saws, and panel saws, Japanese saws are designed to cut on the backward (pull) stroke while Western saws cut on the forward (push) stroke. They also have very finely spaced teeth and a very thin blade so they tend to produce a very clean cut.

- **Panel:** A panel saw is similar to the crosscut saw — with even finer crosscut teeth — but is designed to cut plywood quickly and cleanly. These saws have as many as 12 TPI.

  The panel saw is a great all-around saw, and fine if you can't afford both a ripsaw and a crosscut saw (it takes longer to rip a board than a dedicated ripsaw does, though).

- **Ripsaw:** A ripsaw has straight teeth and very few of them per inch — around 5 TPI. Because you cut with the grain using this saw and the wood fibers run parallel to your cut, the saw doesn't have to slice through the fibers. Instead, it chisels its way through them. The large teeth on ripsaws are designed to plow through the wood very quickly.

Figure 5-11:
A backsaw
has finely
spaced
teeth and
a rein-
forcing bar
designed
to stiffen
the blade.

Making the cut: Handling a handsaw

Follow these steps when using any handsaw:

1. **Hold the saw with your index finger pressed against the side of the handle to give yourself more control over the direction of the blade as you cut.**

2. **Position yourself so that your shoulder is directly behind the saw, and move your arm in a smooth motion as you cut.**

   This position creates less stress on your joints and gives you more power when cutting.

3. **Secure the workpiece with a clamp or vise or by pressing it down with your knees as you cut.**

   If the wood moves while you're cutting it you may hurt yourself, or at the very least, mess up the cut.

4. **Start out by guiding the cut with the thumb of your free hand and pulling lightly backwards until you get into the board ¼ inch or so.**

   Position the saw blade so that it is on the waste side (the part you want to cut off the board) of your mark; otherwise, you cut the board short by the thickness of the cut (the *kerf*).

5. **Support the part of the board that you're cutting off by holding it as you finish the cut, or the waste piece breaks off before you're done and tears the wood.**

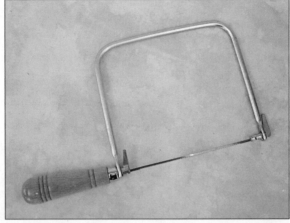

Figure 5-12:
A coping saw helps you cut curves by hand.

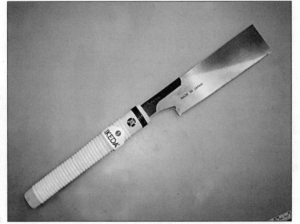

Figure 5-13:
Japanese saws have fine teeth and a narrow blade.

Using Planes: Smoothing the Old-Fashioned Way

Before modern machines were invented, folks used planes to flatten, smooth, and contour wood. Planes have a flat bottom and a sharp blade to cleanly slice off a thin portion of the wood as the plane is moved forward (see Figure 5-14).

Flying through different plane types

You have several different types of planes at your disposal, depending on the type of smoothing, flattening or contouring that you want to do. This section outlines the various plane types:

- **Bench:** A bench plane is the largest of the three basic plane designs. Bench planes have a long body (sole) with a blade that is set at an angle to skim off thin sheets of wood and leave a smooth finish. Bench planes come in several varieties. For example:

  - **Jack planes:** Useful for planing the face surfaces of boards flat, jack planes have a shorter body than a jointer plane, usually measuring around 15 inches.

  - **Jointer:** Also called *try planes,* jointers have very long bodies that create smooth, flat finishes in wood that may have high and low spots. Jointer planes are great for straightening up edges of boards or table legs.

  - **Smoothing planes:** The shortest of the bench planes, measuring around 7 to 9 inches, smoothing planes are designed to create a smooth finish and are often used after the jack plane for wide boards like tabletops. If you have only one bench plane, this is the one to get.

  All bench planes have handles for two hands.

- **Block:** Block planes are small planes designed to be held in one hand. These planes are often used to trim the end grain (the end of the board) of wood and come in two configurations: regular and low-angle.

  The regular block plane has a blade that is set at 20 degrees and the low angle block plane has a blade set at 12 degrees. Both work well on end grain, although the low-angle plane can be a little easier to use on harder woods because it's slicing at, well, a lower angle.

- **Plow:** A plow plane is used to create contours in wood, much like the modern router (Chapter 6). Most woodworkers — except those picky purists — prefer to make their contoured pieces with a router because using a router is much faster and takes less energy (a lot less energy — I'm sweating just thinking about it).

  If you can't use a router (if you live in apartment, for instance), then a plow plane might just be the ticket. You can find plow plane blades that have any number of interesting shapes to them.

- **Rabbet:** This plane is designed to clean up rabbet cuts (Chapter 10) and is able to get right to the edge of an inside corner because its blade goes all the way to the edge of the plane. Due to the rapid increase of power tools in the modern shop, rabbet planes aren't used very much.

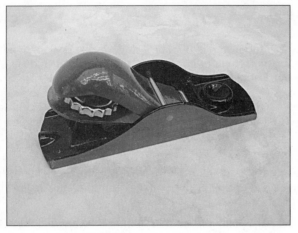

Figure 5-14:
A plane is designed to slice off thin layers of wood.

Getting a clean cut with your planes

Planes are great tools, but they do take some getting used to. Here are the basic steps for using one:

1. **Start with a very sharp blade.**

2. **Set the blade parallel with the sole (bottom) of the plane.**

3. **Stand facing the workpiece with your feet apart.**

4. **Push evenly with pressure applied to both the front and back of the plane, with slightly more pressure on the front.**

   Be careful not to release the pressure until you're finished with the stroke.

Following are some tips for planing edges, flat surfaces, and the end grain.

- ✔ To plane a narrow-edged board, use your front hand to stabilize the plane. Do this by applying pressure to the front of the plane with your thumb while using your fingers to guide the plane from underneath (place your fingers against the side of the board).

- ✔ To plane a surface flat, first plane on a diagonal (going from one corner to the opposite one), and then plane the other diagonal (this pass will be at a 90 degree angle to the first one). After these two passes, plane with the grain.

- ✔ To plane end grain, clamp a support block to the end of the board you want to plane and plane toward it. This keeps you from tearing out the end of the board as your plane finishes the cut.

Charging into Chisels

Chisels are mostly used to cut out joints such as mortises (check out Chapter 9 for more on mortises and other joints). As you'll discover in this section chisels can be used with or without mallets, depending on the type of chiseling you do.

Running down the basic types

Look out for several variations on the chisel and gouge. Each type has its own intended use, which I outline in the following list:

- **Butt:** If I could have only one type of chisel with me on a deserted island populated with woodworkers, the butt chisel would be it, because it's a comfortable size to work with and can do almost any cut. The butt chisel has a blade that's about 6 inches long with a bevel at the tip and along the sides (see Figure 5-15). Butt chisels can be used either by applying hand pressure as you work or by tapping (okay, sometimes pounding) with a wooden mallet.

  Butt chisels come in a variety of widths — from ¼ inch to more than an inch — and are generally sold as a set of four or five chisels.

- **Cranked paring chisel:** The cranked head-paring chisel is dimensionally the same as the paring chisel (see next bullet). The only difference between the two is that the cranked paring chisel has a handle that is angled up from the blade so that you can keep the blade flat to the work surface farther into the board.

- **Paring:** The paring chisel is very similar to the butt chisel. But paring chisels have a longer, wider blade with a shallower angle and longer handle. As a result of the longer blade they are also more fragile, so don't hit them with a mallet. Paring chisels are designed for hand pressure only. Paring chisels are great for trimming wood flush (dovetails, plugs, and such).

Using a chisel properly

As with hand planes (see the "Using Planes: Smoothing the Old-Fashioned Way" section earlier in this chapter), getting used to a chisel takes practice. The main thing to keep in mind when using a chisel is to apply firm, even pressure and to take off only a little bit of wood at a time. You can use a chisel in three ways:

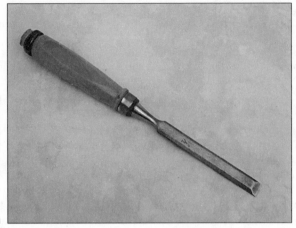

Figure 5-15:
Butt chisels are a must-have for the woodworker.

Paring horizontally

This is a hand-pressure-only procedure that includes the following steps:

1. **Lay the wood flat on your workbench and clamp it securely in place.**

2. **Hold the handle of the chisel with your index finger extended toward the tip of the blade.**

3. **Use your other hand to hold the blade close to the tip (at about the end of the bevel).**

4. **Place your other fingers on the bottom of the blade. With this hand, apply pressure against the workpiece as you push the other hand.**

5. **Gently push the chisel across the workpiece.**

If you need to apply more force to the chisel, lightly tap the top of the handle with the heel of your handle-holding hand while keeping your other hand in its original position.

Paring vertically

Use this technique when you want to trim a little wood off vertically. Vertical paring is especially useful for taking the very edge off a board or cleaning up a mortise joint (Chapter 9 has more on wood joints). Follow these steps to pare vertically:

1. **Hold the handle firmly with your thumb placed across the end of the handle.**

2. **Grip the blade with the thumb and index finger of your other hand.**

3. **Place the palm of the second hand on the workpiece to guide the blade.**

4. **Lean into the blade with your chest and apply even pressure as you slice off a thin slice of wood.**

Using a mallet

Sometimes you want to gouge out a lot of wood with your chisel. In this case, you want to use a butt chisel and a mallet. For example, this technique is useful for clearing wood for a mortise joint. Follow these steps when using a mallet:

1. **Hold the chisel firmly, with your fingers and thumb clear of the end of the handle.**

2. **Place the chisel firmly against the workpiece with the flat side of the chisel against the outside mark for the area you want to chisel out.**

3. **Use a wooden mallet (no hammers, please) and start by gently tapping the chisel squarely on the end of the handle.**

   You may not need to use more force than this, but if you do, tap a little harder.

   If you find yourself really pounding the chisel with your mallet, stop and take some time to sharpen your chisel — forcing the chisel into the wood shouldn't take very much pressure. The next section talks more about sharpening your chisel.

Choosing and Using Sharpening Stones

If you're going to use hand planes or chisels, you're going to need to sharpen them. Yeah, you can take them to a professional, but then you spend all your time driving back and forth (even if it's only a few blocks) because chisels need to be sharpened often. This makes it hard to get any woodworking done. The good news is that sharpening hand planes and chisels isn't very difficult and doesn't take very much time after you get the hang of it.

A dull chisel can be dangerous because without a sharp edge you need to apply extra force in order to slice the wood (in this case you're actually tearing the wood, not slicing it). With this extra force, you're more likely to slip and either cut yourself or damage the wood.

Determining which type works best for you

In order to sharpen your chisel you need a sharpening stone (an abrasive stone). Many types of stones are available, so the first step is finding the right one for your needs. Check out this list of the most common stones:

✔ **Diamond stone:** A diamond stone looks enticing. I mean, what's stronger than a diamond, right? Yeah, well a diamond stone works great for flattening worn oil or water stones, but don't use one on a chisel or plane blade. You won't need one of these for a very long time, so skip it for now.

✔ **Oil stone:** This is the old standby sharpening stone; effective and relatively inexpensive. You cover the surface with oil when you sharpen (hence the name *oil* stone), but unfortunately, oil tends to get on your clothes and/or your workpiece. I have a few oil stones that sit and never get used. Oil stones come in three grades: coarse, medium, and fine.

✔ **Slip stones:** Slip stones are used for sharpening carving tools that don't have a flat edge. You won't need one of these unless you want to do decorative carving (in which case you also need some carving chisels).

✔ **Water stone:** "Water instead of oil?" Oh yeah, this is what I like. "How much for this one?" "What? $100?" "Now where'd I put my oil?" That was my first encounter with a water stone. Yeah, they use water instead of oil. This is a good (no, *great*) thing. No more oil-soaked clothes! No more oily blotches on my wood! No more oily smell contaminating my shop! On second thought, maybe that price wasn't so bad after all; I could go a few weeks without eating. Luckily, I don't need to go without food to afford a water stone these days. Man-made stones have come on the market and they are very reasonably priced ($25 to $30). You can get water stones in a variety of grades (extra coarse through extra fine).

Start with a man-made water stone. Get a combination one. Choose a medium/fine one if you don't let your blades get too dull and, additionally, a coarse/medium one if you wait a little longer before sharpening. This works for your chisels and planes and doesn't cost you an arm and a leg.

Understanding basic sharpening techniques

After you have a couple of sharpening stones (see previous section), then you can start the process of putting an edge on your chisels and plane blades, which is pretty simple. Here are the basics steps to sharpening a chisel or plane blade:

1. **Wet the stone down, following the manufacturer's instructions.**

2. **Hold the handle of your chisel with the bevel side face down and your index finger pointing to the tip of the blade.**

3. **Place two or three fingers of your other hand on the blade close to the tip.**

4. **Put the blade onto the stone (coarse or medium grade, depending on how dull the chisel is) at a low angle so that the beginning of the bevel is touching the stone and the tip is not.**

5. **Gently tilt the blade so that the tip touches the stone.**

   You should feel the entire bevel sit flat on the stone. This keeps the angle of the bevel accurate. You don't want to accidentally change this angle when you sharpen.

6. **Keeping this angle steady, gently move the blade around the stone.**

   The exact pattern of movement is a very personal thing. I go in figure eights. Do what feels good for you but remember to work evenly over the entire stone; otherwise, you wear a groove in the stone over time.

7. **Work until you have a reasonably sharp chisel. Then move on to a finer grade stone.**

8. **Move progressively from coarse to fine stone until your chisel is sharp.**

9. **Turn the chisel over and flatten the backside of the blade by laying it flat on the stone and moving it sideways.**

   This removes the *burr* (sharp metal lip on the back of the blade) that you built up while you sharpened the front of the blade. (You can feel the burr by sliding your thumb across the back of the blade.)

Sharpening is really a pretty simple procedure but may take a while if your blade is really dull.

If you wait too long to sharpen your blades or if you mess up the angle or chip the tip of the blade then you either have to use an extra-coarse stone or a grinder to even up the tip of the blade. If you don't want to have to do this, follow these precautions:

✔ Keep your chisels away from people who might use them as pry-bars.

✔ Don't wait too long to sharpen your chisels. Sharpen them immediately when they start tearing the wood rather than slicing it.

✔ Be careful when you chisel so that you don't take the squareness off the edge; the edge should be at a right angle to the side of the blade. You can check this by using a try square (see the "Measuring angles: Using squares" section earlier in this chapter for more information).

Hammers and Mallets

This section introduces hammers, mauls, and mallets. Most likely you already have a metal claw hammer. This tool is great for driving and pulling nails, but it doesn't substitute for a maul or a mallet.

Handling hammers

Hammers come in many varieties — from small finish hammers with lightweight wooden handles to large framing hammers with titanium heads and shafts. They also range widely in price. A basic wooden handled hammer can run around $10, and a high-tech titanium hammer is close to $200.

Don't go nuts here. Get a basic 14- or 15-ounce hammer with a wooden handle and you're set for most applications. You can spend your money on much cooler things than a high-tech hammer (Chapter 4 has tons of cool tools).

When you use a hammer to drive a nail, don't be a wimp. Use a committed swinging motion from your elbow and hit the nail with the center of the hammer's face. Tapping with a hammer is okay for the first stroke in order to get the nail set, but it doesn't work for driving a nail. Also, swinging the hammer from your wrist is less accurate and often results in missing the nail (and hitting your thumb — ouch!).

Managing mauls and mallets

Hammers are great for driving nails, but they're not suited for hitting other tools or wood. In these instances, use either a maul or mallet.

Mauls are traditionally made of wood and have a very large head as compared to regular hammers (see Figure 5-16). Mauls are basically large wooden mallets that are used to drive chisels. Mallets, on the other hand, are made from rubber or plastic and are mostly used to tap joints into place, although many people use them on chisels too.

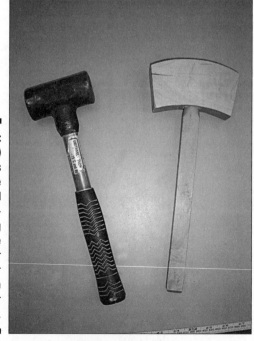

Figure 5-16: Mallets (left) and mauls (right) are essential for wood-working because a regular hammer can ruin tools or wood.

Diving into Drivers

Like hammers (see the previous section), screwdrivers are tools you probably already have lying around your house. And if you're like me, you keep losing them. What's the deal with that? Socks and screwdrivers must be part of some larger conspiracy. Anyway, I digress. Screwdrivers come in three varieties: slotted, Phillips, and square-drive. This section briefly outlines each type.

Each of the following types of screwdrivers comes with different lengths of handles. Short handles allow you to get into tight spaces, whereas longer handles give you more leverage as you screw. Also, the size of the tip of the screwdriver is designed to work with different size screws. Make sure you use the right size for the job; otherwise, you may strip out the head of the screw.

- **Phillips:** These are the "+" looking slots, which are the preferred screwdrivers for woodworking because the driver tends to stay in the slot and you're less likely to strip them out. Just make sure that you use the right size driver for the screw; otherwise, the screw head gets stripped.

- **Slotted:** This is the most common slot design. I avoid slotted screwdrivers when possible because they tend to slip off the screw and gouge the wood. An added nuisance is that this screwdriver makes it easy to strip out the head (ruin the slot) on the screws, and then you're stuck unscrewing the screw (watch out that you don't strip going this way too) and putting a new one in. Can you tell that I just love these screwdrivers? They are handy for opening paint cans, though.

- **Square:** The newest type of screwdriver is the square drive. Square drivers are, well, square, and they have a lot of torque. These drivers often come as driver bits for drills, because you can use a lot of force on them without stripping them out. If you're gong to make carcasses (like kitchen cabinets), a square drive driver is a nice addition to your toolbox.

Holding It All Together: Clamps

Clamps allow you to hold your joints together while the adhesive dries. Without enough or the right kind of clamps, gluing up a project can be a nightmare. Following is a list of commonly used clamps.

- **Bar:** A bar clamp consists of a long bar with an adjustable jaw attached to one end and a moveable jaw on the other end (see Figure 5-17). The advantage of a bar clamp is that you can adjust its size to fit the piece you're trying to glue. Bar clamps come in a variety of sizes, from as short as 12 inches to more than 4 feet.

  Bar clamps are used to clamp everything from tabletops to carcasses to drawers to face frames. Get at least six to eight bar clamps in several sizes. Choose your sizes based upon the size of the wood you want to glue up. For example, if you intend to do tabletops that are 3 feet wide, get at least four clamps that can open 3½ to 4 feet wide. Bar clamps should constitute most of the clamps that you own.

✔ **C-clamps:** C-clamps are made from a "C" shaped piece of metal that has a screw through the jaw (see Figure 5-18). They come in sizes from just over an inch to around 12 inches. These are great clamps for smaller projects; keep at least four on hand (with 4- to 6-inch jaws).

✔ **Hand screw:** Hand screws are old-fashioned clamps made of wood (see Figure 5-19). You don't see many in modern wood shops, but they are one of the most useful (and used) clamps in my shop. Hand screws are great for clamping odd-angled pieces, and I use them instead of C-clamps because they're faster and easier to attach. I recommend that you try one out and see whether you can find some uses for one (or two). I bet you can.

✔ **Miter:** For mitered corners, a miter clamp is a luxury you shouldn't do without (I guess that makes it a *necessity* then). Miter clamps are great for making picture frames, but they can also be useful for face frames that have mitered corners. Don't put miter clamps high on your list of clamp purchases unless you intend to do a lot of mitered-corner work, though.

✔ **Web:** If you end up wanting to glue some odd-shaped projects — octagonal picture frames for instance — then a web clamp is a good investment. Web clamps are made of nylon webbing that loops through a ratcheting housing. To use one, just wrap it around the piece you want to glue and tighten the webbing. The only trick to using a web clamp is to make sure that you don't distort the workpiece as you tighten.

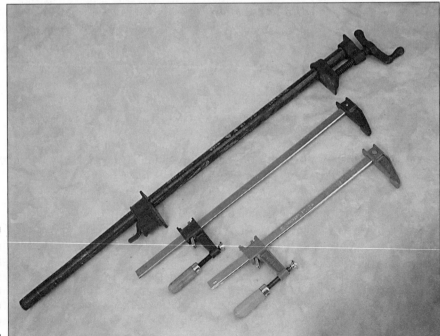

Figure 5-17:
Bar clamps
come in
various
shapes
and sizes.

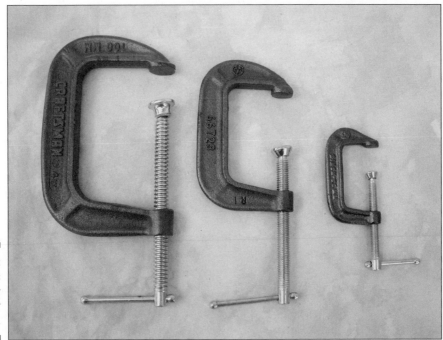

Figure 5-18:
C-clamps
are handy
for smaller
projects.

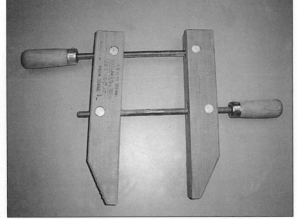

Figure 5-19:
Hand
screws
are often
over-
looked in
the modern
wood shop.

Chapter 6

Peeking at Portable Power Tools

. . . .

. . . .

*M*ost woodworkers think of the big stationary machines (see Chapter 7) as the "go to" tools for the majority of woodworking, but portable power tools are just as useful. Every decent woodworking shop needs a few select portable power tools. In this chapter, I introduce you to the most common portable power tools and show you what to look for when choosing the ones for your shop. In addition, I share some practical tips to help you get the most out of each tool.

To Cord or Not to Cord: The Pros and Cons of Cordless Tools

When you look for portable power tools, you find that many of the most popular tools are available either with cords or without. So which should you use? With the exception of cordless drills, I'm not a fan of cordless tools. I recommend that, unless your woodworking shop doesn't have electricity, you get a corded tool, because cordless tools don't have nearly the amount of power that their corded counterparts possess — and they're more expensive.

On the other hand, if you intend to use these tools in places where a cord might be clumsy or dangerous, then by all means go for battery power. Many of the cordless tools currently on the market are plenty powerful enough for most woodworking tasks, and they'll only get more powerful as new models enter the market.

If you intend to use a battery-operated tool for extended periods of time, invest in a back-up battery so that you can have one charging while you use the other.

Sizing Up Saws

Portable saws are essential if you work with large sheets of plywood or if you can't get the wood to your shop. Cutting the pieces into manageable sizes before you work with them makes life much easier.

Checking out circular saws

If you've done any home improvement projects, I'm willing to bet that you already own a circular saw (see Figure 6-1). If not, run out and get one — this saw is one of the most useful tools to have around. You may not use it every day, but sometimes moving the saw over the workpiece is preferable to moving the workpiece over the saw (as with a table saw).

Circular saws come in a variety of blade sizes — from 4½- to 10-inches — the most common is 7¼-inches. You can also get a variety of blades: for ripping or crosscutting solid wood, for cleanly cutting manufactured boards, and for cutting metal, plastic, ceramic, or masonry.

Circular saws also have a tilting mechanism that allows you to make cuts at any angle between 90 and 45 degrees to the face of the board.

The size of a circular saw's blade doesn't reflect the depth of cut that it can produce. This number is the total diameter of the blade. The actual depth that the blade can cut is less than half that number. For example, a 7¼-inch blade cuts up to 2⅜ inches deep. When you buy a circular saw, make sure that you get one large enough to cut through the largest boards that you intend to use.

Buying a circular saw

When you buy a circular saw, keep the following things in mind:

✔ Hold the saw and make sure that it feels comfortable in your hands. Each manufacturer deals with the handles and weight distribution differently, so one brand may feel more comfortable for you than another.

✔ Look for a saw with a decent exhaust port and dust bag. This way you can either use the dust bag or remove it and connect a wet/dry vacuum to the saw.

✔ Adjust the tilting mechanism to make sure that it moves smoothly. This will allow you to make angled cuts easily.

✔ Also, make sure that the blade guard moves smoothly so that moving the saw through the wood is as easy as possible. A sticky blade guard makes the saw both difficult to use and less safe.

✔ Get a saw with an automatic brake on it. This stops the blade from spinning almost immediately after you turn off the saw.

✔ Get a good carbide-tipped blade. Most saws come with inexpensive steel blades that wear out quickly. A carbide blade cuts better and lasts longer. You can find a carbide-tipped replacement blade for most circular saws at your local home center or hardware store.

Figure 6-1:
A circular saw is handy for straight cuts on large stock.

Using a circular saw

Circular saws are easy to use, but I've included some tips to make it even easier and safer for you:

✔ Never remove the blade guard or wedge it open when you cut. Doing so makes it much more likely that you'll get hurt when you cut.

✔ Wear eye, ear, and breathing protection (see Chapter 3 for more information). Circular saws are noisy and they throw a lot of dust and, very often, wood chips.

✔ Make sure that you have the board you're working on securely supported and clamped on sawhorses so that it doesn't move while you're cutting.

✔ Double-check that the area under your cut is clear of obstructions — you don't want to cut through the sawhorses or the table the wood is resting on.

✔ Use a sharp blade. Dull blades don't cut cleanly and need too much pressure to go through the wood. You're more likely to slip when using a dull blade.

✔ Let the saw do the work. Push slowly and evenly without very much pressure. If you have to apply a lot of pressure to get through the wood, replace the blade.

✔ Use the circular saw to make rough cuts on a large board and then make the final cuts on a table saw (Chapter 7). Circular saws don't make fine cuts as well as a table saw, and getting a straight line — even with a straightedge to guide you — is more difficult.

✔ Use a straightedge as a guide. Doing so helps you achieve the straightest cut you can.

Judging jigsaws

A jigsaw is a great way to cut curves if you don't feel like using your band saw — or if you don't have a band saw. Jigsaws (see Figure 6-2) have a thin, narrow blade that comes in a staggering variety of tooth patterns. You can find ones that cut with or against the grain, that provide speed or a fine finish, and that cut wood, plastic, metal, and ceramic.

Jigsaw blades are cheap. Get a variety so that you don't have to run to the store when you want to cut a board.

Figure 6-2:
A jigsaw
is useful
for cutting
curves.

Spying the specs of a jigsaw

Jigsaws come in two varieties:

✓ With a knob that rotates the blade as you cut

✓ Without a knob that rotates the blade as you cut

This knob is called a *scrolling knob.* It allows you to do finer radius cutting and to make curves without having to turn the entire body of the saw (I actually prefer turning the body of the saw as I make curved cuts in wood, so I go with jigsaws without scrolling knobs).

Take a look at this list before you go looking for a jigsaw of your own:

✓ **Dust port:** Look for a dust port that allows you to attach a wet/dry vacuum to it. Jigsaws don't produce quite as much dust as a circular saw but are messy enough that you should plan on collecting as much dust as possible. See Chapter 3 for a complete discussion of safety and cleanup in your wood shop.

- **Orbital option:** Some saws have an orbital option, which means the blade moves forward on the up stroke and back slightly on the down stroke. Most saws with this feature give you several orbital ranges from which to select. This is a handy feature that can speed up the time required to make a cut, but if you don't see yourself doing much jigsaw work, this may not be a feature that you need.

- **Scroll knob:** Scroll knobs are useful for cutting intricate curves and tight radiuses. A good scroll knob has a solid locking mechanism to keep the blade from moving sideways when you want to cut straight.

- **Variable speed selector:** Check out the variable speed selector (most jigsaws have one). They come in two varieties: with a dial on the handle, or with a trigger switch that varies the speed of the saw based upon your finger pressure (I prefer the latter). Some saws come with both, so be sure you know what you're getting before you buy. Variable speed is helpful when cutting certain types of materials. For example, use a low speed for plastic to keep from melting the material as you cut. If you're only cutting wood, this feature doesn't matter as much.

Getting the most out of the jigsaw

To get prime performance out of a jigsaw, here are some things to remember:

- Choose the best blade for the type of cut and material that you work with. This will save you a ton of frustration. Blade packages are clearly marked with the type of material and cut that they are designed for.

- Jigsaws cut on the up stroke, so the roughest part of the cut (called the *tear-out*) happens at the top. Put the good side of the wood facing down when you cut to keep it looking good.

- Be careful when crossing the grain on hardwoods, because the blade tends to follow the grain pattern and it may climb into the wood on the bottom. Avoid this by using a sharp blade and not applying excessive pressure as you cut curves.

- If you use a scroll knob on a saw, keep the pressure directly behind the blade as you scroll. This often means applying pressure from the side while you turn the scroll knob.

- When you cut tight radiuses, cut the waste section into segments so that they fall off as you work. This keeps your blade from binding.

- Go slowly and let the saw do the work. A sharp blade that is properly chosen practically cuts the wood by itself. Don't fight the saw: If cutting takes too much work, your blade is dull or you're using the wrong blade for the job.

Rallying around the Router

Routers are fairly simple tools that feature a motor with a solid base and a *collet chuck* that holds the bit (see Figure 6-3). A router is one of the most versatile tools in the shop. In fact, if you had a sufficient variety of bits, a solid table with a decent fence, and some imagination, a router could conceivably perform all the tasks necessary to turn a pile of wood into a piece of furniture.

In Chapter 4, I present some safety tips for the router. Be sure to read and follow these suggestions. A router is not only one of the most versatile tools in the shop, but also is one of the most dangerous.

Understanding router specifications

Consider three basic features when choosing a router:

- **Base configuration:** Routers come with both fixed and plunge bases. Plunge bases allow you to position the bit above the wood when you start the router and then use a lever to drop the bit into the wood. Plunge bases also have a spring that brings the bit back up out of the wood when you release the downward pressure. A fixed base, on the other hand, isn't adjustable this way but it's much lighter, so I prefer this type for times when plunging into the wood isn't necessary. Some routers have interchangeable plunge and fixed bases, such as the router shown in Figure 6-3.

- **Collet chuck size:** The *collet chuck* is the mechanism that holds the bit in place. In order for the bit to be held securely, it needs to fit snugly in the collet. Because of this, a router has a collet chuck that holds only one or two (if you use an adapter) sizes of bits (unlike the drill, which I talk about in the "Detailing drills" section later in this chapter). Most routers will come with ¼-inch and ½-inch collet chucks or with a ½-inch collet chuck with an adapter that will also hold ¼-inch bits.

    For your first router (and probably your second and third), choose a router with a ⅜-inch collet chuck.

- **Motor size:** Routers are available with motors that run from under 1 horsepower to 3½ horsepower. But bigger is not necessarily better — depending on what you're trying to accomplish. If you want to use a router for hand-held trimming and shaping, I recommend a 1½ to 2 horsepower router, which gives you plenty of power and yet is still light enough to maneuver by hand. If you want to get a router table and do some serious shaping, then a 2½ to 3½ horsepower model better suits your needs.

Figure 6-3: Routers come with a fixed base (left) or a plunge base or both (right, with plunge base attached).

Some other features that make for a good router include:

- **An exhaust port that allows you to hook up a wet/dry vacuum.** Many routers have ports that don't look like other tools' exhaust ports, because the bit protrudes through the base of the machine. An exhaust port for this type of router is actually an accessory that attaches to the base and catches the chips as they leave the bit.

- **An easy-to-read depth scale with a mechanism that adjusts smoothly and easily.** Getting an exact depth of cut is essential for most router operations. This is no place to skimp on a router (unfortunately, some manufacturers do skimp here).

- **An easy-to-reach on/off switch.** This may seem like a no-brainer, but guess what? I have a router that requires me to take one hand off the machine to turn it on and off. This is unsafe and always makes me nervous. You should have both hands on your router at all times when using one, so find a router with an easy-access switch.

Biting into bits

The router bit does all the work shaping the wood. When you buy a router, you're going to need to buy a few (or a lot of) bits.

You can get router bits made out of three materials:

- ✔ **Carbide-tipped:** Get the carbide-tipped bits. They cut better and last longer. Sure, they're more expensive, but they last much longer than the other types of bits.

- ✔ **High-speed steel:** If you only want to use the bit for one project and money is an issue, then a high-speed steel bit does the trick. Be warned, though, that if you intend to use the bit for more than a few cuts, the savings disappears quickly because you have to replace the high-speed steel bit much — and I mean a lot — sooner.

- ✔ **Pressed-steel:** Of course, you could just go with the cheapest bit on the market, but they don't last very long and they often don't cut nearly as cleanly as the other types of bits.

Following is a short list of the types of bits you can find and what they do (Figure 6-4 shows the cut that each bit makes):

- ✔ **Chamfer bit:** This is like a round over bit except the bit's cutter creates a 45-degree angle rather than a rounded profile.

- ✔ **Cove bit:** A cove bit is used to create a scalloped edge on a board. This bit has a pilot tip that rolls against the edge of the board to guide the bit while the cutter creates the profile.

- ✔ **Dovetail bit:** The dovetail bit is used for cutting dovetail joints (see Chapter 9).

- ✔ **Flush trimming bit:** Like the straight bit, the flush trimming bit has a straight edge. Instead of a flat bottom, however, it has a pilot tip that rolls against the material, allowing you to trim a laminate top or other protruding edge to be flush with the rest of the edge's surface.

- ✔ **Rabbet bit:** This bit has a cutter that extends beyond the pilot bearing on the tip, so that as you run the bit against the edge of the board, the cutter digs into it, cutting a rabbet (Chapter 9 has more information about rabbets).

- ✔ **Round over bit:** This bit rounds over the edge of a board as the pilot tip runs along the edge of the board.

- ✔ **Straight bit:** This bit has a straight-sided cutting area with a flat bottom. Use a straight bit to cut dados and mortises (see Chapter 9) or to clear material for inlays and veneering.

- ✔ **Veining bit.** A veining bit is like a narrow straight bit, but instead of a flat bottom, it has a rounded bottom. This bit is used for creating decorative grooves.

- ✔ **V-groove bit.** This bit cuts grooves in the shape of a "V" and is used for decorative carving, lettering, and engraving.

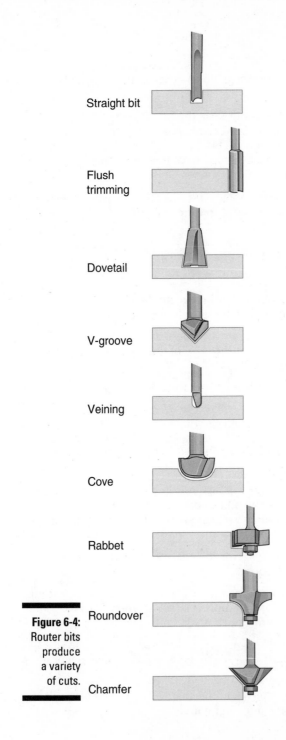

Straight bit

Flush trimming

Dovetail

V-groove

Veining

Cove

Rabbet

Roundover

Chamfer

Figure 6-4:
Router bits produce a variety of cuts.

Getting into routering

Because so many varieties of bits exist, you can use your router many different ways.

The following list touches on some tips to help you with basic tasks. If you want more detailed ideas for using routers, you don't need to look far for many great books on the subject (do a search on www.amazon.com using the keyword **router** to see what I mean).

✔ When routing the outer edge of a board, route the edge with the end grain first and the side grain last. This keeps from creating *tear-out* (splitting the wood at the end of the board).

✔ To cut straight lines within the field of the board, use a straightedge. Clamp a solid, straight board to the workpiece.

✔ If you want to route a groove in the narrow edge of the board, clamp supporting boards to both faces so as to increase the surface area that your router slides along as you cut.

Getting the Skinny on Sanders

I'm not sure you can find a woodworker anywhere that likes to sand (I know I haven't found one yet). Sanding is a messy, thankless job, but undoubtedly a necessary one. You don't ever end up with a smooth, blemish-free finish on your project without first sanding all the scratches, gouges, and uneven surfaces out of the wood before you apply stain or a top coat. This is the job of the sander. Unfortunately, because sanders can take a lot of wood off at a time, they can ruin your project before you know what happened.

Be very careful using a power sander and always finish your sanding by hand with a fine paper (more on this in Chapter 16).

Buying into belt sanders

The belt sander (see Figure 6-5) consists of a round loop of sandpaper stretched between two rollers and spun with a powerful motor. This is the most aggressive sander available and is designed to remove a lot of wood quickly. I try to avoid using this sander unless I have a lot of wood to remove (for instance, if you need to flatten up a tabletop after it's been glued up, but personally, I reach for a plane first).

Considering features

Belt sanders come with several features to consider. They include:

- ✔ **Belt size:** Size is the main thing to look at when you buy a belt sander. As a general guide, the wider the belt, the easier it is to keep the sander flat on the workpiece and the more expensive it is. A wider belt also takes off wood more quickly than a narrower belted model. Belt sizes range from 2⅜ inches wide by 16 inches long to 4 inches wide by 24 inches long. I prefer a sander with a 3-inch-wide belt that is around 21 inches long, which is a good balance between size and cost.

- ✔ **Dust port:** Make sure that the sander you're looking at has a decent dust port that can hook up to a wet/dry vacuum. Most sanders come with a dust bag, but these fill up way too quickly to be of any practical use.

- ✔ **Replaceable belt:** Check to see that the belt is easy to replace. Take the belt off and try putting it back on again. The process should be fast and easy.

- ✔ **Variable speed:** This is not a very important feature to me, but it's available on some models and some people like it. If you just plan on sanding unfinished solid wood, variable speed isn't necessary. But if you intend to sand heat-sensitive materials such as plastic laminate edging, maybe you should consider spending the extra money.

Getting the most out of the belt sander

If you want to use a belt sander, follow these tips and you'll minimize the damage that you can do to the wood.

- ✔ Practice using the belt sander on some scrap wood before you try to tackle a project that you care about. Getting accustomed to this type of sander and its aggressive tendencies takes time and practice.

- ✔ Keep the sander moving at all times. Work in long, even movements both front to back and sideways to avoid digging a trench in the wood.

- ✔ Always sand with the belt running in the same direction as the grain. This prevents you from putting deep scratches in the wood that are difficult to get out.

- ✔ Apply very little downward pressure as you sand. The weight of the sander is sufficient for most applications.

- ✔ Keep the bottom of the sander (called the *platen*) flat on the workpiece as you sand. Due to the force of the belt, when you move the sander, the front of it will want to lift.

Figure 6-5:
A belt sander can remove a ton of wood quickly.

Ogling orbital/Random orbit sanders

If a belt sander seems a bit risky to you or if you don't think you need such serious sanding power, then an orbital sander (also called a finishing sander) may be just the right solution.

An orbital sander, also called a *palm sander,* is designed to fit into the palm of your hand. Orbital sanders have a flat pad on the bottom where you attach sandpaper. The orbital sander moves the sandpaper in a circular motion. This can create circular scratches in the wood that are very difficult to remove. The best way to minimize this is to keep the sander moving at all times when you sand.

Because of their tendency to leave circular scratches, plain orbital sanders have largely been replaced by random orbit sanders (see Figure 6-6). The random orbit sander does what its name says — sands in a random circular pattern. This significantly reduces any difficult-to-deal-with scratches. I use this type of sander 99 percent of the time I sand.

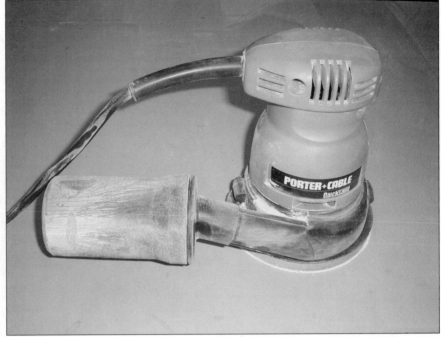

Figure 6-6:
A random orbit sander is less aggressive and easier to use than a belt sander.

Knowing what to look for

When considering a random orbit sander, keep these features in mind:

- ✔ **Dust collection:** Because random orbit sanders are fairly small, they don't have large dust collectors or dust ports. Look for an adapter that connects the small dust port to a wet/dry vacuum. I recommend getting one to reduce the volume of fine dust flying around your shop.

- ✔ **Motor speed:** This speed is listed in rpm's. Most random orbit sanders run around 25,000 rpm's, which is a good speed for woodworking projects.

- ✔ **Paper size:** You can find sanders with any number of size (measured in diameter because the pads are round) pads from 4 to 5½ inches. The larger the pad, the faster it sands; however, this feature doesn't matter much. The difference in speed isn't that great. I recommend that you choose the sander that feels best in your hand.

- ✔ **Sandpaper attachment mechanisms:** Random orbit sanders come with a round pad onto which you attach sandpaper. Some use paper with an adhesive backing, and others have a *hook and loop* (kind of like Velcro fasteners) system. I highly recommend the hook and loop system, which allows you to change paper more quickly, is less messy, and allows you to reuse the paper.

Using a random orbit sander

Although a random orbit sander is much less dangerous than a belt sander, you can still use some tips to make the process faster and easier:

- ✔ Start with a medium grit paper and progressively move up in grade until you get a fine finish.

- ✔ Keep the sander moving as you work. Even a random orbit sander can leave scratches and gouges if left in one place too long.

- ✔ Let the sander do the work. If you have to push down hard on the sander as you work, you need coarser sandpaper for the job.

- ✔ When your surface is smooth and scratch-free, finish the process with a little hand sanding (Chapter 16).

Detailing Drills

Most people already own a portable power drill. Nowadays, drills are used for more than boring a hole in a material. You can use them to drive screws and grind wood, metal, or plastic. In case you don't have a drill or are in need of a new one, this section can help you decide what to buy.

Figuring out drill features

Keep these key features in mind when choosing a power drill:

- ✔ **Chuck size.** This refers to the largest drill bit shank that you can fit in the drill. For most applications, a ⅜-inch size is sufficient, but if you want to get hardcore (if you can be hardcore with power drills) a ½-inch chuck size may be the ticket.

- ✔ **Hammer action.** Hammer action is great for drilling into cement, stone, or brick, because the drill moves the bit in and out as it spins, creating more force to get through tough materials. Hammer action is not necessary for woodworking.

- ✔ **Keyless chuck.** Most new drills have this feature, and in my opinion this is a good thing. With a keyless chuck (the *chuck,* by the way, is the part that holds the drill bit) you don't have to use a tool (called a *key*) to tighten and loosen the chuck. Just adjust it with your hand.

- ✔ **Reversibility.** Being able to adjust the rotation of the drill lets you not only drill and screw into the wood but also unscrew screws and extract a drill bit that may be stuck in the wood; as far as I'm concerned, this is an essential feature.

- **Secondary handle.** Unless you intend to drill through tough materials (not wood), you don't need a secondary handle.

- **Variable speed.** This is an essential feature for power drills. Being able to vary the speed allows you to drill into an almost unlimited variety of materials and to screw in screws without stripping them out.

Defining drill bits

Several types of drill bits exist, and each one has a use in the woodworking shop. The most common are as follows:

- **Bradpoint:** Bradpoint bits are similar to twist drill bits except they have a sharper point on the end and two points at the edge to keep from tearing out the edge of the hole. They are designed for woodworking, but I'm not convinced that they work any better than a sharp twist drill bit.

- **Forstner bit:** The forstner bit has a narrow shank with a large round cutter at the bottom. This bit is designed to drill large, flat-bottomed holes. You can even overlap holes. This is my preferred bit for drilling larger holes (more than 1 inch in diameter).

- **Spade bit:** This bit is flat rather than round and has a sharp tip on the end to keep it from moving sideways as you start the hole. Spade bits come in much larger sizes than twist or bradpoint bits, so they're good for drilling larger holes. The only drawback is that they don't cut the cleanest holes. If this is important to you, choose a forstner bit for the big holes.

- **Twist drill:** The standard drill bit, a twist drill has a pointed tip and flutes, which carry the scrap out as you drill. Twist drills come in sizes from $\frac{1}{16}$ inch to more than 1 inch.

Banking on Biscuit Joiners

A biscuit joiner (also called a plate joiner, see Figure 6-7) cuts a semi-circular slot on wood the perfect size for a biscuit (for more on biscuits check out Chapters 4 and 10). This tool is a recent invention and is great to have if you intend to use biscuits for some of your joints.

Most biscuit joiners have the same features — adjustable guide fence and exhaust port with dust bag, for instance. The main thing to look for is that the tool is easily adjustable and fits into your hand comfortably.

Biscuited joints are great for some things and not so great for others. Once I tried to use biscuits to substitute for mortise-and-tenon joints on table legs. I was in a hurry and needed another table for a party. The table seemed stable until it was slid across the floor. The joint broke loose and the leg bent in (one of these days I'll get around to fixing that table).

Figure 6-7:
A biscuit joiner is great tool for making certain types of joints.

Chapter 7

Introducing the Big Guns: Stationary Power Tools

In This Chapter

▶ Understanding stationary power tools

▶ Getting to know tool specifications

▶ Discovering stationary tool tips

Stationary power tools are staples of most woodworking shops; the number you have will vary, depending on the size of your workshop and budget. (Every shop will probably have at least one stationary tool — if not five or six.) Stationary tools make the process of woodworking faster, easier, and more fun. Cuts are cleaner and more accurate, tasks are quicker, and repeated cuts are a breeze. (Now if I could only find someone to run them for me I'd be all set, but then I wouldn't be doing *any* work at all.)

In this chapter, I introduce you to the most common stationary power tools available for the woodworker. I tell you what to look for when buying tools and go over some practical tips for using them most effectively.

Tuning In to the Table Saw

Of all the modern tools in a wood shop, the table saw is the most used. Countless table saw designs are available, from a basic tabletop version to a contractor's version to a full-blown cabinet saw. As a beginning woodworker, start out with a contractor saw. *Contractor saws* have a large cutting capacity (like the larger cabinet saw), but they have an open base so they're lighter and cost less than an enclosed base cabinet saw. Contractor saws run between $500 and $1000, depending on their features (Figure 7-1 shows a contractor saw).

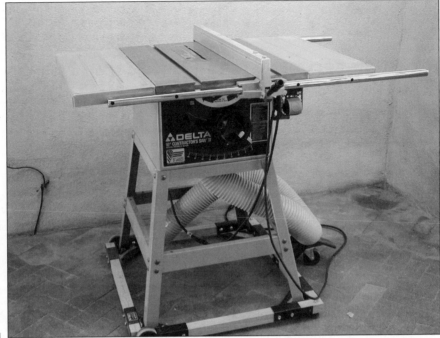

Figure 7-1:
A table
saw is a
wood-
working
essential.

Eyeing table saw specifications

A table saw is an essential tool that can be used for an almost unlimited number of woodworking tasks. Because this is such a versatile and common tool, you have tons of options when buying a saw. This section helps you figure out what features are most important to you.

✔ **Fence (rip fence):** The *fence* (the part that you slide the wood against when you feed it onto the saw) ranks up with the tabletop for its importance in achieving good, accurate cuts. The quality of the fence dictates the price of the saw, so your budget dictates how good your fence is. The main thing to look for in a fence is one parallel with the blade that adjusts smoothly and accurately. Most saws in the contractor category have decent (but not perfect) fences. Starting out with a less-than-perfect fence is okay because you can always add a better fence to your saw later on.

✔ **Left-tilt or right-tilt:** On a table saw, you can adjust the tilt of the blade in order to cut angles. In the past, the vast majority of saws (all except some of the most expensive ones) had blades that tilted to the right. Now you can get saws that tilt either right or left (but not both). The side of the tilt is a very personal thing. (I've actually seen arguments erupt over this issue.)

Some people prefer being able to measure the long side of an angled cut and want a right-tilt saw, although other people prefer the way a left-tilt saw tilts away from the fence so cutting narrow angled pieces is less dangerous. Only you can choose which is best for you. I recommend that unless you intend to do a ton of work that requires mitered cuts, you choose a right-tilt saw because you'll have more options when buying one (right-tilt saws are still more common).

✔ **Miter gauge:** Table saws come with a small t-shaped tool called a miter gauge. The *miter gauge* fits into one of the two slots (called miter slots) machined into the tabletop and it guides wood that you feed through the saw. Most contractor saws come with a decent miter gauge (although not great — again, you need to buy a separate one if you want great). When deciding on a saw, put the miter gauge into the miter slot and try to wiggle it sideways. It should fit snuggly. If it wiggles much, move on to another saw.

✔ **Motor size:** Most contractor table saws have either a 1½ or 2 horsepower motor. Cabinet saws, on the other hand, generally have between 3 and 5 horsepower motors in them. For most applications, the 1½ or 2 horsepower motor on the contractor saw is powerful enough. The trick to getting the most out of the power you have is to feed the wood slowly and use a very sharp carbide-tipped blade.

✔ **Saw blade:** Most table saws have a 10-inch blade, but some of the most expensive cabinet saws have a 12-inch blade. Either works just fine on most tasks. More important than the blade size is the quality and finish of the blade itself. Just like with handsaws, numerous blade designs exist to ensure the best cut possible. You can get blades designed for ripping, crosscutting, both ripping and crosscutting (called a combination blade), cutting dados (see Chapter 10 for more information on dados), and blades specifically made for plywood, plastic laminates, and other man-made materials. I recommend that you start with a good combination blade and a stack dado blade (you'll need to buy the blades separately from the saw). You can add others as you get to know your needs.

Regardless of the blade you get, make sure yours is sharp and clean of pitch when you use it. (For details, see the sidebar "Keeping your saw blades clean.")

✔ **Tabletop:** The tabletop is the most important part of the table saw and needs to be absolutely flat in order to provide the most accurate cut. Most saws have a cast-iron table that has been milled to within 1/1000th of an inch for flatness. I've found that this figure can be deceiving and that you need to check the saw for flatness before you decide to keep it. I've seen some so far from flat that a decent cut is impossible to make. Choosing a saw from a major manufacturer reduces your chances of getting one that doesn't have a flat table (though it doesn't eliminate them).

Even though the tabletop is cast iron on most models, this section covers only about 24 inches of the entire table surface area. The rest of the table consists of wings that can be made of cast iron, molded steel, wood core plastic laminate, or other materials. The size and quality of these table wings (called extensions) dictate the overall price of the machine. I recommend that you start with a fairly basic one, because you can always add table extensions later on.

Keeping your saw blades clean

As your blades cut wood, they sometimes take on small amounts of sap and pitch (resins contained in the wood) from the wood. This stuff can build up over time and make your blades seem dull. Before having your blades sharpened or tossing them in the trash, give them a quick cleaning. You may be surprised how well they cut once the buildup is gone.

You'll find many different techniques and products available for cleaning saw blades, and no matter which you choose you should keep a few things in mind when cleaning your blades.

✔ Don't use files, paint scrapers, chisels, or other hard tools to remove pitch. These may damage the blade and make it dangerous when it spins in your saw.

✔ Read all the warnings on the cleaner you want to use. Some saw blade cleaners are toxic and some will damage certain types of blades (such as those with a Teflon coating on them).

✔ Check with the manufacturer of your saw blades to see what they recommend using to clean the blade. For example, Teflon-coated blades only need a mild soap and water solution coupled with a nonabrasive scrubber (like you use on your nonstick kitchen pots and pans), while other blades can handle a stronger cleaner.

With the large number of products on the market, you're sure to find one that works well for your saw blades. I highly recommend that you do some research (an Internet search using the keywords **saw blade cleaning**, for example) to find the best solution for you.

Using a table saw

You can rip and crosscut boards and cut an almost limitless variety of joints with a table saw. All it takes is some basic understanding of the process involved. This section introduces you to these basic tasks. (For more details on cutting wood joints check out Chapter 10.)

Ripping wood

Ripping wood involves cutting the board along the grain. This is the most common type of cut made with a table saw. The process is pretty simple and is one that you'll undoubtedly get very comfortable with. The basic steps include the following:

1. **Set the rip fence to the width that you want the board by using the ruler located on the front of the saw.**

   Secure it tightly.

2. **Set the depth of cut slightly higher than the thickness of the board (so that the carbide teeth are sticking up beyond the wood) using the depth adjustment handle located on the lower front of the saw cabinet.**

   Set the lock when you're done.

3. **Lay the board on the table against the rip fence, a couple of inches away from the front of the blade.**

4. **Turn on the saw.**

5. **Slowly feed the board into the blade while making sure that it stays in contact with the rip fence.**

6. **After the back end of the board is fully on the table, use push sticks (for more on push sticks, see Chapter 8) to guide the wood through the blade.**

   One push stick (in your right hand) feeds the board from behind, while the other (in your left hand) pushes the wood against the rip fence. (I have the push sticks in my hand when I start feeding the wood so that I can keep the board moving as I switch to using the sticks.)

7. **As the end of the wood is cut, keep pushing until it fully clears the blade.**

   I generally push the waste material (wood on the left side of the cut) off to the side as I move it past the blade. For long material, either ask someone to stand on the other side of the saw or provide a flat table the same height as the tabletop so that the wood doesn't fall off the back end of the saw.

8. **Turn off the saw.**

In no time flat, you'll become an expert at doing rip cuts on your table saw.

Crosscutting

Crosscutting involves cutting the wood across the grain. Because a board is generally longer than it is wide, feeding the wood against the rip fence causes it to twist away from the fence as it goes through the blade. So when cross-cutting wood on a table saw, use a miter gauge, a crosscut table, or a panel cutter (you can find plans to make a panel cutter in Chapter 8). Following is the basic procedure for making crosscuts using a miter gauge.

1. **With the saw turned off, measure your cut.**

   You can do this either by marking your board with a sharp pencil or marking gauge (Chapter 5 details this procedure) or by placing the board against the miter gauge and moving the board until it touches the edge of the blade.

   Use your ruler to measure from the left side of the board to the left edge of the blade. This is the length of your cut. The scrap goes on the right of the blade. Alternately, you can use the rip fence as a guide for length. Do this by attaching a short piece of wood to the rip fence so that it ends before the blade starts. Set the rip fence to the desired length minus the width of the board you attached to the fence. Position your board against the wood attached to the rip fence and supported by the miter gauge.

2. **Move the miter gauge with the board to cut away from the blade.**

3. **Turn on the saw.**

4. **Slowly move the miter gauge forward while holding the board firmly against it.**

5. **Move the board past the saw.**

6. **Turn off the saw.**

With these skills, you'll be a crosscutting pro in no time.

Joining the Jointer

The jointer is a great tool for squaring up the edges of a board. You can also use one to flatten the surface of a narrow board or to make rabbet cuts (Chapter 10 has more on rabbets — and not the floppy-eared kind). A jointer is a large tool that will take up quite a bit of room in your shop (see Figure 7-2), but if you intend to glue up any tabletops, you'll need one.

Digging into the details of a jointer

Jointers are common tools in woodworking shops, with quite a few products on the market. Keep the following specifications in mind when looking at which jointer to buy:

- **Base configuration:** Jointers come with an enclosed base or an open stand. Because the enclosed base doesn't cost that much more and it offers quite an improvement in noise level reduction and dust collection abilities, I recommend going this route if you can afford it. A closed base will cost about $50 more than an open-stand model.

- **Blade size:** Jointers come in both 6-inch and 8-inch sizes. This measurement describes the width of the blades. For most amateur woodworkers, a 6-inch jointer is sufficient. An 8-inch jointer is nice, but at almost twice the price, it's not worth the cost for most people.

  The only other consideration you have regarding blades is that they should be as easy as possible to change and adjust. Depending on the model of jointer that you buy, you will use either jackscrews or springs to do this. Both work, but I prefer jackscrews because I'm used to them. Whichever of these you end up with, after you get the hang of it you'll be able to adjust your blades without too many problems.

  When you buy a jointer, order an extra set of blades. They aren't that expensive. This way you'll have some on hand when you need them, and you won't be stuck waiting for blades or cutting with dull ones.

- **Fence:** Having a high enough *fence* (the metal piece that you slide the wood against) to support the wood as you feed it through the jointer — and being able to adjust it accurately — is essential if you want flat edges at the desired angle. A good fence system is easy to adjust (with positive stops at 45- and 90-degree angles so you can joint beveled edges), locks tight in place, stays flat and doesn't bend, and supports the wood as you feed it through the jointer. Look for the highest fence you can get that has an adjustment system that works smoothly. The major manufacturers of jointers all have their own way of adjusting fences. No particular one is significantly better than the other (contrary to what some woodworkers will tell you). Just choose the one that you like best.

- **Motor size:** For the most part, mid-level jointers have either a ¾ or 1 horsepower motor in them. A ¾ horsepower motor works okay, but if you can afford it, go for a 1 horsepower model, which is heartier and works better if you plan to use the jointer often.

- **Table:** Because the flatness of the final cut is directly related to the flatness of the table, this is a very important part of the jointer. You want your table (also called a bed) to be as flat as possible. Unfortunately, tables that aren't flat are common — even those from major manufacturers — so check the table before you buy the jointer.

The other consideration when you buy a jointer is the length of the table. Here I recommend the longest table you can get. Most 6-inch jointers have around a 46-inch table length. This is long enough to safely and accurately joint a board around eight feet long (twice the length of the table, although most manufacturers recommend a maximum length of 1.5 times as long as the table). An 8-inch jointer will have a considerably longer table (around 60 inches or so), so if you plan on jointing very long boards, an 8-inch jointer might be worth the (considerable) extra cost.

Figure 7-2:
The jointer is great for making square edges on a board.

Getting used to the jointer

Running wood through a jointer is easy: Just lay the wood flat on the table and firmly against the fence, turn on the machine, and run the wood through slowly and smoothly. The tricky part to using a jointer is getting it set up properly. I touch on this topic in Chapter 8.

Cutting Curves with the Band Saw

If you do any cutting that requires curves, you'll quickly tire of the slow inaccuracy of the jigsaw (see Chapter 6). In this case, a band saw is for you. A band saw has a long blade (around 8 feet for most 14-inch band saws) that is made into a big loop. This loop is fitted on the saw across two large wheels. The motor then turns these wheels, spinning the blade.

A band saw (see Figure 7-3) makes quick work of cutting curves and tenons, ripping and crosscutting wood, and slicing boards (called *resawing*) into veneers.

Figure 7-3:
The band saw is a useful tool for a variety of cutting tasks.

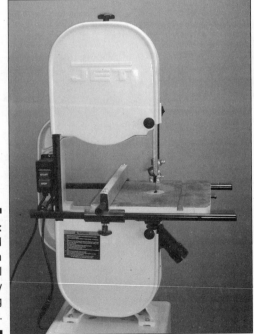

Getting into band saw features

Following are the main features of band saws and how they relate to the quality of the machine.

✔ **Blade:** With a band saw, you should be able to remove and replace blades quickly and easily, especially if you intend to do a variety of tasks with your saw. Not all band saws feature easy-to-take-on and -off blades, so read tool reviews to make sure the saw you like is user-friendly. Most woodworking magazines do tool reviews. Chapter 21 has a list of the most common magazines.

As with any saw, choosing the right blade makes the job easier, faster, and more accurate. Make sure you pick up a selection of blades when you buy your saw so that you'll be able to jump right into different projects. I suggest that you start with the following:

- **Standard tooth blade ⅛-inch wide with 14 TPI (teeth per inch):** This blade allows you to cut some pretty tight curves without binding. This tooth pattern cuts smoothly, but not very quickly.

- **Hook tooth blade ¼-inch wide with 6 TPI:** This blade is great for overall cutting — ripping, crosscutting, cutting joints, and so on. You'll still be able to make some curves with this, but not as tight as you can with the standard tooth blade.

- **Skip tooth blade ⅜-inch with 4 TPI:** This blade is good for general resawing. For more hardcore resawing or for resawing thinner stock, choose a wider blade — ½-inch or larger (make sure you know the widest blade that your saw will take before buying a super wide one).

✔ **Motor size:** 14-inch band saws have between ¾ and 1½ horsepower motors in them. Most common are 1 horsepower motors. As with any machine, the larger the motor, the more power the band saw has, but this factor should only be part of your decision when buying a saw.

✔ **Rip fence:** Many band saws come with a rip fence that allows you to rip board or do resawing accurately. If you intend to do any ripping or resawing, make sure that the saw you're considering comes with a fence or has one readily available. A good fence should be sturdy and lock securely in place (this seems obvious, but you'd be surprised how many fences don't lock).

✔ **Saw size:** This measurement is the basis for how a band saw is made and marketed. For the most part, home-workshop band saws have a 14-inch reach; professional models are 16 to 20 or more inches. What this measurement indicates is the distance from the saw blade to the arm that separates the wheels and allows the blade to run from one wheel to the other. This means that you can rip a board up to 14 inches (slightly less on some machines). Saws with a 14-inch reach run from around $300 to $900, depending on the manufacturer.

✔ **Table:** As with all stationary machines, the flatness of the table is a major consideration when choosing a band saw. And like the rest of the tools I describe in this chapter, flatness varies from manufacturer (and saw) to manufacturer (and saw). Be sure to check your tool when you get it to make sure that it's flat.

You should be able to secure the table and lock it in place across the range that the table will tilt (band saw tables tilt so that you can cut angles).

Making the band saw easier to use

Techniques for using a band saw vary, as do the tasks that you can use them for, but take a look at some general tips that can make the process easier:

✔ Make sure that your blade is installed and adjusted properly. This procedure will vary from brand to brand, so I can't go into detail here. Read your owner's manual and take some time getting accustomed to the process. Your saw needs to be adjusted periodically as you use it, so you'll become a master in no time.

✔ Use the fence for straight cuts whenever possible. The blade tends to wander a bit, so using a fence will give you a finer cut.

✔ For tight inside curves, cut relief cuts in the waste stock to within 1/32 inch of the cut line before you cut into the curve. This way, the waste will peel off as you go around the corners, minimizing the possibility of binding the blade.

✔ For tight outside curves, trim the waste off in sections as you round the corner. This involves starting at your cut mark and sawing away from it to the edge of the board, then coming back and doing another pass. This may seem like it takes more time, but it is actually faster in the long run.

✔ Take your time and listen to the motor as you cut. If it starts to bog down, ease off on the cut until it speeds up again.

✔ Turn off the saw before you back the wood out of a cut. If you don't, you could pull the blade out of alignment and off the wheels and cause it to spin out of control.

✔ If the blade breaks, shut off the saw and stand back. The blade tends to whip around until it stops.

✔ Keep your fingers away from the blade. I know this seems obvious, but when you're focused on the cut, you sometimes forget where your fingers are in relation to the blade.

✔ When resawing or ripping any narrow board, use a push stick to feed the wood into the saw (you can find out how to make push sticks in Chapter 8).

Making a Case for the Miter Saw

The miter saw (see Figure 7-4) is made for crosscutting wood. Miter saws are very useful and accurate (I love mine). They come in three varieties: regular, compound, and sliding compound. I discuss all three in more detail in the "Recognizing types of saws" section.

Recognizing types of saws

All three types of miter saws crosscut wood, but each one varies in the size of wood that it handles and the number of angles it cuts. Here's a rundown on these differences:

- **Compound miter saw:** This saw can cut angles on two planes. In other words, the saw not only rotates, but it also tilts, which is handy for cutting complex angles such as those on cove moldings.

- **Regular (conventional) miter saw:** This saw can cut angles from 90 degrees to 45 or 60 degrees off center. This is an inexpensive way to cut angles on a single plane.

- **Sliding compound miter saw:** This saw is pictured in Figure 7-4. It cuts compound angles just like the compound miter saw, but the motor and blade slide out from the back of the workpiece to accommodate a wider board (up to 12 inches in most cases). If you intend to crosscut wide boards, get this saw.

Managing miter saw features

You have a variety of features to consider when buying a miter saw, which I introduce in the following list.

- **Accuracy:** Accuracy is the one area that many woodworkers complain about regarding miter saws. Miter saws were originally developed for construction work, where absolute accuracy isn't as important as speed and ease of use. Some of the earlier miter saws didn't cut accurately enough for the most demanding woodworkers. But this is changing as more saws enter the marketplace and manufacturers try to meet the demands placed on them. I have a miter saw that is very accurate; the cuts I get using it are more accurate than those I can get by using my table saw and miter gauge.

  Read some reviews to see how the saw you're considering ranks in this area. A good place for tool reviews is in woodworking magazines (or their Web sites). Chapter 21 has a list of the most popular magazines.

- **Adjustability:** What you want to look for in adjustability is the ease with which the saw adjusts and the accuracy of the angle. Most decent saws have *positive stops* (the saw clicks into place) for the most common angles such as 90, 45, and 30 degrees. Even without the positive stops, the saw should lock tight at any angle.

- **Cutting capacity:** The cutting capacity of a miter saw depends on the size of the saw blade and whether you have a sliding compound saw.

  Miter saws come with 8-inch, 10-inch, or 12-inch blades. All three sizes will cut a board 3 inches to 3½ inches thick. They vary in how wide a board they can cut. The 8-inch blade will cut a board up to 5 inches wide, the 10-inch blade will cut a board up to 5½ inches wide, and the 12-inch blade will cut a board up to 8 inches wide.

  If you go with a sliding miter saw, you can cut 12-inch-wide boards because the motor and blade housing slides out.

- **Fence:** Because miter saws were developed for construction job site work, they don't come with the type of fence that most discerning woodworkers prefer (because the fence is the part of the saw that positions the wood so that you get an accurate cut). The fences on miter saws tend to be short and low. The only way to deal with this design deficit is to build your own saw fence (check out Chapters 19 and 21) or buy an extension fence (most woodworking supply stores will have some).

Figure 7-4:
Miter saws
crosscut
wood
accurately.

Using a miter saw

Miter saws are simple to use. Just put the wood up against the (rather short) fence, mark it, and cut. The only problem you typically encounter with this type of saw is that it needs to be adjusted properly to be truly accurate. Unfortunately, miter saws often don't come accurately adjusted, so you'll have to dig into your owner's manual and do the initial adjustment before you start cutting. And remember to check the saw periodically and readjust it when needed.

Read your owner's manual before you cut any important furniture parts and spend some time getting your saw adjusted as best you can. This process doesn't take very long and saves you tons of headaches later on.

Partying with the Planer

The planer (also called thickness planer) is designed to create boards with parallel faces (the wide part) and to allow you to get several boards to the same thickness (this is important for making tabletops). Figure 7-5 shows a thickness planer.

Figure 7-5: Planers allow you to quickly and easily create the thickness of wood you want.

A planer consists of a set of blades that cuts the top of the board as it's fed through the machine. On either side of the blade are rollers that press the board flat against the bed of the planer as they feed it through the machine. What you get is a board that is parallel on the top and bottom, but not necessarily flat. This is because as the rollers press the board against the planer bed, any twists or warps are temporarily flattened out. After the board comes out of the planer, it returns to its original twisted or warped shape (with perfectly parallel faces, though).

Perusing planer features

When looking to buy a planer, you should consider several features. I present the most important in the following list.

- **Cutter-head speed:** The speed at which the cutter spins and the rate at which the planer feeds the wood through determine how many cuts the blades can make over an inch. This often (but not always) translates to how the cut looks. The most popular 12-inch planers have cutter speeds between 8,000 and 10,000 rpm and they have two knives in the cutter-head.

- **Depth of cut indicator:** This helpful new feature consists of a gauge on the front of the planer that tells you how much you're cutting off in each pass. It helps keep you from cutting too much off in one pass and bogging down the machine.

- **Depth stop:** You need this feature if you have boards of different thicknesses that you want to plane down to the same thickness. A depth stop lets you select the lowest thickness that you can plane to. For example, say you have four boards of varying thicknesses that you want to plane down to ¾ inch. Just set the depth gauge at ¾ inch and then plane each board starting at the thickness of that board. Keep running passes with that board until you hit the depth stop. Move on to the next board.

  Without this feature, you have to find the thickest board and start planing it until you reach the thickness of the next thickest board. Then plane those two down until you get to the thickness of the next thickest board, and so on until you get to the final thickness that you want.

- **Knives:** Some planers come with single edge knives (blades) and others have reversible knives. The advantage with the reversible knives is that you can, well, reverse them when they become dull. This effectively doubles the life of each set of blades. You can't resharpen planer knives on most planers, so when they get dull you have to buy new ones.

  Another consideration regarding knives is how easy it is to change them. I have an older model planer, and I spend an hour each time I have to replace and adjust the knives. Newer models are much easier to use in this regard. All the major brands of planers have decent systems, including a magnetic knife adjustment tool, that make changing and adjusting the knives fairly easy. Check the major woodworking magazines for up-to-date tool reviews. (You can find a list of these magazines in Chapter 21.)

✔ **Planer size:** Planers are sized according to the width of the board that they'll plane. For most amateur woodworkers, a 12-inch planer is the way to go (planers in this category actually cut between 12- and 13-inch-wide boards, depending on the manufacturer). These planers are small — often fitting on a benchtop — and are reasonably inexpensive. You can expect to pay around $300 to $400 for a good one.

✔ **Tables:** Older model planers, such as mine, have in-feed and out-feed tables that aren't attached to the planer (instead they're just clipped to it). Avoid getting one like this, because it requires an absolutely flat bench for the planer to sit on. Most newer planers have in-feed and out-feed tables that are permanently attached to the planer and hinge up and down. This helpful feature does a better job at feeding the wood through the machine. With a good in-feed and out-feed table, snipe (see the "Ending snipe: Getting the best cut with your planer" section for an explanation of snipe) is reduced.

Look for long in-feed and out-feed tables that are sturdy and flat.

Ending snipe: Getting the best cut with your planer

Planers are very useful tools and make *thicknessing* (getting wood to the thickness you want) any wood much faster and easier than the old-fashioned way (by hand planing).

The only real problem with planers is that they sometimes create an uneven surface at the front and back ends of the board, called snipe. *Snipe* refers to a slight indentation cut into the board as it enters and leaves the planer. Snipe happens when only one roller is pressing down on the board while the knives cut it. As a result, the board may not be totally flat against the table, and because the knife mechanism is part of the two rollers, the knife may sit slightly lower than when both rollers are touching the wood.

Older planers had a lot of problems with snipe, but newer designs have helped in this regard. Still, snipe happens. The good news is that you can minimize snipe by the way you plane your boards. Here are some suggestions:

✔ **Plane extra-long boards and cut out the snipe when you're done planing.** Sure, this is a waste of wood, but if you plan your projects, you're prepared when you lose a piece of your project to snipe. Add about 3 inches to each end of the board and cut the ends off to get to the finished length of your material.

✔ **Use sacrificial boards.** Take some scrap material of the same thickness as the board you're working on and feed it into the planer right before and right after the good board goes through. Make sure the sacrificial boards are touching your important board as they travel through the planer one after the other so that the sacrificial board gets any snipe.

✓ **Create a train of boards.** In this approach, you link all the boards you want to plane in succession (assuming you want to plane more than one board to the same thickness), leaving no gaps between them as you feed the boards through. You can still use a sacrificial board at the beginning and end of your train. You do need another person to grab the boards as they come out of the planer. You could also place a long table, set at the same height as your planer tables, up against the out-feed table to catch the boards as they come out of the planer.

Detailing the Drill Press

A drill press consists of a motor attached to a stand with a lever that allows you to bring the bit up and down toward the table. On most drill presses, the table is also adjustable so that you can fit wood of varying heights between the bit and table.

A drill press, like many other tools in the modern woodshop, has a lot of uses. You can drill straight holes with it much easier than with a hand-held drill, you can attach sanding drums to it to sand curved parts, and you can even buy a mortising attachment for drilling square holes.

Detailing drill press features

When buying a drill press, you have to consider various features, including:

✓ **Chuck size:** Most drill presses have a ½-inch *chuck* (the part that holds the bit) that allows you to use a greater variety of drills than a ⅜-inch hand-held drill does. I wouldn't even consider buying a drill press without this feature.

✓ **Depth gauge:** This handy feature allows you to set the depth of your cut, which is helpful if you want to drill successive holes at the same depth (for mortise joints, for example).

✓ **Drill press base:** The base of the drill press is what holds the machine up. It needs to be sturdy and heavy enough to keep the drill press from tipping. Some drill presses are on bases that sit on the floor, but others have shorter bases that allow you to place the drill presses on a workbench. Either one works fine, but the floor stand models are more expensive.

The advantage with a floor-standing drill press is that you'll have greater ability to adjust the distance between the worktable and the drill bit, thus allowing you to work with higher stock. If this feature is important to you, then you may want to get a floor stand model.

✔ **Maximum depth:** This is the amount that the feed lever moves (the *feed lever* is the handle that you use to move the bit into the wood). Drill presses will often have maximum depths between 2 and 3½ inches.

If you want to drill a hole deeper than the maximum allowed, all you have to do is drill partway, turn off the drill, and then raise the worktable up until the bit is almost touching the bottom of the hole that you just drilled. Turn on the drill — making sure that your workpiece is securely fastened to the table — and drill again.

✔ **Variable speed:** Almost all drill presses have a variable speed selector. Definitely go for this option, because some materials (plastic, for example) and some operations (drilling large holes) require a slower speed. Look for a drill press that can go as slow as 450 rpm and as high as 3,000 rpm.

✔ **Worktable:** The worktable is the table where you put your workpiece (naturally). This table will have a height adjustment mechanism. Make sure that it is solid and easy to move up and down. The table itself should be flat and adjustable to different angles.

Operating the drill press

Using a drill press doesn't require any special skills or instructions. But do keep a few things in mind when using one:

✔ Make sure that you have the workpiece secured against the table, because the spinning bit will want to spin the wood with it.

✔ Don't wear loose clothing, because it can easily get caught in the spinning machine. This caution holds true for all power tools.

✔ Use sharp bits. Dull bits don't cut cleanly and require too much force to do the job.

Chapter 8

Setting Up Your Workshop and Maximizing Your Tools

In This Chapter

▶ Taking inventory of your workshop

▶ Finding the best space for you

▶ Tuning up your tools

▶ Making some jigs to improve tool use

*N*o doubt about it: Woodworking takes up a lot of space and creates quite a mess. So one of your primary considerations is figuring out how to work in a way that minimizes both of these potential problems. The best way to deal with the mess is to keep your shop clean as you work. I discuss this topic in detail in Chapter 3.

In this chapter, I explain how to best use your space. You can examine the core issues of electricity, lighting, and tool and wood storage. You can also delve into some common shop scenarios, such as the apartment, basement, or garage shop. Finally, I introduce you to jigs, which are tools you can construct that will make using *other* tools more effective and efficient.

Considering Core Issues

No matter how big, small, high tech, or low tech your shop is, you need to consider certain things before you actually start working. These things include electrical and lighting issues, wood storage, and tool storage.

Managing electrical requirements

Most home shops run on 110 volts (normal household current), and most professional cabinet-making shops run on 220 volts. Likewise, most consumer-grade tools run on 110 volts and the larger professional-grade machines require 220 volts. For most woodworkers, 110 volts is sufficient; just make sure that you have enough power (amperage) to plug in and run all the tools that you want.

If you find yourself eyeing a large machine such as a cabinet saw or an 8-inch jointer, you may end up installing 220-volt power. But don't try to install 220-volt power yourself. Tinkering with your electrical system is a very dangerous process that needs to be handled by a professional.

Your amperage (amount of power going through the wires in a given time) requirements are going to be more of an issue than the 110/220 volt one if you're looking at most non-professional new machines because most run on 110-volt systems. A typical table saw or jointer can draw a lot of power (amps) and if your shop isn't up to it you could be spending your time running back and forth to the circuit-breaker instead of milling wood.

If the building you work in has 100-amp service (you can find this out by looking at the circuit breaker box that serves your building), you should be in fine shape. If you can, try to ensure that the room you work in has several circuit breakers. If an organized electrician installed the circuit panel, everything should be labeled so you generally won't have to check all the circuit breakers in the panel. But if your circuit breakers aren't labeled, turn off the breakers one at a time and check each of the light switches and outlets in your room. This tells you which light or outlet is wired to which circuit breaker.

After you know which circuit breaker feeds each outlet and light switch, you can develop a plan to plug everything in. Try to plug each major tool into a separate circuit breaker. That way if you have more than one tool running at a time, they're not all pulling off the same circuit. If you don't have separate breakers in your room, don't worry — as long as you don't trip circuits all the time, you're doing okay. But if you frequently trip circuits as you work, you need to upgrade your electrical system or reduce the amount of power you draw at one time. The easiest way to do this is to limit your use to one machine at a time and use low wattage lighting (such as the fluorescent shop light I describe in the "Letting in the light" section).

Letting in the light

Many people put their workshop in the garage or the basement. (See the section, "Sampling Some Shop Setups" later in the chapter.) Neither of these workshop situations generally offers much in the way of natural lighting, however. I'm a real advocate of getting as much light into my workshop as possible. For very little money you can get some shop lights — long fluorescent lights (48 inches) paired in a simple fixture that can throw quite a bit of light without running up your electricity bill. I recommend that you get enough of these so that you're bathed in enough light to easily see all that you're working on.

How much light is this? Only you can be the judge of that, but a good guideline is to plan to have one shop light per 160 square feet or so of shop space. For example, in my 18-x-24-foot shop I have three sets of lights. I also have four large windows and two skylights. On bright days (which is most of the time) I don't have the lights on at all because I'm well bathed in light. But, when the sun goes down and I turn on my three lights, my shop is at about the same brightness as it is during the day with the bright sun outside.

Storing your tools

One thing's certain in woodworking: You'll always buy more tools. By getting into woodworking you have just excavated your own money pit. Congratulations! Now you need to start figuring out where to put all your expensive new friends. You want to find a place for your tools that will keep them both handy and relatively clean. This can be tricky because for most people space is at a premium.

Open shelves are nice if you have the wall space, but dust will collect on your tools. And I'm not just talking about that wimpy, light dust that collects on all the knick-knacks in your house (do woodworkers even have knick-knacks?). No, I'm talking about some serious dust. Stuff so thick and heavy you may not even know what tool is hiding beneath it. So open shelves aren't the best idea. Just put doors on those shelves and you're all set.

If wall space just doesn't exist in your shop, build worktables with closed storage underneath (check out Figure 8-1 for a worktable/storage cabinet that I built for my shop). You can easily find plans for these types of tables — look in Chapter 21 for some options.

Figure 8-1:
A work-bench with closed storage underneath keeps your tools clean and handy.

When designing your worktable tool storage, think about when and how each of your tools will be used and try to put the tools close to where you'll use them.

Storing wood

You've gotta have wood to work with, but workshop space is so valuable that storing wood in it seems like an awful waste of space. Most people just lean their boards against the wall, but you can find more efficient and much safer ways to store your wood:

> ✔ **A horizontal rack** is your best solution for the long boards (see Figure 8-2). Making a horizontal rack is simple: Just buy or make some L brackets and screw them into your walls at every other stud. This puts them 32 inches apart. Make sure that you screw them into the studs because they'll end up carrying a lot of weight. You may have to do some searching to find the studs if your walls are covered with drywall or plaster.

I prefer to hang racks about 6 feet off the ground so that the space underneath is usable (I can roll an unused tool or bench underneath). Some woodworkers prefer to have two or three levels of racks starting a foot from the floor and spaced every 2 feet or so.

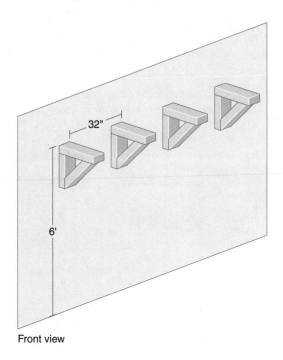

Front view

Side view

Figure 8-2:
Brackets hung from the wall are great for long board storage.

✔ **Vertical bins** are the way to go as far as sheet good storage goes (see Figure 8-3). These bins can be made any depth but 3 feet is optimal to hold full size sheets of plywood (the plywood will stick out one foot from the bin).

Try to have at least one bin a full 8 feet high so that you can store full, uncut sheets. The number of divisions you make depends on your available space and how much plywood you think you'll store in your shop. Having several bins helps separate the different types of plywood. This makes them easier to find and get at.

As you're cutting wood, you need a place to put your scrap. I recommend two bins about 12-x-24-x-24-inches (see Figure 8-4). Or you can get a couple of sturdy trashcans. I use one bin for larger scrap that can be used for other projects and the other for small pieces that will either be recycled or used for small projects like children's toys. Really small pieces that have no use go directly into the trash or recycling bin.

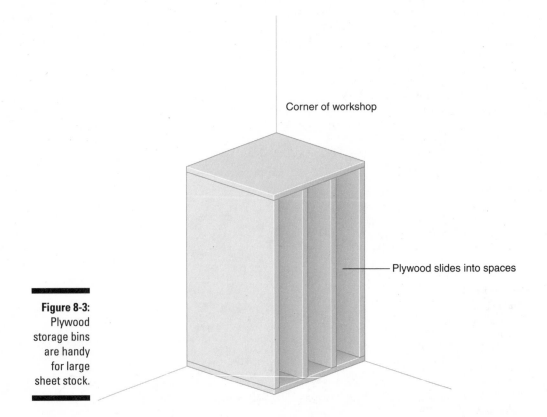

Corner of workshop

Plywood slides into spaces

Figure 8-3:
Plywood
storage bins
are handy
for large
sheet stock.

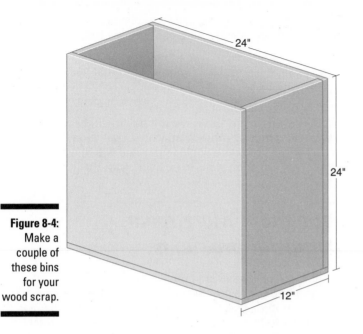

Figure 8-4:
Make a couple of these bins for your wood scrap.

Sampling Some Shop Setups

Woodworking shops come in many different flavors: the small apartment shop, the basement shop, the garage shop, and the dedicated shop, to name just a few. In this section, I outline these four types of shops and offer some suggestions for getting the most out of them.

The apartment shop: Small but efficient

If you live in apartment you can still work with wood. But you probably won't be able to have many large tools (if any), and you may want to avoid power tools altogether unless they're really quiet.

Here are a few things to consider when going this route:

- ✔ Size your projects to your space. If you live in a small apartment, don't try to make an armoire or an entertainment center.

- ✔ If your living area and workshop share the same space, spend more time and energy on stuff that will keep the dust down. A good air cleaner and a shop vacuum with a good filter are essential (see Chapter 3). Also, try to work in a way that doesn't produce much dust, for instance by using hand tools.

- Buy small pieces of wood and only buy what you need at the time. This can be a pain, but you'll find it even more of a pain to store wood in a small space.

- Set up your workbench and large tools on wheels so that you can move them around easily.

- Avoid using solvent-based finishes (see Chapters 17 and 18 for more information about finishes). The fumes are not healthy to be around for very long (or at all without lung protection, which I talk more about in Chapter 3). A finished piece takes a while to dry and will off-gas (release fumes) for a long time. You don't want to be living with this.

The basement shop: More room, but some potential problems

When I was a kid, my dad had a basement shop. I remember it fondly. All the dust drifting up the stairs into the rest of the house, the back-wrenching trips down the stairs with the wood (a 4-x-8-foot sheet of plywood had to be held close to the ground in order to fit down the stairs — talk about hard on the back). And I won't even mention the trouble getting that plywood around the corner at the bottom of the stairs (oh, I guess I just did). Then you have to carry the finished project back up the stairs (make sure before you assemble it that it will, in fact, fit up the stairs). Yeah, I loved that shop.

The only really good thing about it was that I could easily go downstairs to watch or help out and the neighbors didn't complain all that much about the noise because most of the shop was underground. Oh, did I mention that when my dad was working it was almost impossible to talk upstairs without shouting? Oh yeah, I loved that shop.

In spite of all the potential problems with the basement shop (did I mention that the dampness of a basement is not very good for your valuable wood?), a basement shop is not at all uncommon, especially with the cost of real estate nowadays.

So what do you do if your only option is to build your workshop in your basement? Well, I'm glad you asked. Take a look at these tips:

- Buy a good dehumidifier and always keep it running. This reduces the dampness of the basement and keeps your wood from warping, cupping, or twisting.

- Make sure you have enough ventilation. Basements usually only have a few small windows that often don't function properly, so you may need to install an exhaust fan to blow the dust and fumes out of your basement.

✔ When you work with large lumber such as full sheets of plywood, cut the larger pieces down to a manageable size with a circular saw (see Chapter 5) before you drag them downstairs.

✔ Always make sure that your final project will fit back up the stairs when you're done (I know I already mentioned this but it bears repeating). If the project won't fit, you'll need to do the final assembly and finishing outside the shop.

The garage shop: A great solution for many

A garage shop is my favorite kind of shop (well, except for the full-blown dedicated, stand-alone shop with tons of really big, expensive machines). One of the greatest things about a garage shop is that you can get your truck right up to the door and you don't have to carry wood, tools, or your finished projects very far.

Garage shops do have some quirks to consider, though:

✔ Heat and air conditioning often don't exist. If you want to work during cold or hot times, you may get uncomfortable. If you end up doing a lot of woodworking, you may want to insulate your garage and install a good HVAC system (heating, venting, and air conditioning). At the very least a wood-burning stove (properly installed, of course) can allow you to work in the winter. An added benefit to this is that you can burn some of your scrap wood for heat (just don't burn manufactured products like MDF or plywood because they emit toxic fumes when burned).

If you don't want to go that far, a good space heater may work well enough in the winter and opening the garage doors may work in summer. That is, if your neighbors don't mind the noise (most do) or if you live far enough away from your neighbors (most don't).

✔ Uninsulated garages can be noisy (for your neighbors). If you get a lot of complaints about the noise when you work, you'll likely have to insulate your garage. Doing so can get costly, so try to work during the day, keep the windows and doors closed, and get on really good terms with your neighbors (consider making them something once in a while).

✔ In most cases, the garage shop has to share space with a car or two. In this case, I suggest putting your benches against the wall and putting everything on wheels. This way, you can drive out the car and roll out the tools when you want to work. When you're done, roll the tools against the walls again and you have room for the car.

✔ If your garage has open rafters, you have a great place to store your long boards. Just make sure that they're secure, because you don't want them falling onto your car, your tools, or you.

The dedicated shop: For the lucky few

I just recently finished building my dedicated workshop. My shop's not very big, but for the first time ever, I get to keep my tools out and have a project sitting out *while* I work on it. No more putting everything away at the end of the day (or weekend).

Before you start thinking "I could never afford a dedicated shop", let me assure you that this type of shop doesn't have to be big or elaborate. For example, one of my neighbors has a 10-x-12-foot shed for a woodworking shop. He has windows positioned at tabletop height that open up to let the large pieces of wood pass through while he cuts, making the space seem much bigger than it is. It didn't cost him much money to build and it fits all his tools compactly but comfortably.

If you get a chance to build a dedicated shop, here are some things I did (or wish I had done) to make using the shop easier and more efficient:

✔ Place most of your outlets at countertop height. This allows you to access the outlets without having to crawl around on the floor, and provides more flexibility in where you can put your workbenches.

✔ Put some outlets in the floor as well or run some electrical boxes down from the ceiling so that your machines in the center of the room don't need to have extension cords running to the walls.

✔ Provide easy access for your wood by building your shop right next to a driveway or access road. (Okay I didn't do this; I have to walk more than 50 feet with the wood and projects to get them to and from the truck.) Save your back and plan ahead on this one.

✔ Consider installing a whole-shop dust collection system. One of the great things about a dedicated shop is that your tools can be kept in one place. This makes creating permanent dust collection connections to each of your tools easy and inexpensive.

✔ Consider setting up a separate finishing room in your shop so that you can keep on building stuff while your finished project dries. This can be as a simple as sealing a corner of the room with plastic sheeting or as complex as building a completely separate room outfitted with air exchangers (see Chapter 3 for information on air cleaners and exchangers).

Tackling Tool Set-ups

When you get your tools into your shop (no matter what kind of shop you may have), always spend a few minutes fine-tuning their settings so they cut as accurately as possible. Doing this extra step will save you a ton of headaches later on.

Every manufacturer treats each tool differently so I can't go into detail on how you should set up your tools. Check out your owner's manual and follow the instructions on how to set each one up properly. I also recommend periodically readjusting each tool to ensure that it always functions optimally.

Check out the following list for the main things you want to check when tuning up your tools.

- ✔ Check that the blade is set square to the tabletop. For planers, table saws, band saws, and joiners (see Chapter 7), the blades should be parallel with the tabletop.

- ✔ Check that the *rip fence* (a guide that keeps the edge of a workpiece a set distance from the blade) is set parallel to the blade.

- ✔ Make sure the blade spins evenly and doesn't wobble back and forth.

- ✔ Put a coat of car wax on the in-feed and out-feed tables. This will keep them smooth and help the wood slide as you work.

- ✔ Check the cords for your motors. Make sure that they aren't frayed and that the protective outer wrap isn't pulling away from the motor or plug.

- ✔ Make sure that your blades are sharp and clear of *pitch* (the residues from the wood including sap).

Journeying into Jigs

Jigs are like extra hands. *Jigs* allow you do things with a tool (a table saw, for instance) that will either make the task safer or more accurate (or both). In this section, I introduce you to some basic jigs and show you how to make them for your shop.

You often hear woodworkers talking about jigs, but technically two classes of tool helpers exist: jigs and fixtures. Jigs hold a tool and fixtures hold a workpiece. Throughout this book, I call all jigs and fixtures jigs because that's what you'll likely hear from other woodworkers when they talk about these tool helpers.

Producing a push stick

A push stick is one of the most useful jigs. With one of these, you can keep your hands away from the blade when you feed wood into a table saw, router table, jointer, or band saw. As you can see in Figure 8-5, a push stick is simply a piece of wood cut to fit in your hand comfortably with a notch that holds the wood as you push it through the machine.

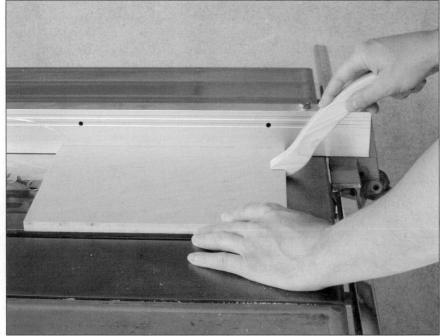

Figure 8-5:
A push stick allows you to keep your hands away from the blade.

The jig shown in Figure 8-5 is made out of ¾-inch stock. Any wood will do. Just find a scrap about 9 x 4 inches. You want to use either a jigsaw (see Chapter 6) or a band saw (see Chapter 4) to cut the push stick, because you need curved cuts. It also feels better in the hand if you round over the edges of the handle. Do this with a router fitted with a round-over bit or with a sander.

To make this jig:

1. **Draw a grid with 1-inch squares on a piece of paper and draw lines between the squares like those shown in Figure 8-6.**

2. **Cut out the drawing from the paper and use that to trace the push stick onto a board.**

3. **Cut along the lines.**

I highly recommend making a bunch of these and keeping two with each of your stationary tools.

To use the push stick, feed the wood into the saw with your hands. When the back end of the board is on the table, use the push stick to feed the wood past the blade.

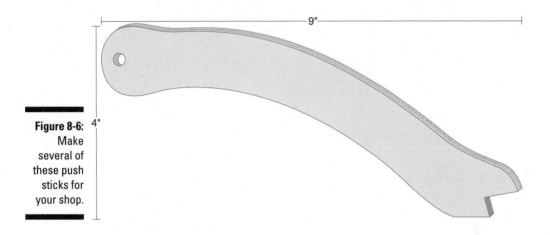

9"

4"

Figure 8-6:
Make
several of
these push
sticks for
your shop.

Fashioning a featherboard

A featherboard (see Figure 8-7) is used to keep wood against a fence and to prevent kickback. I recommend that you make several and keep them in easy-to-reach spots around your shop.

Figure 8-7:
A feather-
board is
used to
keep wood
tight up
against a
tool's fence.

Making a featherboard is easy. Check out Figure 8-8 for the dimensions. Any solid wood will do for this jig. The dimensions don't need to be exact, just close enough so that the fingers of the featherboard bend easily when feeding wood past it and keep the wood from coming back out at you.

Featherboards can be used to hold the wood against both the fence and the table. Either way, you want the wood to bend the fingers of the featherboard slightly as you feed the board past the featherboard. For this to happen, you need to have the featherboard positioned slightly closer to the opposing surface (fence or table) than the wood that you're cutting, and you need to clamp the featherboard securely so that it doesn't move when the wood is fed past it.

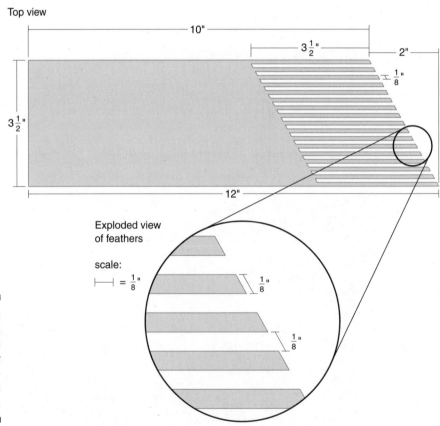

Top view

10"

$3\frac{1}{2}$"

2"

$\frac{1}{8}$"

$3\frac{1}{2}$"

12"

Exploded view of feathers

scale:

$\longmapsto = \frac{1}{8}$"

$\frac{1}{8}$"

$\frac{1}{8}$"

$\frac{1}{8}$"

Figure 8-8:
You can never have too many feather-boards in your shop.

Creating a portable circular saw guide

One of the problems with circular saws is that they aren't very accurate. But with a circular saw guide, you can minimize the deficit. A circular saw guide is simply a straightedge with a guide for your saw (see Figure 8-9).

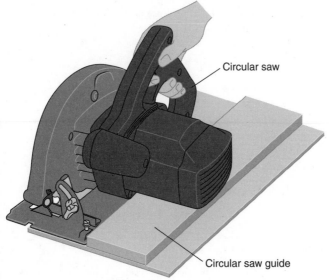

Circular saw

Circular saw guide

Figure 8-9:
A circular saw guide makes getting straight cuts on your circular saw easy.

This guide is very easy to make and consists of a 4-inch wide piece of ¾-inch plywood, an approximately 8-inch wide piece of ¼-inch Masonite (the exact width depends on your saw), and (16) ¾-inch flathead screws. Check out Figure 8-10 to see how this jig is made.

When you have your wood cut to the dimension in Figure 8-10, follow these steps to put it together:

1. **Use the screws to attach the ¼-inch plywood to the ¾-inch plywood 2 inches in from one side by driving the screws through the thinner plywood into the thicker plywood.**

   The ¼-inch plywood extending 5 inches from the ¾-inch plywood will need to be trimmed down to fit your saw. To do this:

   a. **Clamp the jig down to a piece of plywood or a pair of saw horses by putting the clamps against the ¼-inch plywood on the 2-inch side of the thicker board.**

   b. **Get out your circular saw and set the depth of the blade slightly deeper than the plywood.**

   c. **Position the saw with the base on the ¼-inch plywood and the left side of the base up against the ¾-inch plywood guide.**

   d. **Turn on your saw and run it down the jig, keeping the saw's base tight up against the ¾-inch plywood.**

Now you have a custom-sized jig for your saw. Making accurate cuts using a circular saw just got easier!

Materials list
$\frac{1}{4}$" X 12" X 96" (or 48") plywood or masonite.

$\frac{3}{4}$" X 5" X 96" (or 48") plywood

(16) $\frac{3}{4}$" flathead screws

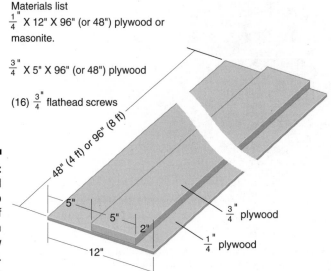

Figure 8-10:
You need only two pieces of wood for a circular saw guide.

Tackling a table saw panel cutter

A table saw panel cutter is one of the most useful jigs for your table saw. With a good panel-cutting jig you will be able to make accurate crosscuts and mill perfectly square panels for tabletops and carcasses. Figure 8-11 shows you a picture of a panel-cutting jig.

The panel cutting jig is made from the following materials:

- ✔ (1) ¾-x-24-x-24-inch plywood
- ✔ (1) ¾-x-1½-x-36-inch good hardwood such as oak or cherry

Figure 8-11:
A panel-
cutting jig
helps you
make
accurate
crosscuts
on a table
saw.

✔ (1) ⅜-x-¾-x-36-inch hardwood such as oak or cherry. The exact size of this piece depends on the size of the miter slot in your table. Most are ⅜-x-¾ inch.

You can also use a piece of aluminum or other metal (this is what my panel cutter uses).

✔ (3) ¾-inch flathead screws for attaching the miter slot board onto the bottom of the 24-inch panel

✔ (2) 1½-inch flathead screws for attaching the backing board onto the panel

Figure 8-12 shows you how to make this jig and the specific procedures are as follows:

1. **Cut all pieces to size.**

   Check to make sure that the 24-x-24-inch board is perfectly square (or as close as you can get).

2. **Measure the distance from the left side edge of your saw blade to the close edge of the miter slot located to the left of the saw blade (opposite the fence).**

   On my Delta contractor's saw this distance is 4¼ inches.

3. **Attach the ⅜-x-¾ inch board one quarter of an inch further from the edge of the 24-x-24-inch board than the saw blade is from the miter slot (for my saw this would be 4½ inches).**

   Use the ¾-inch screws and drive them through the narrow board into the thicker one. Make it as close to parallel with the edge as possible.

4. **With the saw blade lowered all the way, put the jig on the table with the narrow strip of wood in the miter slot to the left of the saw blade.**

5. **Pull the jig back so that the blade can be raised without hitting the jig and raise the blade to slightly higher than the jig.**

6. **Turn on the saw and slide the jig along the miter slot and through the blade.**

   You should have cut off about ¼ inch of the ¾-inch plywood and have an edge that is perfectly parallel with saw blade.

7. **Drill pilot holes through the ¾-x-1½-inch board (backing board).**

   One hole goes three inches from the end and the other 21 inches from that same end. The first hole should be drilled slightly smaller than the size screw you use and the second should be elongated slightly to allow movement for fine-tuning the backing board.

8. **Attach the screw on the right side of the jig and tighten it down securely enough that the backing board doesn't move easily.**

   Using a square, set the backing board perpendicular with the left edge of the panel (the freshly cut side).

9. **Drill the second screw through the elongated hole and into the panel below.**

   Double-check that the backing board is in the proper position.

Finding jig plans

You can find several good books on making jigs for your shop. One particularly good one on the subject is *Making Jigs and Fixtures* by Nick Engler. This book is part of "The Workshop Companion" series by Rodale press (1995). My one small complaint about this book is that some of the jig designs are more elaborate than necessary to get the job done.

Jig plans are also periodically published in the various woodworking magazines. You can find a list of these magazines in Chapter 21.

Top view

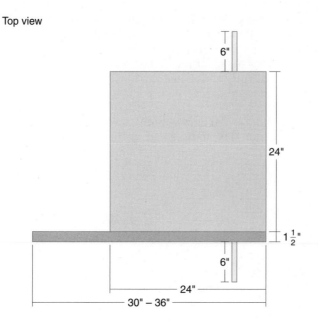

6"

24"

$1\frac{1}{2}$"

6"

24"

30" – 36"

Back view

36"

24"

$\frac{3}{4}$"

$\frac{3}{4}$"

Support strip on back set perfectly square to saw blade

Plywood base

Hardwood strip fits in miter slot $\simeq \frac{3}{8}$"

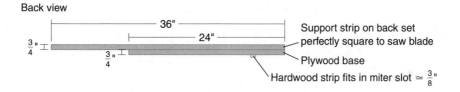

Attaching the backing board to the panel

Figure 8-12: A table saw panel cutter takes very little time to make.

Drill elongated hole through top board only (allows for fine tuning of backing board)

Check with a square

3"

3"

21"

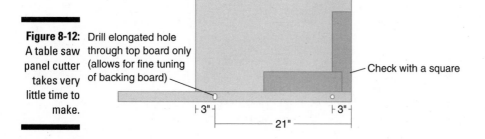

To check the panel cutter for square, put a board on the cutter and run it through the saw. Check that freshly cut board with your square. If the board's square, you're set to go. Just make sure that both screws holding the backing board are tight. If your panel cutter isn't square, just loosen the screw with the elongated hole slightly and adjust the backing board. Test again and re-adjust until your cut is square.

If you use this jig a lot (as I'm sure you will), I recommend that you check the accuracy of the jig from time to time and readjust as needed.

Part III
Together Forever: Basic Wood Joinery

The 5th Wave   By Rich Tennant

In this part . . .

Binding two pieces of wood together successfully is essential to making anything out of wood. This part details the process for you — from understanding adhesives, to making wood joints, to using mechanical fasteners.

Chapter 9

Stuck on You: Using Adhesives and Glues

To make strong furniture, adhesives are essential. Only a few years ago, you didn't have many choices for adhesives, but nowadays the options are almost limitless. In this chapter, you discover the most commonly used adhesives for woodworking. You also examine when and how to use each of them, as well as how to clean up when you're done.

Cluing into Gluing: Understanding the Essential Role of Glue

Adhesives work one of two ways: mechanically or chemically. The type you choose depends on what material you glue and the type of joint you're gluing.

For the most part, chemical bonding requires that the surfaces being glued together have even contact without gaps. This is because they require undisturbed surface area in order to bond properly. That said, these glues *will* work with some voids but not substantial voids. Chemical bonding adhesives include carpenter's glues (yellow and white) and hide glue.

If the items you want to glue together do have large gaps, you're better off using an adhesive with mechanical bonding characteristics. These types of adhesives include epoxies and plastic resins. Their advantage is that they can actually fill the voids between the joints and create a lasting bond when gluing less-than-perfect joints. As for which type of adhesive to use on a specific joint, I explain that in the sections that follow.

Working with Carpenter's Glue

White carpenter's glue is the standard for gluing up wood. The stuff is inexpensive, easy to work with, and it creates a strong, lasting bond. Technically, white glue is a polyvinyl-acetate (PVA) adhesive and creates a chemical bond, but white glue is just so much easier to remember.

Yellow carpenter's glue is really just a newer version of white glue. However, yellow glue is slightly thicker, dries quicker, and is more resistant to heat and moisture.

Knowing when to use carpenter's glue

White and yellow glues are chemical bonding glues so they require joints with a substantial surface area and few voids. If you machine your joints with some degree of care and use the best joint for the job (see Chapter 10 for more information about joints), you can use carpenter's glue without hesitation for nearly all your woodworking tasks.

If you intend to expose your finished project to moist conditions, then choose a waterproof yellow glue.

Applying carpenter's glue for best results

To apply carpenter's glue, wipe or brush a thin, even coat on both surfaces of the joint. Don't put so much on that the glue drips out of the joint when you clamp the pieces together (a little oozing is good, though). Apply the glue and work fairly quickly, because the glue will start to set up in a few minutes. After the glue is applied, securely clamp the surfaces together for several hours (or preferably overnight).

When clamping the joint, apply enough pressure to pull the joint firmly together and to hold the piece securely in place, but not so much that you squeeze all the glue out of the joint. If the joint starts to distort from your clamp pressure you can be sure you're using too much.

Cleaning up

You can clean up both yellow and white glue with water when they're still wet. Use a damp rag or towel and wipe down the outside of the joints after you've glued up the joints. After the glue has dried, it's a pain to remove and will ruin the final finish, so take some time before the glue dries to wipe all exposed surfaces free of extra glue. Trust me, doing so will save you tons of time and frustration later on.

If you miss some glue and it dries, you'll need to sand the glue off the wood or scrape it with a scraper or chisel. Unfortunately, you'll probably end up taking quite a bit of wood off in order to get all the glue, because it does soak into the pores of the wood.

Handling Hide Glue

Made from ground up animal bones and skin (I know, not the most appealing thought, is it?), hide glue has been around for centuries. Hide glue is becoming less common, but it still has admirers. One advantage of hide glue is that it can be softened up again with a little heat, which can be handy if you're restoring old furniture.

Knowing when to use hide glue

To be honest, I only use hide glue if I'm restoring an old piece of furniture and I want to use the same glue that was used on the rest of the piece. Otherwise, I just use yellow glue.

The only other time I consider using hide glue is when I glue something that I can't hold with a clamp and I know that my finished piece won't be exposed to hot or moist conditions. In this instance, hide glue's quick set time comes in handy, because I can hold the joint by hand until the glue sets up a bit.

Applying hide glue for best results

Traditionally, hide glue is sold in pellets that need to be melted down in order to work. However, nowadays you can find some hide glue available in ready-to-use liquid form. If you use the pellets, you need a double boiler and a thermometer to get the glue to the right temperature to melt (check the package the glue came in for specific instructions). When it's melted, or if you use the new ready-to-use liquid, you apply it the same way you do yellow or white glue: Spread an even coat over both surfaces and join them together.

Because hide glue dries quickly as it cools down, you need to work fast. The good news is that if you don't have clamps to hold the parts together, you can just hold them by hand until the glue has cooled (hardened) enough to hold itself. This often only takes a few minutes.

Cleaning up

Clean up any extra glue with a damp rag while it's still soft or with a scraper or sander after it has hardened.

Choosing Contact Cement

Contact cement is a solvent or water-based adhesive that must be allowed to dry before you put the pieces together.

Knowing when to use contact cement

Contact cement is great for applying plastic laminates to wood (or MDF), which is really the only time I use it. Contact cement is not all that good for wood-to-wood gluing.

Applying contact cement for best results

To apply contact cement, coat both surfaces with a thin layer, using a rubber roller, and let it dry until tacky. Then carefully position one surface over the other before letting the surfaces touch. Try putting some scraps of wood, small diameter dowels, or cardboard between the two surfaces and then removing the cardboard after you have everything where you want it.

The main drawback with contact cement is that after the coated surfaces touch one another they're locked in place. Ordinarily, you can't readjust them. However, some newer versions of contact cement do allow some readjustment.

Contact cement is solvent based so it's toxic, smells unpleasant, and is very flammable. Only use this stuff with adequate ventilation and always wear a respirator (see Chapter 3).

Cleaning up

Solvent-based contact cement needs to be cleaned with a solvent-based cleaner such as paint thinner or turpentine.

Relying On Resin Glues

Several types of resin glues are on the market, and all of them use a two-part system. The major types of resin glues are

- ✔ **Epoxy resins:** Epoxy resin adhesive consists of a two-part formula that is mixed together to get it to harden. Many formulas are available, which vary in their set time and strength.

- ✔ **Resorcinal-formaldehyde:** This formula consists of a powdered substance that you mix with a liquid hardener. To use this adhesive, you first mix the two parts together in prescribed proportions and then apply to the workpiece. This type of adhesive is waterproof so it's great for outdoor furniture and other places where the project will be exposed to a lot of moisture.

- ✔ **Urea-formaldehyde:** This type of epoxy has good gap-filling abilities. Although it comes in two parts, one powder and one liquid, you mix the powder with water and apply to one side of the joint. Then you apply the liquid part to the other side. This type of adhesive is water resistant so you don't want to use it on outdoor projects.

Knowing when to use resins

Resins aren't your everyday adhesives. They're most useful when you need gap-filling capabilities or when you need the ultimate in watertightness. The downside to these adhesives, however, is that they're

✔ A pain to mix

✔ Much more expensive than carpenter's glue

✔ Toxic

You need to work in a well-ventilated area and use gloves and lung protection when working with resin.

Applying resin for best results

Each brand and type of resin adhesive is a little different. Some require you to mix the two parts before applying it to your joints and others need to be applied separately. Follow the instructions that come with the adhesive.

Cleaning up

Resin adhesives are toxic and you need to clean them with solvent-based cleaners, such as acetone. Follow the guidelines described on the adhesive's packaging to find out the best way to clean the particular formula that you use.

Honing In on Hot Melt Glue

Hot melt glue comes in sticks that you melt in a glue gun and squeeze out onto your project. You can find a variety of glue formulas made for glue guns. You can also find veneer strips with hot melt glue attached to them for quick and easy edge veneering (Chapter 13 talks more about veneer strips and veneer edging).

Knowing when to use hot melt glue

Hot melt glue is fast and easy but not the best solution for permanent projects. However, I highly recommend it for making mock-ups of cabinets because the glue dries quickly and holds well enough for that purpose.

The hot melt glue used for edge veneers is good but I still recommend that if you want to edge veneer you use a good carpenter's glue instead. (But that's just me. My dad had no problem with the hot melt veneer edging and he was a better woodworker than I'll ever be.)

Applying hot melt glue for best results

Using a hot melt glue gun is easy: Just put the glue in the gun, wait a few minutes for the glue to melt, and squeeze the trigger to apply it. The only drawback is that it comes out as a thick droplet and tends to go on thick as well.

To use hot melt veneer edging all you have to do is put the edging where you want it and run a hot iron across it until it melts. Remove the iron and press the veneer down with a rubber roller until the glue hardens. This takes only a few seconds.

Cleaning up

Depending on the type of glue stick you use, you can clean up with a damp rag or a dull chisel, just like carpenter's glue (see the section, "Working with Carpenter's Glue" earlier in the chapter for more information).

Cedar is one of several softwoods used for furniture. Rough sawn cedar is often used for outdoor projects.

Fir is common for construction but can also be used for furniture if chosen wisely.

Pine is the most commonly used softwood for furniture.

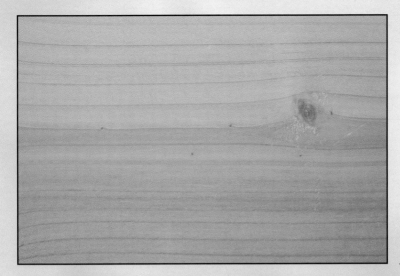

Redwood is an outdoor project staple. It's easy to work with and looks great.

Ash is a white-colored hardwood with a straight, pronounced grain.

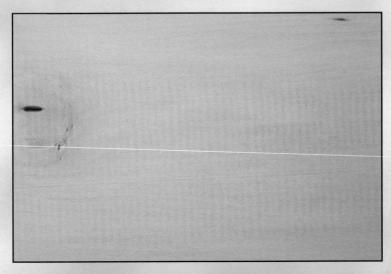

Basswood is a soft hardwood that has a white color and fine texture.

Birch is a pale brown or off-white-colored hardwood with medium to hard density.

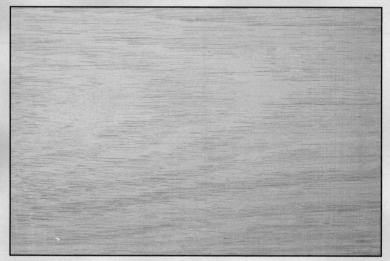

Brazilian cherry has a darker color than North American cherry.

Cherry is one of the most popular hard-woods for furniture. It has a pronounced sapwood that needs to be darkened or cut out for best appearances.

Red oak is common for woodworking. It has more open pores than white oak and doesn't tolerate wet conditions well.

White oak is one of the most used hardwoods for furniture and can be purchased quarter sawn (shown).

Mahogany has a reddish color and is getting harder to find.

Maple is a hard, white-colored wood that can be found with a variety of grain patterns such as bird's eye (shown).

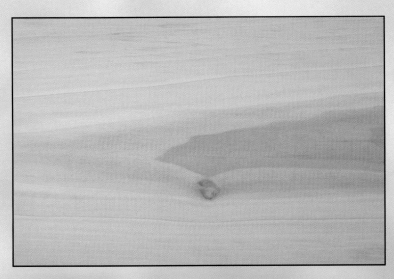

Poplar is a great wood for painted projects because it paints well and is inexpensive.

Teak is one of the more sought-after woods. It works extremely well for outdoor projects but it's expensive and hard to find.

Walnut comes in a variety of colors depending on where it's from. It ranges from light brown to almost black. This is a premier wood for furniture.

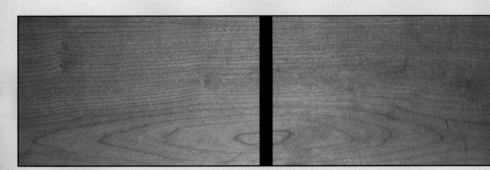

Pigment stains accentuate the grain. Left has a sanding sealer applied before the stain and right has the stain applied directly to the wood without the sealer.

Dye stains give an even appearance. Left has a sanding sealer applied before the stain and right is without the sealer.

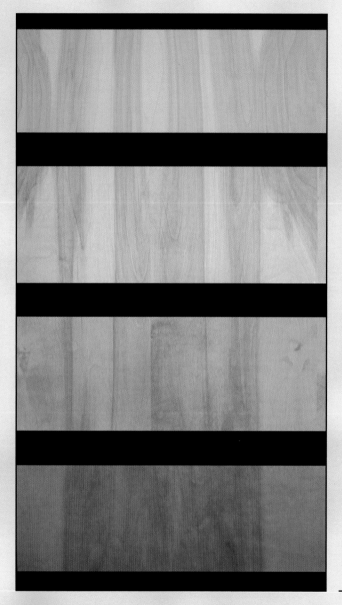

Each variety of shellac adds its own color to the wood. Pictured on birch are (top to bottom): bare wood, blond shellac, orange shellac, garnet shellac.

Chapter 10

Working with Wood Joints

*W*ood joints involve fastening two pieces of wood together in the most appropriate way for the job it needs to do. With the right joint, your project will be strong, stable, and last a lifetime (or more). With the wrong joint, however, your project won't stand up.

Wood joints are the backbone of woodworking, but as you can probably guess, there's more than one way to join wood. Knowing which joint to use in a given situation isn't hard. In fact, joints fit into three general categories based on the job they're doing: edge to edge, carcass, and frame. In this chapter, you see how each of the joints is used in modern woodworking, and discover the best applications for each joint as I explain how to cut them (the fast and easy way, of course!).

Choosing the Right Joint for the Job

For the most part, choosing the right joint for a job isn't hard. You only have so many joints to choose from, and most of them have been around for a long time. As long as you stick with customary joints, you'll be just fine.

The key to a good, solid joint is surface area. In others words, you want as much wood-to-wood contact as you can get. How much contact you actually need depends on the types of stress the joint will be subjected to.

For example, a chair leg needs a stronger joint than a tabletop does because it needs to handle a lot more stress. When choosing a joint for a part of your project, you want to make sure that the strength of the joint coincides with the area where the greatest force against the joint is going to occur. A mortise-and-tenon joint, for example, is great for places that have a lot of lateral stress, such as table or chair legs, whereas an edge-to-edge butt joint on a tabletop handles the pressure placed on it quite well because there isn't nearly as much lateral stress put on the wood.

All the joints presented in this chapter will do the job they're designed to do. All you need to decide is which joint fits your working style best. I try to help you figure this out as well.

Easing into Edge-to-Edge Joints

An edge-to-edge joint involves gluing the narrow edge of one board to another, such as those used to create a tabletop. Make sure that you have straight, flat edges on all your boards; you can do this using either a hand plane or a jointer.

When gluing up narrow boards to make a wider surface, alternate the growth rings so that you get the stablest board possible with the flattest surface. Check out Figure 10-1 to see how this is done.

Figure 10-1:
Alternating the direction of the growth rings gives you a more stable board.

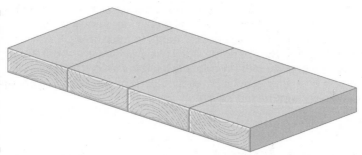

Take great care in selecting the wood you use for making wide surfaces out of narrow boards. Choose the wood based upon color, grain pattern, and overall beauty. See Chapter 12 for more information about this topic.

Butting in about butt edge joints

The *butt edge-to-edge joint* involves gluing together boards with flat edges. This joint is plenty strong for most applications (see Figure 10-2). In fact, the glue is actually stronger than the wood itself.

Figure 10-2:
A butt joint has two flat edges glued together.

To make a butt edge-to-edge joint, cut each board to width and joint the edges on the jointer. If the edges don't match up perfectly when you put two boards together, they aren't perfectly straight, so you need to return to the jointer. You can use a hand plane to square up the edges, but getting them perfect takes skill and time. If you choose to go this route, use a plane with a long bed and plane the board with long smooth strokes. Oh, and be patient.

Grooving on tongue-and-groove joints

If you're searching for more strength than you can get from a butt joint, then a *tongue-and-groove* joint will work well for you (see Figure 10-3).

Figure 10-3:
A tongue-and-groove joint.

The easiest way to make a tongue-and-groove joint is with a table saw. Follow these steps to make a tongue-and-groove joint:

To create the tongue:

1. **Set your blade height to the depth that you want the groove to be.**

   For a ¾-inch board, ¼ inch is deep enough.

2. **Adjust the fence so that you cut the side of the tongue farthest from the fence (this would be on the left side of the board on most saws).**

   For a ¾-inch board, your fence will be set ½ inch from the edge of the blade that is closest to the fence (the right side on most saws).

3. **With the face of the board against the fence and the edge of the board that you want to cut the tongue into on the table, feed the wood through the saw.**

   Make sure to hold the face against the rip fence at all times. If the wood comes away from the fence during the cut, the tongue will turn out thinner than you want. To make this less likely, use a featherboard to hold the wood against the fence (Chapter 8 has plans to make a featherboard).

4. **Turn the board around so that the other face is against the fence, and run it across the saw blade.**

   You should now have two cuts in the edge of your board that are exactly the same distance apart as the groove is wide. If you're using a ¾-inch board, the cuts should be ¼ inch apart (see Figure 10-4, top).

Top

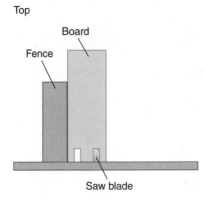

Bottom

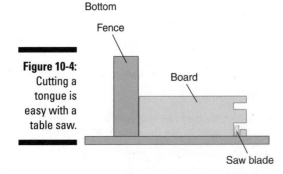

Figure 10-4:
Cutting a tongue is easy with a table saw.

5. **With the face of the board on the saw table and the tongue side of the board facing the blade, adjust the fence so that the blade is right against the board.**

   Then adjust the depth of cut (height of the blade) so that the blade is up to the bottom of the tongue. For a ¾-inch board your blade will be set at ¼ inch. This is the distance from the edge of the board to the beginning of the tongue.

6. **Adjust the fence so that you cut the edge of the board that has the tongue to where the blade cut it in Steps 3 and 4.**

   For a ¾-inch thick board, this will be ¼ inch. So if your board is 4 inches wide, you set the fence 3¾ inch from the edge of the blade closest to the fence (see Figure 10-4, bottom).

7. **With the face of the board against the saw table, run the board across the saw.**

8. **Flip the board over and run the other face against the saw table.**

   Make sure you're cutting the edge that has the tongue, not the opposite edge. You now have a tongue that will fit your groove.

Only put a tongue on one edge of each board. The other edge gets a groove.

To create the groove (see Figure 10-5):

1. **Set your blade height to the depth that you want the groove to be.**

   For a ¾-inch board, ¼ inch is deep enough.

2. **Set your fence so that your blade cuts ⅓ of the way into the board.**

   For a ¾-inch board, set the fence ¼ inch from the edge of the blade closest to the fence.

3. **With the face of the board up against the fence, run the edge of the board through the saw.**

   Once again, to give yourself the best cut, use a featherboard to hold the wood against the fence. If the wood comes away from the fence the groove will be too wide.

4. **Put the opposite face against the fence and run the same edge through the saw.**

   If you're grooving a ¾-inch board and you have a blade with a ⅛ kerf (width), you're done. You now have a groove that is perfectly centered and is exactly ¼ inch wide.

Figure 10-5:
A table saw makes quick work of cutting grooves for tongue-and-groove joints.

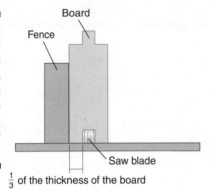

Board

Fence

Saw blade

$\frac{1}{3}$ of the thickness of the board

If your blade is narrower than ⅛ inch or if your board is thicker than ¾ inch, then you may have a thin sliver of wood left in the center of the groove. Don't remove it until you put this basic groove in all the boards you want to cut. This way you won't have to reset your saw more than once.

When you have cut the basic groove into all your boards, move your fence out until your saw blade is set to cut this sliver away. Run your boards through the saw. For really thick boards, you may need to do this more than once.

I highly recommend using a piece of scrap wood (with the same thickness) and making adjustments to the saw to ensure that the tongue fits snugly in the groove before you cut all your boards.

'Splaining spline joints

A *spline joint* (also called a loose tongue) is similar to a tongue-and-groove joint (see previous section), except instead of one side of the boards having a tongue and one side a groove, both sides have grooves. The tongue is created by a third piece of wood, called a *spline*. Figure 10-6 shows a spline joint.

Figure 10-6:
A spline joint.

Splines are generally made of plywood, so you want to make sure to create a groove that is as wide as your chosen plywood is thick. For a ¾ grooved board the groove is ¼ inch. In this case, you use a ¼-inch piece of plywood.

Keep in mind, however, that plywood sold as ¼-inch may not be exactly ¼-inch thick because plywood is generally thinner than it says it is. Always measure the plywood's thickness before you cut your grooves.

Then all you have to do is cut its length to that of the boards you'll be splining and the width to that of double the depth of the groove. For a ¾ board your spline will be ½ inch wide.

Taking a bite out of biscuit joints

A good way to reinforce a basic edge-to-edge butt joint is to use biscuits. *Biscuits* are oval-shaped pieces of wood placed inside a joint to increase the joint's surface area. To make a biscuited joint, you need a special tool to cut the proper size hole for the biscuit. This tool is called, appropriately enough, a *biscuit joiner* (see Chapter 6 for a description). I highly recommend getting a biscuit joiner because it makes fast work of joining wood. (The biscuit joiner isn't for all applications, but for edge-to-edge gluing it can't be beat.)

Figure 10-7 shows a biscuit edge-to-edge joint.

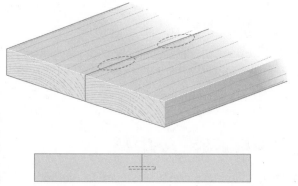

Figure 10-7:
A biscuit
joint.

To make a biscuit joint, follow the guidelines for creating butt edge-to-edge joints described earlier in this chapter, then arrange the boards the way you want them to join. Then follow these steps:

1. **With the boards lined up next to each other, make a mark across the joint about 4 inches in from the edge of each board, and another such mark every 6 to 8 inches for the length of the boards (see Figure 10-8).**

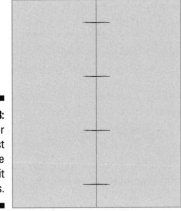

Figure 10-8:
Mark your
boards first
to make
biscuit
joints.

2. **Take your boards apart and set the depth of your biscuit joiner so that the blade cuts into the middle of the edge of the board.**

3. **Adjust your biscuit joiner for the size biscuit you're using.**

4. **Line up the guide mark on the biscuit joiner with the mark you made on each board.**

5. **Make the cut on all the boards.**

When you glue up the board, fill the biscuit cut with glue and insert the biscuit. The biscuit will swell into the hole as is absorbs the moisture from the glue.

Constructing Carcass Joints

When making a *carcass* you have one board meeting another at a right angle. In this case you use a carcass joint (pretty logical, huh?). You find carcass joints on cabinets, dressers, and drawers. You can choose from several joints to make this connection as strong as possible.

Even though these joints share some of the same names as the joints in the edge-to-edge joint section, the process is different because you're joining an edge of a board to the face of another board instead of an edge to an edge.

Building with butt joints

Because of the small amount of surface area and the stresses imposed on a carcass, butt joints aren't the best choice for carcass building, unless you reinforce them somehow. But you may find yourself using one or more of these joints in a project because they're quick and easy to make and they may be strong enough for some applications. Following the guidelines I present in this section will help you to make the best of these less-than-perfect joints.

There are two kinds of carcass butt joints: square and mitered.

Square

A *square butt carcass joint* (see Figure 10-9) consists of two boards meeting at a right angle. The butt carcass joint needs some sort of reinforcement in order to be strong enough to last. I use this joint only on carcasses that won't be seen from the side (kitchen cabinets, for example) and I always use screws to reinforce them (see Chapter 11 for more about screws).

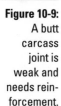
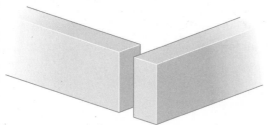

Figure 10-9: A butt carcass joint is weak and needs reinforcement.

If I want the ease and speed of the butt carcass joint and can't use screws because the side of the carcass will be seen, then I use either dowels or biscuits, as follows, to reinforce the joint:

✔ **Doweled:** By adding some *dowels* (small round pieces of wood) to the butt carcass joint, you increase its strength considerably. Figure 10-10 shows a doweled carcass butt joint. To make this joint, drill holes in each of the boards to be joined and insert dowels into the holes. The only tricky part of this procedure is getting the holes lined up perfectly. Fortunately, you can find doweling jigs that make easy work of this process.

✔ **Biscuited:** Ten years ago I doweled my basic butt joints, but now I use biscuits because they're faster and easier to use (see Figure 10-11). Sure, you need a special tool (the biscuit joiner, see Chapter 6), but after you get used to using it (which won't take long at all) you can burn through a bunch of joints in no time flat. Making a carcass butt joint with a biscuit joiner is as simple as marking where the biscuits go in each board and cutting the holes with the joiner.

Figure 10-10:
A doweled butt joint is strong enough to last.

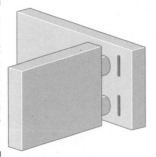

Figure 10-11:
A biscuited butt joint is easy to make (if you have the right tools) and is very strong.

Mitered

Sometimes you may want the look of a mitered joint when building carcasses. The look of two boards meeting with a 45-degree angle (check out Figure 10-12) is very refined.

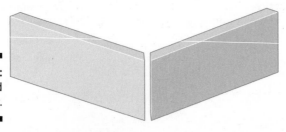

Figure 10-12:
A mitered butt joint.

Like the square butt carcass joint, the mitered butt carcass joint needs reinforcement in order to be truly useful; you can either use a dowel or a biscuit. The process is the same as with the square butt carcass joint except your dowel or biscuit goes in at a 45-degree angle to the face of the board (just like the cut).

Running after rabbet joints

For carcass boards that meet at the corners, you can't go wrong with a rabbet joint. The basic *rabbet joint* consists of a square cut on one board and a shoulder cut (notch) on another. Figure 10-13 has a picture of a basic rabbet joint.

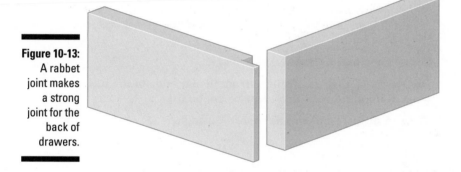

Figure 10-13: A rabbet joint makes a strong joint for the back of drawers.

Because the boards share two surfaces, this joint is extremely strong. You can also use this joint on the back of drawers, although it's really not strong enough for the front of drawers (for this, use the dovetail joint detailed later in this chapter).

To make a basic rabbet joint on a table saw, simply cut one board square and the other board the following way (Figure 10-14 shows you the process):

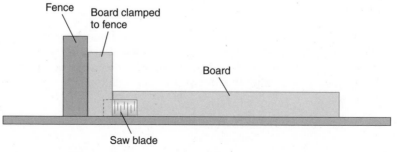

Figure 10-14: Making a rabbet joint is easy on a table saw.

Fence

Board clamped to fence

Board

Saw blade

1. **Outfit your table saw with a dado blade (see Chapter 7) that is slightly wider than the thickness of your first board (the one cut square).**

2. **Clamp a piece of scrap wood against the fence of your saw.**

3. **With your saw blade fully lowered, adjust your fence until the outer edge of the blade is exactly the distance from the fence as the square cut board is thick.**

   This will mean that the blade will be recessed slightly into the scrap board that you clamped against the fence.

4. **Turn on the saw and slowly raise the blade until it cuts into the piece of scrap wood that is clamped to the fence.**

   Raise the blade slightly higher than the depth that you want to cut your rabbet (just eyeball it, you don't need to be precise).

5. **Turn off the saw.**

6. **After the saw blade has completely stopped spinning, adjust the height of the blade to ⅔ of the thickness of the board you want to cut the rabbet into.**

   For a ¾-inch board this would be ½ inch.

7. **Double-check that the distance from the far edge of the blade to the fence is the thickness of the square cut board.**

8. **Turn on the saw and run the board through.**

Getting down and dirty with dado joints

A dado joint is like a rabbet joint except that it doesn't fall on the end of a board but anywhere within it. Dado joints come in two basic varieties: through dado and stopped dado. These two are the bread and butter carcass joints, because they have a large amount of surface area, which translates into strength.

Through

A *through dado* (see Figure 10-15) consists of a groove cut into one board into which another board fits.

Cutting a dado is easy. All you need to do is set your blade to the depth you want to cut (usually ½ of the thickness of the board) and cut a groove the width of the thickness of the joining board. The easiest way to get a cut the thickness of your adjoining board is to use a dado blade and set the width accordingly.

Figure 10-15:
Strong,
easy-to-
make
through
dado joints
are the
standard
carcass
joints.

TIP

If you don't have a dado blade, you can use your regular blade and start by making a cut at the outer edges of where you want the groove to go and then either chisel out the remaining material or use the saw (by making cuts, one right next to the other, until you have a clear groove).

Stopped

A *stopped dado* (see Figure 10-16) is a dado joint that you can't see from one side. This is a good joint to use if you want to hide the joinery from view at the front of a bookcase, for example.

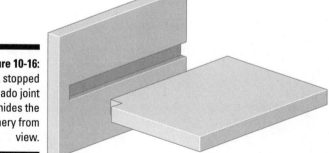

Figure 10-16:
A stopped
dado joint
hides the
joinery from
view.

Because the dado doesn't go all the way through the board, you can't cut it with your table saw the way you do a through dado. However, you can still make this cut on a table saw. The procedure is as follows:

1. **Set your dado blade to the width of the adjoining board.**

2. **Set the depth of cut to your desired depth.**

   This is generally ½ the thickness of the board you're cutting into.

3. **Place a piece of tape on your saw's fence where the front edge of the blade is, and mark the exact spot with a pen or pencil.**

   You want this mark to extend high enough up the fence so that you can see the mark when you feed your board into the saw.

4. **Mark the spot where you want your dado to end (stop) on the face of the board where it will slide against the fence.**

   This is often about ½ to 1 inch or so. When you cut, you'll feed the board until this mark matches up with the mark indicating the front edge of the saw blade.

5. **Set your fence so that you cut the dado where you want it and turn on your saw.**

6. **Feed the wood through the saw, until the mark on the board and the mark for the front of the saw blade match up.**

   Make sure that you keep the end of the board tight against the rip fence (or use a miter gauge to keep the wood from twisting as you feed it through the saw).

7. **Without moving the wood from this location, turn off the saw.**

8. **You're left with a dado that ends with a rounded edge, which you need to square up.**

   The easiest way to do this is with as sharp chisel (see Figure 10-17).

Figure 10-17:
The stopped dado requires a bit of chiseling to get a square edge in the groove.

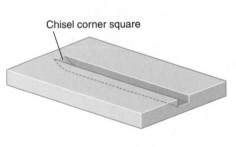

Chisel corner square

After you have the dado, you need to create a notch in the adjoining board where that dado stops. To do this, simply measure the distance from the edges of the dadoed board to the end of the dado and cut this amount out of the adjoining board to a depth equal to that of the depth of the dado.

When cutting dadoes with a dado blade in your table saw, you may end up with an uneven bottom in the groove (this really depends on the blade). I like to clean them up with a sharp chisel. Sure, cleaning the dadoes takes some time, but you end up with a better joint.

Detailing dovetail joints

Dovetail joints are one of the staples of a fine woodworker. You can often tell the skill of a woodworker by the quality of her dovetail joints. *Dovetail joints* consist of interlocking wedge-shaped fingers. This feature creates a really strong joint. The dovetail joint boasts many variations and I could write an entire book about all of them, but in this section I detail only the three most common: sliding, through, and half-blind.

Sliding dovetail

The *sliding dovetail joint* is similar to a dado (see the section, "Getting down and dirty with dado joints" earlier in the chapter), but instead of having a square cornered groove, it sports a dovetail-shaped one. And instead of having a joining board with a square cut, it has a dovetail cut on the end that slides into the groove cut into the other board. Figure 10-18 shows a sliding dovetail joint.

Because of the interlocking nature of the dovetail shape, this joint is much stronger than a dado. It also takes more time to make. The easiest way to create a sliding dovetail joint is to use a router fitter with a dovetail bit. This gives you the proper angles from which to cut the joint.

Cutting the groove for this joint with a router involves the following steps (see Figure 10-19):

Figure 10-18:
A sliding dovetail is a stronger alternative to a dado joint for carcasses.

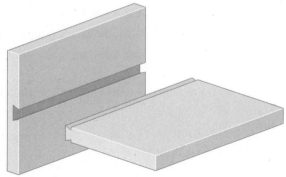

Figure 10-19:
Cutting the
groove for
a sliding
dovetail is
easy with a
router and a
straight-
edge.

1. **Put the board you want to cut the groove in on your workbench with the to-be-grooved side up and mark where you want the groove to go.**

   The size of the dovetail groove should be the same width as the thickness of your joining board at its widest point.

2. **Clamp a straightedge to this board at a distance from the cut marks so that your router bit will cut at this mark when the edge of your router base slides against the straightedge.**

3. **Set the depth of cut to the depth that you want the groove to be.**

   This is usually about ½ of the thickness of the board you're cutting.

4. **Turn the router on and run it along the straightedge as you cut the groove.**

   You may need to adjust the straightedge and make more than one pass if your groove is wider than your router bit.

The simplest way to cut the dovetail in the joining board is to use a router fitted in a router table. In this case, follow these steps (Figure 10-20 shows the process):

1. **Set the height of the cutter to equal the depth of the groove in the board you're joining to.**

2. **Set your router table fence so that the narrowest part of the bit doesn't quite cut the board as you feed it across the table.**

3. **Lay your board up on end with the face against the fence and slowly feed it into the bit.**

4. **Turn the board around with the other face against the fence and feed it through the bit.**

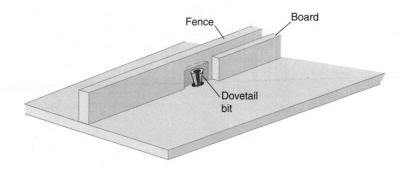

1st cut

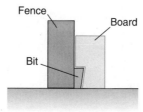

Figure 10-20:
Cutting the
dovetail
from the
joining
board is
best done
on a router
table.

2nd cut

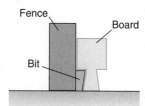

I highly recommend that you do this procedure first with a piece of scrap wood the same thickness as your board and test to make sure that the dovetail you cut fits snugly in the groove. You want the dovetail to slide smoothly into the groove but not be so loose that it wiggles around. Be patient and take your time, because you'll probably need a few tries before you get it just right.

Through dovetail

A through dovetail (see Figure 10-21) is a staple for making drawers that have drawer fronts on them. This joint is also used for making boxes and box-shaped projects, such as cradles and chests. The through dovetail is a beautiful joint that shows off your woodworking skills.

In the old days, this joint was made by hand and if you're a purist that's how you'll still do it. I'm not a purist, so I use a dovetailing jig and a router to help me (see Figure 10-22).

Dovetailing jigs aren't very expensive (around $100) and they make the process much easier. I know what you're thinking: I'm cheating, right? I should make through dovetails the proper way. Well, I don't think I'm cheating. In fact, I can make a joint just as strong and beautiful using a jig as I could cutting it by hand. And using a jig takes me a *lot* less time. This is just the efficiency expert in me speaking. After all, who cares how the joint was made as long as it looks and works correctly? I know I don't (now I'll go off and cut a couple of dovetails by hand as penance).

To make a through dovetail joint with a jig, just put a dovetail bit in your router, set up the jig according the manufacturer's guidelines, and cut away.

Here are some tips to help you make the best cut using a jig:

- ✔ Go slow and be careful not to tear out the wood as you cut.

- ✔ Wear eye and ear protection (see Chapter 3) and cover yourself with (not loose) clothing. Because you have to bend down to make the cuts and you're close to the router, you'll get covered in sawdust.

- ✔ Get a dust collection hood for your router to minimize dust.

Figure 10-21:
A through dovetail joint is great for drawers that get a face front.

Figure 10-22:
A dovetail
jig and a
router make
easy work
of making
through
dovetails.

Half blind dovetail

A *half blind dovetail* is a modified dovetail joint that hides the joint from one side (see Figure 10-23). If you make drawers that aren't fitted with a face front, this joint is preferred. This joint is just as durable as the through dovetail, and although harder to cut by hand than the through variety, it's no more work when using a jig. The process for making the joint is the same as the through dovetail version with some minor variations in settings (your jig manual will spell out the setting you need).

Figure 10-23:
A half blind
dovetail
joint
is hidden
from view
on one side.

Figuring Out Frame Joints

Frame joints are found in face frames, chairs, doors, and tables. Because of the lateral (sideways) stresses present in these types of furniture, frame joints need to be strong. These types of joints consist of lap, bridle, and mortise and tenon. As well, you can have frame joints that consist of a basic butt joint reinforced with a biscuit, dowel, or spline.

Lapping up lap joints

Lap joints are joints where half the material is cut from each board being joined and the pieces are joined together in a number of configurations. Common lap joints include cross, corner, and "T"(see Figure 10-24).

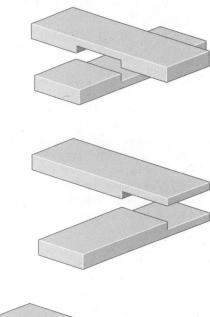

Figure 10-24:
Lap joints are great when two boards cross one another.

The easiest way to cut lap joints is with either a router or table saw (see Figure 10-25). On a table saw, use your dado blade and follow these steps:

1. **Mark your boards where you want them to cross.**

   To measure the size of the groove you need to cut out of each board, place the other board over the top and mark it with a marking gauge.

   Don't use a pencil (unless it's very sharp) or pen. The mark won't be right at the board and it will be too thick, resulting in a groove that's too wide.

2. **Set the depth of cut of your saw at exactly half the thickness of your boards.**

3. **Using your miter gauge, line up the cut and feed the wood through the saw.**

   If your groove is wider than your dado blade, you'll need to make more than one pass.

4. **Run the other board through the saw.**

5. **Clean up the bottoms of the grooves with a sharp chisel.**

Figure 10-25:
Cutting a cross lap joint on a table saw is easy with a dado blade and your miter gauge.

Due to the large amount of surface area in these joints, they're pretty solid, However, I tend to put dowels in them to add to their strength. I also like the way dowels look. The procedure for adding dowels to a joint is as follows:

1. **Glue and clamp the joint and let it set overnight until you can remove the clamps.**

2. **Using a brad-tipped drill bit the size of your dowel, carefully drill a hole through one board and halfway into the other board.**

    Be very careful not to drill too deep. You don't want to go through the board. I recommend wrapping the bit with a little tape at the depth you want to drill to (refer to Figure 10-25). Use a drill press, because you want the bit to drill the wood perpendicular to its surface. If you can't get a drill press, use a square to help you drill straight. Hold the square against the wood and estimate whether it's going in straight as you drill (see Figure 10-26).

3. **Drop a little glue in the hole, and gently tap the dowel into place.**

4. **Using a Japanese saw (see Chapter 5), cut the dowel down close to the board.**

    I prefer Japanese saws, because they don't have teeth set out at an angle from the blade. This keeps you from marring the wood when you saw flat against a board.

5. **With a damp rag, wipe up any excess glue that squeezed out of the dowel hole.**

6. **Sand the dowel flush.**

    Chapter 16 gives details on sanding.

Note: This procedure works for bridle joints and mortise and tenons too. I describe those two types of joints later in this section.

Fashioning bridle joints

Bridle joints are a cross between a lap joint and a mortise-and-tenon joint. Bridle joints are stronger than lap joints but more difficult to make because you need to cut out a tenon from one piece and a slot (called a *mortise*) in the other. Figure 10-27 shows a bridle joint.

Both of these parts can be cut on a table saw if you have a tenoning jig, but I prefer to cut the tenon on a table saw and the mortise with a drill press and chisel or a mortising machine.

To cut the tenon on a table saw, follow these steps:

1. **Mark the cut on both sides of the board to be tenoned.**

2. **Set the depth of cut to ⅓ the thickness of the board.**

3. **Using your miter gauge, line up the cut and feed the wood through the saw.**

   If your groove is wider than your dado blade, you'll need to make more than one pass.

4. **Run the other side of the board through the saw.**

5. **Clean up the tenon with a sharp chisel.**

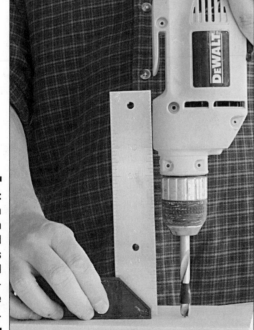

Figure 10-26:
Using a square with a hand-held drill helps you to drill perpendicular to the board.

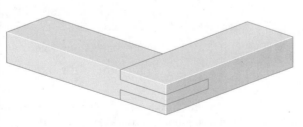

Figure 10-27:
A bridle joint is a cross between a lap joint and a mortise-and-tenon joint.

After the tenon is cut, I like to make the mortise using a benchtop mortise machine. (This tool is like a drill press except it drills square holes. Check out Figure 10-28.) If you don't have access to one of these machines, then you can use a drill press and a chisel to square up the holes, or you can cut the mortise by hand. (Don't worry, this method is really easy and almost as fast as using a power tool.)

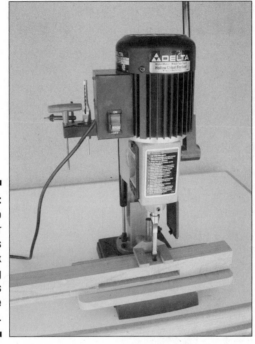

Figure 10-28:
A benchtop mortiser makes quick work of cutting the mortises for a bridle joint.

Here are the steps for creating the mortise by hand (see Figure 10-29 for a look at the process):

1. **Clamp your board securely in a vise, and mark where you want to cut the mortise.**

2. **With a drill (a hand-held one is fine here), drill a hole halfway into the board at the inner edge of the mortise.**

   Use a bit as close to the width of the mortise as possible.

3. **Turn the board over and drill from the other side until you meet your first hole.**

4. **Turn the board up on its end and saw (a backsaw is great for this cut) down along one side of your mortise markings until you reach the hole.**

5. **Cut along the other line to the hole.**

   The material should fall out of the mortise.

6. **Turn the board back down and use a chisel to square the inner part of the mortise.**

Tending to mortise-and-tenon joints

Mortise-and-tenon joints are one of the strongest and most used joints in woodworking. Mortise-and-tenon joinery is used for almost any project that has frame construction and needs to be as strong as possible. Chairs and tables fit this category as does almost all Arts and Crafts and Mission style furniture.

Mortise-and-tenon joints come in several types — stopped/blind, through, angled, wedged, and many more — but they all consist of the same basic parts: a mortise (a recess cut into a piece of wood that accepts a tenon) and a tenon (a tongue at the end of a board that fits into a mortise).

Drill hole here first

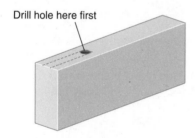

Cut along these
lines next

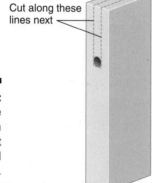

Figure 10-29:
Cutting the
slot for a
bridle joint
by hand
is easy.

In this section, I show you how to make three of the most common mortise-and-tenon joints — stopped, through, and angled. You can make any of these joints with one or a combination of techniques. If you end up doing much woodworking at all, I guarantee that you'll become an expert at making these joints regardless of how you do it.

Tenons can be made with or without *shoulders* (a squared off notch on a tenon; see Figure 10-30). Which way you choose to do them depends on the design of the piece and your skill at making the joints. **Hint:** A shouldered tenon can hide less than perfect joinery.

Figure 10-30:
A tenon can be made with (left) or without (right) shoulders.

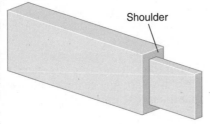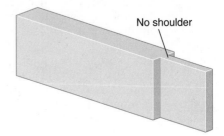

Shoulder

No shoulder

Stopped/Blind

A *stopped (blind) mortise-and-tenon joint* is one in which the tenon is hidden fully in the mortise (see Figure 10-31). This type of tenon is often used on table and chair legs or anywhere else that you don't want to see the joint.

To cut the mortise with a benchtop mortiser:

1. **Mark the mortise on your board.**

2. **Choose a mortising bit that matches the width of your mortise as closely as possible (without going over).**

3. **Set the fence so that your workpiece is positioned correctly under the bit.**

4. **Set the depth of cut on the tool.**

5. **Drilling slowly, make your first hole at one end of the mortise.**

6. **Make the next pass at the other end of the mortise.**

7. **Overlapping by half the width of the bit, drill/chisel out the rest of the mortise.**

8. **Clean the hole up with a chisel if necessary.**

   This will depend on your bit and the model of tool you have. Some cut cleaner than others.

For mortises that are wider than your bit, you need to repeat this procedure after adjusting the fence to clean out the rest of the joint.

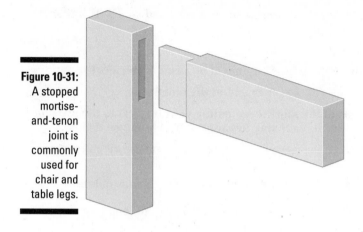

Figure 10-31:
A stopped mortise-and-tenon joint is commonly used for chair and table legs.

To cut the tenon on a table saw:

1. **Mark the cut on both sides of the board to be tenoned.**

2. **Set the depth of cut to the thickness that you want the tenon in the center of the board.**

3. **Using your miter gauge, line up the cut and feed the wood through the saw.**

   If your tenon is longer than your dado blade is wide, you'll need to make more than one pass.

4. **Turn the board over and do the other side.**

5. **Clean up the tenon with a sharp chisel.**

If you want to include a shoulder on the tenon, repeat this procedure only put the board on its edge instead of its face.

Be sure to reset the depth of cut for the shoulders.

Through

A *through mortise-and-tenon joint* is essentially the same as the stopped mortise and tenon except that the tenon goes entirely through the mortised board to be revealed on the other side (see Figure 10-32). The through mortise and tenon is a staple of Arts and Crafts furniture from the early 1900s.

The following steps show you how to make this joint with a drill press and chisel and a table saw using a tenoning jig.

To cut the mortise with a drill press and chisel:

1. **Mark the mortise on your board.**

2. **Choose a drill bit that matches the width of your mortise as closely as possible (without going over).**

3. Set the fence so that your workpiece is positioned correctly under the bit.

4. Set the depth of cut on the tool.

5. Drilling slowly, make your first hole at one end of the mortise.

6. Make the next pass at the other end of the mortise.

7. Drill out the rest of the mortise by setting your bit next to the previous hole and progressively moving toward the first hole you drilled.

   Don't overlap the holes because this puts stress on the bit and creates uneven holes.

8. Clear out the rest of the wood in the mortise with your chisel.

To make the tenon on a table saw with a tenoning jig (a tenoning jig helps you hold the board vertically; check out Figure 10-33).

If you don't have a tenoning jig, follow the steps for the stopped/blind tenon to cut a through tenon on a table saw.

1. Mark your board for the cuts.

2. Set the depth of cut for the tenon.

   This is generally ⅓ of the thickness of the board.

3. Using the miter gauge in the left-hand slot, run the board through the saw to cut a single-saw-blade-wide cut at the mark.

4. Turn the board over and cut the other side.

5. Take your miter gauge out of the miter slot and replace it with the tenoning jig.

6. Clamp the board vertically in the jig.

7. Raise the blade to the height of the tenon.

8. Run the board through the saw (refer to Figure 10-33).

9. Turn the board around and repeat the process.

Figure 10-32:
A through mortise-and-tenon joint is one of the most beautiful joints that you can make.

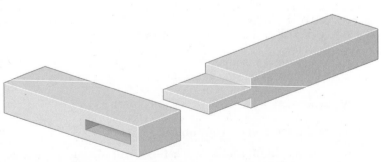

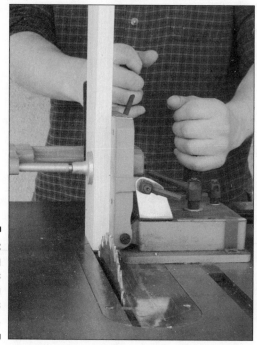

Figure 10-33:
A tenoning
jig makes
cutting
tenons
really easy.

Angled

An *angled mortise and tenon* is commonly used for chairs because the rail comes out of the leg at an angle (see Figure 10-34). However, this angle makes the joint tricky. You can create an angled mortise and tenon in two different ways: by angling the tenon or by angling the mortise. Which one you choose will depend on your style and the project you're working on. I explain both of the options in this section.

You don't need to angle both the mortise and tenon, just one or the other.

For me, the easiest and most accurate way to make an angled tenon is by hand. These are the steps I follow:

1. **Mark your tenon as shown in Figure 10-35.**

2. **Cut the shoulder cuts first using a handsaw.**

3. **Cut the cheek cuts (the wide sides of the tenon).**

To make an angled mortise:

1. **Place the piece to be mortised on an angled piece of wood and clamp it to the bench.**

2. **Cut the mortise as you would cut a regular mortise, with your chisel, drill press, or benchtop mortiser perpendicular to the table (see Figure 10-36).**

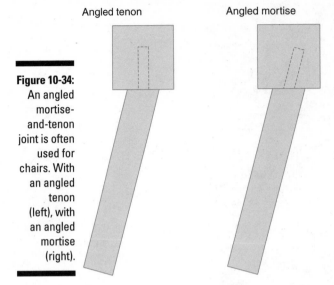

Angled tenon   Angled mortise

Figure 10-34:
An angled
mortise-
and-tenon
joint is often
used for
chairs. With
an angled
tenon
(left), with
an angled
mortise
(right).

Speeding things up with modern frame joints

With all the joints woodworkers already have at their disposal, you might not expect them to come up with new ones, but they do. In fact, a few have become very popular, including doweled and biscuited joints, which are both fast and easy to make. They may not do for all purposes (I wouldn't use them on chairs, for instance), but they're useful in a lot of places.

Dowel joints

Like the dowel joints I present at the beginning of this chapter, dowel joints for frame construction have a definite job to do (see Figure 10-37). Dowel joints aren't as strong as a mortise and tenon, but for some things such as lightweight doors for cupboards, they can work very well.

To make this joint, line up and cut your boards for a butt joint (see the section, "Butting in about butt edge joints" earlier in this chapter), mark where you want the dowels to go, drill the holes in both boards, and assemble. The only tricky part about making these joints is getting the dowel holes lined up properly. You can buy inexpensive jigs to help you do this.

Biscuit joints

Another common modern joint is a biscuit joint (see Figure 10-38). Biscuit joints have a little more room for error and are nearly as strong as doweled joints. I wouldn't use a biscuit on a chair or table leg but for any other joint that I'd consider for a bridle or dowel joint I'd use one of these. Biscuits are especially useful for edge-to-edge gluing (such as the biscuit reinforced butt joints in the section "Taking a bite out of biscuit joints" earlier in this chapter) and for assembling face frames (see Chapter 13).

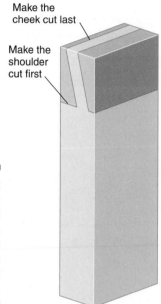

Make the
cheek cut last

Make the
shoulder
cut first

Figure 10-35:
To make
an angled
tenon,
cut the
shoulders
first and the
cheeks next.

Figure 10-36:
To make
an angled
mortise,
support your
workpiece
at an angle
and cut as
usual.

You do need a special tool (called a biscuit joiner) to make the cuts for the biscuits. But with the speed at which you can work, you'll never wonder why you bought the machine. Joining wood is as easy as marking the wood and cutting the slot for the biscuit. The only disadvantage I see with this type of joint is that making them is so fast and easy you'll be tempted to use them when you should use a stronger joint.

Figure 10-37:
A dowel frame joint can work well for lightweight doors or face frames for dressers.

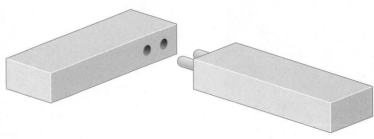

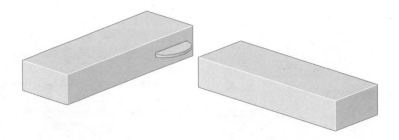

Figure 10-38:
A biscuited frame joint is great for places where you don't need all the strength of a mortise-and-tenon.

Slot

Biscuit

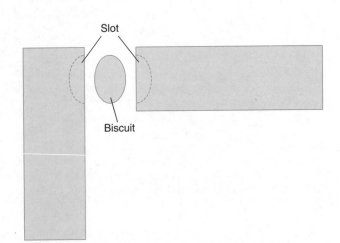

Chapter 11

Making the Most of Mechanical Fasteners

*N*othing beats a good solid wood joint, but sometimes even the most diehard woodworker needs to resort to mechanical fasteners (nails and screws). For instance, if you're reinforcing carcass joints, holding joints in place while glue dries, attaching tabletops, or installing hardware, you may need to turn to mechanical fasteners. In this chapter, I go over the different types of mechanical fasteners and help you find the best ones to use in a given situation.

Understanding the Role of Mechanical Fasteners

Screws and nails aren't usually used in fine furniture-making except for attaching hardware or for decoration. In most cases, wood joints do the job better than screws. However, sometimes a screw or nail can make joining wood easier and faster. Also, adding a screw or nail to a wood joint can increase the joint's strength or make assembling the project easier.

For example, when building a carcass with dado joints, I often send a nail (with a nail gun) into the joint to hold it while I put the rest of the dados in place. I run the nail at an angle to the joint from the inside of the carcass. If I use a square to hold the joining pieces at a 90-degree angle while I nail, I often end up with a perfectly square carcass before I even attach the clamps.

Another time I find mechanical fasteners handy is when I make a carcass out of medium density fiberboard (MDF). Attaching a screw from the outside of the dado joint and into the shelf piece adds a considerable amount of strength to the joint in this less-than-strong wood. If you try this, make sure you pre-drill the hole before screwing in the screw; otherwise, you'll split the MDF.

Securing with Screws

Screws come in many sizes and configurations. Knowing which screw to use in a particular situation isn't rocket science. But I do have some general guidelines that you can follow to help you get the best securing force for the job. Wood screws consists of three parts:

- ✔ **The threads:** The threads draw the screw into the wood and hold it in place. This section takes up about ⅔ of the length of the screw.

- ✔ **The shank:** The shank is the unthreaded section further up toward the head that acts like a dowel and allows the two pieces of wood to be pulled together.

- ✔ **The head:** The head serves two purposes, as follows:

  - Gives you a place to apply the torque necessary to drive the screw

  - Keeps the screw from being pulled into the wood

Handling head shapes

Screws come with a variety of head shapes. Here's a closer look at the three most common shapes (see Figure 11-1):

- ✔ **Flat.** Flat-headed screws have flat tops and tapered bottoms. This structure allows you to *countersink* (a beveled hole allowing the head to sit even with the surface of the wood) the head so that it doesn't stick out above the wood. The flat-head screw is the most common wood screw and is used for joinery such as the carcass screwing procedure I describe in the "Understanding the Role of Mechanical Fasteners" section earlier in this chapter.

- ✔ **Round.** The round-head screw has a rounded top and a flat bottom. This type of screw is used most often for attaching a tabletop to its base. With the flat bottom to the head, this screw can be used with a washer to give you some room for movement when the hole for the screw is slightly larger than the screw itself.

- ✔ **Oval.** Oval-head screws are a variation on the flat-head screw and are most commonly used on hardware. With the tapered bottom, the screw needs to be countersunk, but the rounded head will protrude above the surface. This gives a more traditional look to the hardware.

Figure 11-1:
Screws have
a variety
of head
shapes, with
the most
common
being flat,
round,
and oval.

Eyeing the sizing

When you choose a screw, you have two dimensions to consider: the length and the diameter. The length is simply listed in inches or millimeters, and the diameter is listed in what seems to be an arbitrary sizing number, such a #6.

Sizing numbers go from 0 to 20 with the lower number indicating a smaller diameter. The most common sizes for general woodworking are from #4 to #12. I find myself using the #6, #8, and #10 the most. Most screws are in even number sizes. Odd-number screws are hard to find. But don't worry about this, because with the even-numbered sizes you still have plenty of variations to choose from.

Screw lengths run from ¼ inch to over 5 or 6 inches. Choose a length of screw that is at least ⅛ inch shorter than the combined thickness of the boards you want to screw together. If the screw's tip comes too close to the surface of the wood, it creates a bulge.

Selecting drive slots

The head of the screw has a slot into which you put your driver to drive the screw. You can find a variety of different drive slot shapes; the three most common are slotted, Phillips (cross-head), and square. Take a look at Figure 11-2 to see what they look like.

I try to avoid slotted drive wood screws because they can't handle nearly as much torque as either Phillips or square drive screws.

Whichever slot style you choose, make sure that you match the screwdriver size to the screw. If the driver doesn't fit snugly in the screw head slot, you increase the chances of stripping out the slot, which will make your screw useless and difficult to remove.

Figure 11-2:
Common wood screw drive slots are slotted, Phillips, and square.

Using screws on furniture

If you use screws for making furniture, you need to know about three main processes:

- **Pre-drilling:** To keep from splitting the wood when you drive the screw in, you need to drill a small hole (called a *pilot hole*) to make room for the screw. The pilot hole should be slightly smaller than the narrowest part of the screw between the threads. Drill this hole as deep as the screw is long.

  In order for the screw's shank to fit into the hole and not bind up, you need to drill the top third of the hole a little wider than the pilot hole. This is called the *shank (free) hole.* The shank hole should be the same diameter as the shank of the screw.

- **Countersinking:** If you use flat- or oval-head screws, you need to countersink them so that the head sits flush with the surface of the wood. You can countersink with a special countersinking drill bit that drills both the pilot hole and the countersink at the same time. Or you can use a separate countersink tool. These tools come in both hand-driven and drill-bit formats. A countersink bit drills a shallow hole at the same angle as the head of the screw.

- **Counter-boring:** If you want to hide the screw head completely from sight, you need to drill a wider hole for the entire head to go into. This hole is called a counter-bore and is generally about $\frac{1}{4}$ inch deep by $\frac{3}{8}$-inch diameter and filled with a piece of wood after the screw is inserted. This piece of wood can be a dowel or a *plug* or *button cap.* A plug is a piece of wood cut out from a board with the grain running in the same direction as the surface of the wood you're screwing together. You can buy a special drill bit that will drill plugs from your scrap wood. This type of bit is called, logically enough, a *plug-cutting bit.*

Getting Down to the Nitty-Gritty of Nails

I'm not a big fan of nails. I think screws do a better job securing joints with less chance of splitting or damaging the wood. The only exception is the nail gun.

I find it to be indispensable for building carcasses quickly. With that said, this section gives you the lowdown on nails and when and where woodworkers use them.

Digging into brads

Brads are small diameter nails with tiny heads not much larger than the diameter of the nail itself. Brads come in sizes from ½ inch to 2 inches long and are mainly used to attach plywood cabinet backs to the carcass or to attach trim pieces such as moldings.

Finding finish nails

Finish nails are similar to brads except they're larger in diameter. They have the same overall shape with a small head that can be sunk into the wood to hide it. Finish nails come in sizes ranging from 1 inch to many inches long and are listed according to a *penny system,* where each larger nail size is slightly wider and ¼ inch longer. In this system, a 2d nail is 1 inch long, a 3d nail is 1¼ inches long, a 4d nail is 1½ inches long, and so on.

Brads and finish nails need to be set below the surface to hide the nail. You do this with a tool called a *nail set.* When you drive the nail, leave the head up about ⅛ inch and drive it into the wood ⅛ inch or so below the surface with the nail set.

If you don't have a nail set the right size, another nail turned upside down and pressed against the head of the driven nail (the nails will be head to head) will do the trick. Just tap it flush with the surface with a hammer. Then turn the nail around and use the dulled tip to drive the head ⅛ inch below the surface.

Nailing nail guns

A nail gun is one of those optional shop tools that most people wait a long time before buying only to slap themselves on the forehead and say, "I can't believe I waited so long to get this." (At least, this was the case for me.)

Nail guns are one of the truly handy options for the woodworking shop. I don't even use regular nails any longer. "A nail gun or nothing" is my motto. If you build a lot of carcasses, I highly recommend that you try a nail gun out. I'm sure you'll see what I mean.

Nail guns use compressed air (or hammer action) to send the nail at high speed into the wood. As you may expect, this can be very dangerous. All nail gun manufacturers have safety mechanisms in place on their guns, but accidents still happen. For example, it's not uncommon for a nail to blow out of the wood by deflecting off the grain of harder woods and shooting out the side of the wood. Or a nail can get you in the finger if you're holding the wood when you nail. Use nails guns with caution and follow the safety guidelines presented by the manufacturer.

You can find tons of nail guns. Some require an air compressor to work, whereas others are electrical or use rechargeable batteries.

Getting What You Need: Stocking Up on Your Screw and Nail Selection

So, with all the different types of nails and screws available, what should you have around? This section lists some of the must-haves so that when you want to fasten something mechanically, you'll have something usable around.

Screws

Make sure you have a selection of lengths of #6, #8, and #10 wood screws with either Phillips-head (cross-head) or square-drive slots. Good lengths to have are ¼-inch increments of screws between ¾ inch to 2 inches. This will cover most woodworking applications.

Make sure that you have screwdrivers that fit these screws.

Nails

Stock up on brads that are ⅝ inch, ¾ inch, and 1 inch long. Make sure you have finish nails that are 1¼ and 2½ inches long. The sizes of the finish nails will be 3d, 4d, 5d, and 6d. These nails should cover you for finish work as well as making mock-ups of projects. If you want some nails for general household stuff, get a few sizes of common nails. Common nails have flat, wide heads that are much bigger than the diameter of the nail itself.

Part IV

Getting Your Hands (and Shop) Dirty: Turning Raw Wood into Furniture

The 5th Wave   By Rich Tennant

"...and this is no off-the-showroom rack either. Lars made this one himself."

In this part . . .

One of the best parts of woodworking is that after all your hard work you end up with something of value. Something that you can point to and proudly say, "I made that." In this part, you get a chance to build some projects. I'm not talking about some useless junk, but some valuable, lasting projects that you'll be proud of.

To start you off, Chapter 12 guides you through the wood-working process and helps you makes sense of all the details involved in building furniture. In Chapter 13, you discover the ins and outs of making bookcases and other storage units. Chapter 14 shows you how to make tables, and Chapter 15 introduces you to the process of putting together dressers and cupboards, including making doors and drawers. In each of these chapters, I also give you insights into creating your own unique variations on the projects listed.

Chapter 12

Understanding the Building Process

A woodworking project involves a very definite process. From choosing the wood and milling it to size to assembling the piece properly, each step needs to be done correctly, or your project won't be successful. In fact, it may not even go together at all.

In this chapter, I guide you through the entire process of building a project and give you a chance to see how the various steps along the way lead to success. You can explore all the details of a project plan — the diagrams, dimensions, and procedures. You get to know the best way to choose the part of the board from which to cut each piece, and you walk through the assembly process from dry fitting to gluing up in sections.

Following Plans: Making Sense of Diagrams, Dimensions, and Procedures

Unless you build on the fly and can visualize every step of the cutting and building process, you need plans from which to work. Plans make the building process easy, because they spell out exactly how much, what kind, and what size of wood to cut for each part of the project. In addition, plans tell you how to put those parts together.

If you can accurately follow a set of plans, you can make any project for which you have the skills and tools. The main parts of a project plan are the

✔ Material list

✔ Measured drawings

✔ Procedures

I outline each of these parts in this section.

Checking out your material list

The material list gives you a rundown of all the wood, fasteners, and hardware you'll need to build a project. By glancing at this list, you can quickly determine what you need to buy before you get started. Figure 12-1 shows a typical material list for a table. It runs down the parts for the project, their quantity (bordered by parentheses), and their cut size in thickness (T), width (W), and length (L).

Figure 12-1:
A material list tells you what you need to make a project.

Material list				
	Qty	T	W	L
1. Legs	(4)	2" x	2" x	29"
2. Short rail	(2)	3/4" x	3" x	35 1/4"
3. Long rail	(2)	3/4" x	3" x	71 1/4"
4. Top	(1)	1" x	36" x	72"
5. Cleats	(8)	3/4" x	1 1/2" x	2"
6. Screws	(8)	1 1/4" #8		

Numbers, give me numbers: Measured drawings

Measured drawings are the heart and soul of a project plan. A measured drawing details each and every board, screw, nail, and piece of hardware that goes into a project *and* where each of these things goes. With this drawing, you should be able to build a project even without the other two sections of a project plan.

You may need some time to get used to how a measured drawing organizes a project, but soon you'll be able to glance over a measured drawing and tell right away whether you want to tackle the project. And with a little experience, you'll likely also be able to tell how much time you will need to build it.

A measured drawing shows a project from several angles to give you a better idea of how the finished project will look. However, the level of detail varies depending on who created the drawing. Some designers detail everything and include full-size drawings of joints or unusually-shaped parts (the back of a chair, for instance). Other designers provide very simplistic drawings that just show the overall dimensions of a part, its position in the scheme of things, and the overall view of the project. Figure 12-2 shows this kind of detail. (Because this is how I draw plans for myself. Oh, and I'm not a very good draftsman.)

Top

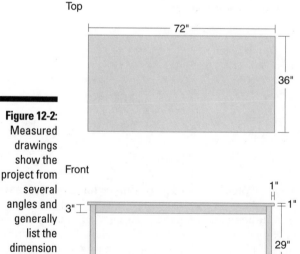

Figure 12-2:
Measured
drawings
show the
project from
several
angles and
generally
list the
dimension
of each part.

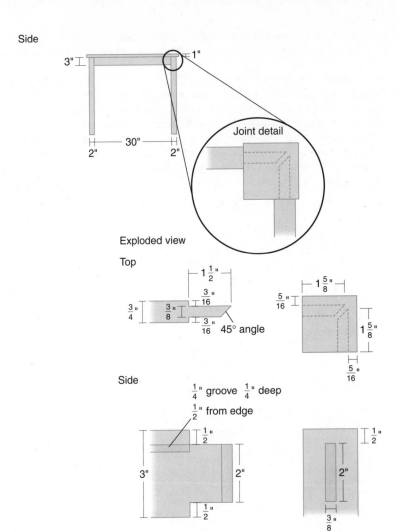

Side

3" 1"

Joint detail

30"

2" 2"

Exploded view

Top

$1\frac{1}{2}$"

$\frac{3}{16}$"

$\frac{3}{4}$" $\frac{3}{8}$"

$\frac{3}{16}$" 45° angle

$1\frac{5}{8}$"

$\frac{5}{16}$"

$1\frac{5}{8}$"

$\frac{5}{16}$"

Side

$\frac{1}{4}$" groove $\frac{1}{4}$" deep

$\frac{1}{2}$" from edge

$\frac{1}{2}$"

3" 2"

$\frac{1}{2}$"

$\frac{1}{2}$"

2"

$\frac{3}{8}$"

If you don't buy project plans (Chapter 21 has some resources for buying plans), I highly recommend that you make your own drawings to work from. Creating the drawings will alert you to difficult sections in the project and help you to determine how much wood you need. You don't have to be elaborate; just draw something simple. If the project includes any tricky parts (curves, unusual angles, and so on), then draw those sections full size so you can clearly see what you're up against. In fact, I suggest that you make a template.

A *template* is a pattern for the part recreated in full size, which you can use over and over again. Templates are generally made out of ¼-inch plywood or

Masonite. Templates are really handy if you need to make more than one copy of a particular part (chairs, for instance, because many people make more than one chair at a time).

Speaking of templates, I highly recommend making templates for any full-size drawings that are part of the plans you buy. Templates make milling the part to the right size much easier, and you'll always have them on hand. See the section entitled "Making the Cut" later in the chapter for more information about milling.

Putting the pieces together: Using a procedures list

The procedures list is the section that walks you through the process of assembling your project into its final form. Keep in mind that the procedures list is not included in all project plans, because many people assume you can figure out the best way to put something together just by looking at the measured drawings.

Procedures lists can really be helpful for beginning woodworkers though, so I highly recommend that you find plans with detailed procedures lists when you first start out. Doing so will make life a lot easier for you. Figure 12-3 shows a typical procedures list. This one is pretty simple, but some plans will have very detailed lists.

Procedures

1. Choose, dimension, and assemble boards for top leaving 1" extra in width and length.
2. Dimension legs and stretchers.
3. Cut groove in stretchers for cleats.
4. Cut 3/8" x 2" x 1 3/4" mortises in legs.
5. Cut 3/8" x 2" x 1 5/8" tenons in stretchers.
6. Sand legs and stretchers to 150 grit.
7. Assemble short stretcher to legs.
8. Assemble glued up leg assemblies to long stretchers and check for square.
9. Cut tabletop to its final dimensions.
10. Sand top.
11. Finish sand leg/stretcher assembly.
12. Apply stain.
13. Apply top coat.
14. Attach top to leg assembly using cleats.

Figure 12-3:
A procedures list helps you keep track of what you have to do.

If a set of plans that you buy doesn't include a procedures list, make one before you start to build. Create your procedures list by carefully looking over the material list and drawings. Then walk yourself through the building process, writing down the steps you need to take. When you actually start to build, you won't get confused and miss a joint or mill a part twice. (This is really easy to do.)

Creating a Cut List

Before I start building anything, I take my measured drawing, pull out the wood I have on hand, and mark where each part of the project is coming from with pencil or chalk. This minimizes waste and also helps to plan the beauty of a project. For example, if I have a dresser with four drawers, I want the wood I use for the drawer fronts and the face frame (if there is one) to match. I want the color and grain patterns to create a visually pleasing arrangement. The only way to make sure this happens is to look at each board and carefully consider where it should go. This will take some time, and you may end up rejecting a few boards in order to find a composition, which is why I always recommend buying more wood than you need for a given project. (See Chapter 2 for more about choosing wood.)

Check out Figure 12-4 for a look at a cut list. The drawing on the left shows parts cut out of a solid board, and the drawing on the right shows how the parts of a *carcass* (the box for a cabinet) would be cut out of a sheet of plywood.

Selecting the best section of the board

Not only do you need to consider the look of the wood you use for a given part of the project, but you should also think about how that wood will behave in response to moisture changes. Check out Figure 12-5. It shows how a board expands and contracts with changes in moisture. You want to make sure that any boards that meet will expand and contract in such a way that they won't tear apart a joint or weaken your project.

On the whole, wood moves more against the grain than it moves with it. So as humidity changes, you'll see less change along its length and more along its width. Also, because plain-sawn boards have growth rings that run at a close angle to the face of the board, you may see more movement on one side of the board over another. This can cause warping, twisting, or cupping if the change in humidity is extreme. (Chapter 2 has more about warping, twisting, and cupping.)

Figure 12-4:
A cut list shows where you plan to cut your parts from a board (left) or sheet of plywood (right).

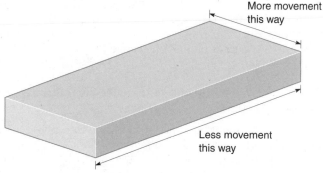

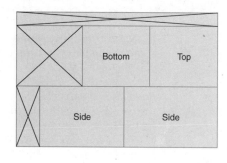

Figure 12-5:
Consider how wood expands and contracts when you choose it for a project.

More movement this way

Less movement this way

Organizing your cut list

After you've chosen the wood from which to cut all the parts of your project, your next step is to decide in what order you want to cut these boards. I usually organize my boards according to the type of cuts they need and what tool I'll use to cut them. I start with the largest pieces, cut the pieces to size, and then work on the actual joints (see Chapter 10 for a complete discussion of joints). I also usually proceed in stages and, if I'm working on a large project, I work on one section at a time.

If you don't already have the wood at your shop, take your cut list with you to the lumberyard and mark off the parts of the cut list as you choose your wood. Doing this helps you choose the right boards for your project and ensures that you end up with the right amount of wood. In fact, I recommend that you mark the boards that you buy while you're still at the store. This will save you time when you get home.

Preparing the Board for Milling

Before you cut your wood down to its final size, I recommend that you do some preliminary cutting to prepare the wood for its final milling. This is called (logically enough) pre-milling.

Pre-milling means cutting the board down to near its final dimensions so that the wood can acclimate to its new size. I can't tell you how many times I've had a nice straight board twist slightly when I cut it in half. This is the nature of wood: You can't predict what's going to happen after you change its shape. So cut the boards down to size (well, almost), and wait to see what happens.

I usually pre-mill the board down to its final length and width plus an inch and down to its final thickness plus an ⅛ inch (if possible). Then I let the boards rest for a day or so before I do the final milling. After the boards have rested for a day, I check to see that they're still flat and straight. If they aren't, then I need to flatten them out. This process involves using a jointer and a planer to flatten and square the board (Chapter 7 has more on planers and jointers). Here are the steps to follow:

1. **Run one of the faces of the board (the wide part) through the jointer until the board is flat.**

   This may take a few light passes. Pay attention to running the stock over the jointer with proper grain direction to avoid tear-out. If you don't know which direction to feed the board into the jointer to avoid tear-out, use a scrap piece and run it through first in one direction and then the other to see which provides a cleaner cut.

2. **Turn the board up on its edge and run it through the jointer with the flat face (the one you just made) against the fence.**

3. **Flip the board over and do the other edge.**

   Again, the freshly flattened face should be against the fence.

4. **Take the board over to your planer and run the board through with the flat face against the bed of the planer until it's flat too, once again paying attention to proper grain direction to avoid tear-out.**

   This may take a few passes.

5. **Now you should have a flat, straight board again.**

After the board is straight and flat, you can move on to the actual milling stage, which I describe in the next section.

Making the Cut

Milling is just an extension of the pre-milling stage and consists of doing the final cutting to the board to make the final part for your project. This includes all the joints, routing (like rounding over the edge of the board), and rough sanding of all the parts so that everything is ready for assembly.

I follow this process when milling a board:

1. **Cut the board to width plus ¹⁄₃₂ inch.**

2. **Run the freshly cut edge through the jointer until it's at its final width.**

   Set the jointer to take off ¹⁄₃₂ inch or less and only take 1 or 2 passes off the edge to get your final width dimension.

3. **Thickness plane the board to its final thickness.**

4. **Crosscut a square edge on one end of the board.**

5. **Cut the board to length, measuring from the freshly squared end (the total length includes any tenons or other joints).**

6. **Cut out any joints such as mortises or tenons.**

7. **Cut any curves or other shaping such as routing.**

   Always do all shaping, such as rounding over the edge of a board, after all the joinery is done, so that you do not lose any straight line references that you need at various machines against fences, jigs, and so on.

 After all my parts are milled, I go over them with a random orbit sander (see Chapter 6) and sand them smooth using 150 grit sandpaper (see Chapter 16). This saves me a ton of time later on and makes getting at inside corners easy — because they aren't inside corners yet. Be careful not to sand the joint parts such as tenons, because this will change how well your joints fit.

Putting It All Together

You can approach the assembly and milling process in several ways. Some people mill everything and then assemble, whereas others prefer to mill a section of the project, assemble it, mill the next section and assemble it, and so on. Personally, I usually combine the two and mill according to cut type. Depending on the size of the overall project, I sometimes assemble in sections. I'm sure that as you do more projects you'll find the way that works best for you.

Preparing for assembly

After you get all the parts milled (or at least those for the section you're working on), the next step is to lay those parts out on your workbench. This will confirm that you have all the parts that you need and help you to visualize the assembly process. As you lay the parts out, double-check your material list and your drawing to see that everything is there and that all the parts are milled properly.

Next get all your assembly materials ready:

- **Clamps.** Bring all the clamps you think you'll need (plus a couple extra, just in case) over to your bench and put them where they'll be easy to reach.

- **A damp rag** and a **dull chisel.** You use these to remove any extra glue that squeezes out of the joints when you add the clamps (more about this in the "Cleaning up your mess" section later in this chapter).

- **Glue and glue brush.** You can't glue without the glue! When I use carpenter's glue (see Chapter 9), I always use an *acid brush* (a small metal-handled brush) to apply it. The acid brush helps me achieve an even coat and it's also small enough to get into mortises and other joints.

- **A rubber mallet.** This will allow you to tap any joint into place and to make adjustments to the square of the piece if necessary.

- **A straightedge.** When you glue up boards edge to edge (a tabletop, for example) a straightedge allows you to see if your assembly is flat. (The section "Squaring up the parts and verifying flatness" later in this chapter has further details about this.)

- **A tape measure.** This will allow you to check that your work is square when it's glued (see the section "Squaring up the parts and verifying flatness" later in this chapter for more information).

Before you start, make sure that your work area is clean and free of clutter. Gluing up a project is nerve-racking, and you don't want to trip over a tool or a board when you're working. I also recommend keeping all other parts of the project away from your assembly area until you need them. This will eliminate any possible confusion as you work and will keep you from accidentally gluing up the wrong parts.

Dry fitting

After the glue is applied to your parts, you have only a few minutes (about 5 or 10 with white or yellow carpenter's glue) in which to get everything to fit properly. Because of this time limit and the stress that you'll undoubtedly feel as a result, I highly recommend that you do a *dry fit* and run through the glue-up process before you actually break out the glue.

Walk yourself through the process of assembling the parts in front of you by putting each of the joints together, applying the clamps, and checking for square (you can follow the steps in the sections that follow). This will ensure that all the parts fit as they're supposed to and that you have a clear idea of what steps are involved in putting the joints together.

Time yourself as you dry fit the parts. If it takes you more than 10 to 15 minutes, consider breaking the assembly down into several smaller assemblies *(sub-assemblies)* that you can glue together in stages. Or at least plan on applying the glue in stages so that each joint is put together before the glue starts to set.

When you're comfortable with the process, disassemble everything, take a few breaths, and break out the glue.

Applying the glue

If you've done a dry fit of your parts (see previous section), then you just need to redo the process, this time using glue as you go. You shouldn't have any new surprises along the way. Remember that when you work with the glue, you only have a little time in which to get everything to fit back together again. (For more on applying adhesives, go to Chapter 9.)

Here are some other things to consider when you glue up your parts:

- ✔ **Don't use too much glue.** People often use too much when they first start out. A thin coat is all you need on each part of a joint.

- ✔ **When gluing up veneers, apply glue only to the backing material and not the veneer itself, because the veneer will curl and become difficult to work with.**

- ✔ **After you assemble a joint, push (or tap with the mallet) or clamp the joint fully in place; otherwise, the joint may lock up partway.** This is especially important with tight-fitting mortise-and-tenon joints. When joints are wet with glue, the wood swells, and the joints require more force (clamp pressure) to assemble.

- ✔ **Don't panic.** Yes, gluing up can be nerve-racking, but if you panic then you'll end up with a partially assembled piece and will likely have to start over (this is why dry fitting is so important).

Clamping

The trick to clamping is applying just enough pressure to pull the joints tightly together but not so much that you squeeze all the glue out. Clamps hold the joints together until the glue has a chance to dry.

Some other things to consider when clamping include:

- **Make sure that your clamps are perpendicular to the workpiece and not angling off one way or another.** This is especially important when doing edge-to-edge joints (see Chapter 10) because the angled clamps will pull the boards out of alignment.

- **Double-check that you don't apply so much pressure that you warp the workpiece with the pressure.**

- **Make sure that your clamps are centered on the board so that they apply even pressure.** If your clamps aren't centered, they will more easily warp the workpiece. Ideally, the clamp pressure should be applied down the centerline of the joint.

- **If you think you need to use an additional clamp, use it.** You can never have too many clamps (within reason, of course).

Squaring up the parts and verifying flatness

After everything is glued and clamped up properly (see previous sections), you need to make sure that all your parts are square and flat.

Checking for flatness

When you edge-glue a bunch of boards into a tabletop, you want to make sure that those boards remain flat. If you did a good job creating perfectly straight and square edges on each of the boards, the boards will want to lay flat. The only trouble you might have is with too much clamp pressure or an uneven benchtop.

To check for flatness, run your straightedge against the top of the boards. If you can see light through the straightedge as it passes over the boards, they aren't flat. To straighten, adjust the clamps (see the "Clamping" section). If edges are sticking up, you may need to tap them down with the mallet.

Checking for square

In order to check that your assembled parts are *square* (that is, they have 90 degree corners), you need a tape measure. The process is really simple and involves the following steps:

1. **Measure diagonally from the upper right to the lower left corner.**

2. **Measure diagonally from the upper left to the lower right corner.**

   If these numbers match, you're square.

   If not, then you need to square it up. Follow these steps:

   a. **Gently push the upper corner of the measurement that was longer than the other toward that other corner.**

      If this doesn't work (which it often doesn't) try this:

   b. **Take another clamp and run it diagonally from the corners that have the longer measurement and tighten the clamp until both diagonal measurements are equal.**

You can also use a square inside a carcass to check for square in all four corners.

Cleaning up your mess

Ugh, cleaning up is my least favorite part of the assembly process (and I'm sure I'm not alone). After all the stress and work of getting everything to fit properly, all I want to do is sit back and admire my work (or break for a beer). So trust me when I say this: A little work now will save you tons of work later.

Glue is much easier to remove when wet. To clean up glue spills and seepage, follow these steps:

1. **Use a dull chisel or a scraper and gently scrape off the beads of glue that formed around all the joints.**

   Go with the grain and be careful not to gouge the wood.

2. **Take a damp (not wet) cloth and rub around all the joints until you're down to bare wood.**

   Depending on how much glue spillage you have to deal with, you may need to rinse your rag out. I usually keep two rags available. Because I live in a very dry place, I also find that I have to keep a bucket of water right next to my workbench so that I can dampen the rag right before I need to use it. I just make sure that I ring it out so that I don't have any water dripping when I rub the wood.

3. **Be sure to do both sides of your workpiece.**

   Don't forget to clean up the bottoms of drawers and tabletops and insides of carcasses (or anywhere that can't be easily seen).

4. **Double-check that you get all the joints completely clean before you quit.**

Letting it sit

I like to plan my assembling for the end of the day so that I'm not tempted to take the clamps off too soon. I always let the assembled parts sit in the clamps overnight before I try to remove them. This minimizes any chance that the glue hasn't cured enough before I remove the pressure.

Chapter 13

Banging Out Bookcases

· ·

· ·

*B*ecause you bought this book on woodworking, I'm willing to bet that you're also going to buy a few more woodworking books before you're done. So what better first project to make than a place to store these books? Not only are bookcases functional, but they can also be beautiful. And the best part? They're easy to make.

In this chapter, you get a chance to get your hands dirty by building a basic bookcase. Don't worry about being bored with a project that's too easy; if you have a few more skills or just want to push your limits, you can alter the basic bookcase plan to meet your design aesthetic and woodworking experience. To top it off, this chapter also helps you understand the ways that bookcases can be built so that you can design your own unique project.

Parts Is Parts: Breaking Down Bookcases

Bookcases and basic storage units have essentially the same components, which include the carcass, the shelves, and the face frame. The following list explains each of these components in more detail:

✔ **The carcass:** The carcass consists of the sides, top, bottom, and back. It can be made with either sheet products (plywoods) or solid wood. You can use many different joints to make a strong carcass (see Chapter 10 for a complete rundown of the different kinds of joints), but the goal is to build a solid, square box.

✔ **The shelves:** Use either fixed or adjustable shelves. Fixed shelves attach much the same way as the rest of the carcass and can add a lot of strength to the bookcase. On the other hand, adjustable shelves allow flexibility. Many bookcases have both fixed and adjustable shelves. Having one or two fixed shelves can add to the robustness of the bookcase, and including some adjustable shelves gives you flexibility in the way you can set it up.

Shelves are constructed of either solid wood or plywood. Solid wood shelves are strong, but they have a tendency to change size as the moisture in the room changes. If you use solid wood, make the shelves by gluing up fairly narrow boards into the width of the shelf, and make sure you arrange the grain so that the finished board won't warp or twist with changes in moisture.

Also, make the adjustable shelves slightly narrower than the space available for them (⅛ to ¼ inch is a safe amount) if you're using a face frame on the shelf unit. Make them about ¹⁄₁₆ to ⅛ inch shorter in length than the inside width of the bookcase — this will keep the shelf from binding up inside the bookcase if the moisture level gets higher in the room. (Wood expands as moisture levels increase. Check out Chapter 2 for more information.)

For the shelves on bookcases, I prefer to use plywood because it's stable with moisture changes. Lumber-core plywood (see Chapter 2) is best because it's strong enough to handle the weight it'll be subjected to when loaded down. Plywood shelves require some sort of edging on at least the front edge to hide the core of the board. You can use either veneer strips, such as those in the basic bookcase design in the "Making Your Own Simple Bookcase" section later in this chapter, or you can use thicker strips of wood if you choose.

✔ **The face frame:** Face frames attach to the front edges of the top, bottom, and sides to hide the edges, to add a design element to the bookcase, and to make the carcass more rigid. Not all bookcases have face frames.

Making Your Own Simple Bookcase

This section focuses on building a simple bookcase out of furniture-grade plywood. It doesn't include a face frame. Instead, the front edges of all pieces are dressed up with thin veneer edging. If this project seems too easy for you or if you don't care for the design, check out the variations later in this chapter.

Figure 13-1 shows the bookcase detailed in this section, which has adjustable shelves. The structural strength and rigidity of the bookcase comes from the fixed top and bottom, which are rabbeted and dadoed (Chapter 10 has details about these joints) in place. The ¼-inch plywood back adds quite a bit of rigidity to the bookcase.

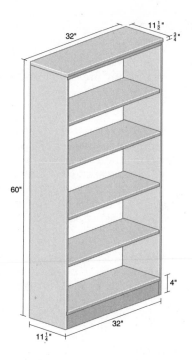

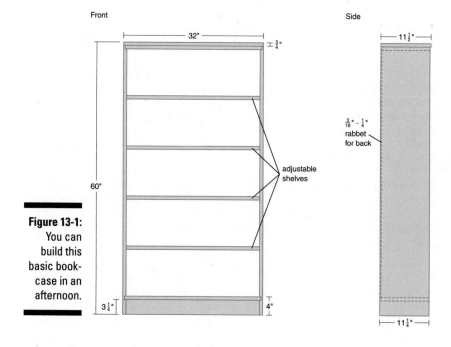

Front

Side

adjustable shelves

$\frac{3}{16}$" – $\frac{1}{4}$" rabbet for back

Figure 13-1:
You can build this basic bookcase in an afternoon.

Going over the basics

The simple bookcase shown in Figure 13-1 can be made in a day (except for the finish) and doesn't require any previous woodworking experience.

Tooling up

For this project, you need a table saw or a circular saw with a cutting guide (like the one I show you how to make in Chapter 8). Aside from the main tool, you need the regular woodworking tools such as a tape measure, clamps (four to six bar clamps), a block plane, and sanders (for more on these and other tools, go to Chapters 5 and 6). In addition, if you use veneer edging with hot melt glue, you need an iron (a regular household iron is fine) to melt the glue. You also need supplies such as sandpaper and glue.

Knowing what techniques to use

To build this bookcase, all you need to be able to do is cut plywood panels square (not into squares), cut rabbet and dado joints (discussed in Chapter 10), and assemble the parts so that they fit properly (Chapter 12 explains this process). Each of these skills will easily develop as you dig into the project.

Assembling your materials list

This basic project uses a single 4-x-8-foot sheet of ¾-inch hardwood veneer plywood and a little under a half 4-x-8-foot sheet of ¼-inch plywood of the same hardwood veneer. You also need about 50 feet of veneer edging in the same species of wood as the plywood veneer to cover the edges of the plywood.

Depending on the type of plywood you want, you can get it at most home centers. If you want mahogany or cherry, however, you'll likely need to go to a decent lumberyard. The veneer edging isn't available at home centers. You need to get the veneer from either a decent lumberyard or a mail-order wood-worker's supplier (check out Chapter 21 for some resources).

Managing your cut list

One of the great things about working with plywood is that all you have to do is cut your pieces to size. You don't have to sort through stacks of boards to find straight and flat pieces from which to cut, and you don't need to spend the time and energy pre-milling the wood after you've chosen it (Chapter 12 has more on pre-milling).

Figure 13-2 shows how to lay out the cuts on the plywood for this bookcase.

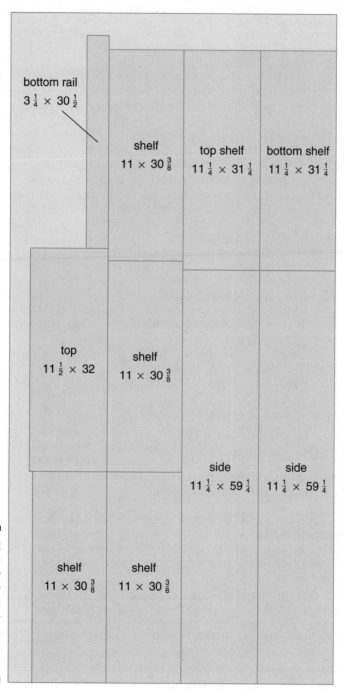

bottom rail
$3\frac{1}{4} \times 30\frac{1}{2}$

shelf
$11 \times 30\frac{3}{8}$

top shelf
$11\frac{1}{4} \times 31\frac{1}{4}$

bottom shelf
$11\frac{1}{4} \times 31\frac{1}{4}$

top
$11\frac{1}{2} \times 32$

shelf
$11 \times 30\frac{3}{8}$

side
$11\frac{1}{4} \times 59\frac{1}{4}$

side
$11\frac{1}{4} \times 59\frac{1}{4}$

shelf
$11 \times 30\frac{3}{8}$

shelf
$11 \times 30\frac{3}{8}$

Figure 13-2:
Before you
cut any
parts, lay
out the cuts
for your
bookcase
on the
plywood.

Before you cut, take a close look at the plywood's grain patterns and choose the best areas for the sides. Because the sides are only 11¼ inches wide, try to find places where you won't have a seam in the middle of the piece (or anywhere, for that matter). Your piece will look best if you have book-matched grain patterns on the sides, which means that the grain patterns are mirror reflections of each other — as though the sides were cut from the same board that was split in half. Figure 13-3 shows what book-matched grain patterns look like.

When you lay out the cuts, make each piece a little larger than it's going to be when you're finished. (I like to use a pencil to lightly draw each of the cuts on the plywood.) Doing so gives you some room for error in case you end up with a less-than-perfect cut from muscling the large piece of wood around on your table saw or from using a circular saw to get the sheet down to a manageable size. I like to give ½ inch or so extra in both directions. So, the sidepieces would be laid out and roughly cut to 11¾ x 60 inches, which gives you ½ inch extra in width and ¾ inch extra in length.

Building the bookcase

After laying out your cuts on the plywood (see the "Managing your cut list" section), cut them using a circular saw and saw guide or your table saw. I recommend using the table saw only if you have someone to help you, a series of tables or roller stands, or an outfeed table that you can position near your saw to handle the weight of the full sheet.

Making the cut: Dimensioning your wood

To make cuts from the plywood sheet, I like to start with the crosscuts and then do the rip cuts. Crosscuts tend to tear out the edge of the wood, so by making them first, you can cut off the tear-outs and have the cleanest cut possible. Make sure that you have a good, sharp carbide-tipped blade in your saw. Use either an all-purpose or a sheet stock blade.

Cut the plywood with the good side of the board facing up. The worst tear-out occurs at the bottom.

Table 13-1 shows what your final cuts should be.

Table 13-1	Final Cuts for Basic Bookcase		
Name of Part	*Number Needed*	*Dimensions*	*Material*
Sides	2	¾" x 11¼" x 59¼"	Plywood
Fixed top and bottom	1 each	¾" x 11¼" x 31¼"	Plywood
Adjustable shelves	4	¾" x 11" x 30⅜"	Plywood

Name of Part	Number Needed	Dimensions	Material
Top	1	¾" x 32" x 11½"	Plywood
Bottom rail	1	¾" x 3¼" x 30½"	Plywood
Back	1	¼" x 31½" x 55½"	Plywood

Figure 13-3:
Choose the places to cut your board based upon the grain pattern.

Finagling the fit: Making the joints

This bookcase uses rabbet and dado joints. The dados are only cut in the sides for the fixed top and bottom (see Figure 13-4), but the rabbets are cut in the back inside edges of the sides, the top, and bottom to accept the ¼-inch plywood back (see Figure 13-5).

You can cut the dados and rabbets with a dado blade set to the correct width; with a dado blade you only need to cut once. You can also use a regular blade to nibble out the cut by making several passes with the wood and adjusting the fence each time.

✔ **Using a dado blade:** If you use a dado blade, be sure to test the width of your cut and don't rely on the measurement of the dado. A piece of ¾-inch plywood isn't necessarily ¾ inch thick. It may actually be ¹¹⁄₁₆ or ²³⁄₃₂ inch thick.

If you cut the dado ¾ inch and the wood is ¹¹⁄₁₆ inch, your joint will be too loose to work effectively. I know this seems obvious, but you'd be surprised at how often people make this error. Rather than take a measurement of the thickness of the board and trust it, make a test cut in scrap wood and make adjustments until the joint fits tightly. You may need to use spacers with your dado blade to get the correct width. (*Spacers* are slim metal shims that go between the blades in the dado stack. You may have to purchase these separately from the dado blade itself.)

✔ **Using a regular blade:** If you use a regular blade to cut your rabbets and dados, start by cutting the outsides of the joint and then nibbling away at the middle. With this approach, you should still test your joint with scraps so that you don't cut the dado too wide.

Front view joinery detail

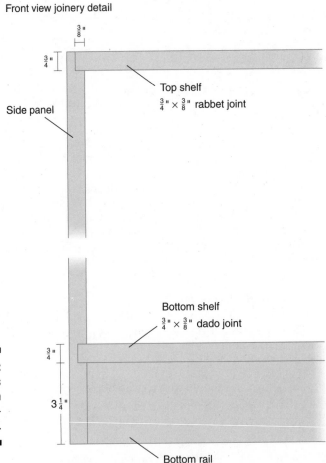

$\frac{3}{8}$"

$\frac{3}{4}$"

Side panel

Top shelf
$\frac{3}{4}$" × $\frac{3}{8}$" rabbet joint

Bottom shelf
$\frac{3}{4}$" × $\frac{3}{8}$" dado joint

$\frac{3}{4}$"

Figure 13-4:
Dado joints
are cut in
the side-
pieces.

$3\frac{1}{4}$"

Bottom rail
use butt joints

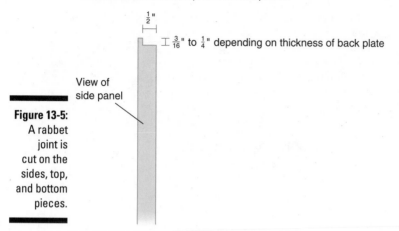

Rabbet in back of side, top, and bottom pieces

$\frac{1}{2}$"

$\frac{3}{16}$" to $\frac{1}{4}$" depending on thickness of back plate

View of side panel

Figure 13-5:
A rabbet joint is cut on the sides, top, and bottom pieces.

For the rabbets, you don't need to worry about using the exact width of the dado blade if you use a sacrificial fence (Chapter 10 has more on using dado blades). Just make sure you check the ¼-inch plywood's thickness. The last sheet I bought was only ³⁄₁₆ inch thick. You want the rabbet cut so that the plywood is flush with the back edge of the sides, top, and bottom.

Creating the adjustable shelves

To make the adjustable shelves, you need to drill a series of ¼-inch holes in the inside of the sidepieces for the shelf supports. The easiest way to drill these holes is to make a jig. Figure 13-6 shows a simple jig made out of ¼-inch plywood or hardboard (such as Masonite) and a strip of ¾-inch plywood. The ¼-inch wood has a series of holes spaced 1 inch apart and 2 inches in from the ¾-inch board. The ¾-inch board is used as a guide.

To use the jig, place it against the front or back edge of the side piece, clamp it to the workpiece, and load a ¼-inch drill bit into your power drill with either a piece of tape or a depth collar set to ¾ inch. This will create a hole ½ inch deep in the side of the carcass into which you can put shelf holders like those shown in Figure 13-7.

Be sure that the front set of holes (2 inches in from front edge) and the back set of holes (2 inches in from the back edge) on both sides are at the same level. Use a square to strike a pencil line starting from the lowest hole on both sides and work your way up the bookcase sides, drilling and rechecking for hole alignment as you move the jig and clamp it in place.

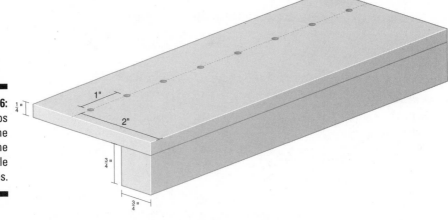

Figure 13-6:
A jig helps you drill the holes for the adjustable shelves.

Figure 13-7:
Shelf clips fit into the hole to hold the shelf up.

Don't bother drilling holes less than 8 inches from the top and 12 inches from the bottom. You'll rarely place a shelf closer than that to the top or bottom.

Assembling the parts

When making this bookcase, you have to glue only the sides, top, and bottom pieces in at the same time, because the rest of the shelves are adjustable.

Before you add any glue to the joints, do a dry fit of the carcass to give you a chance to rehearse your moves and to ensure that all the parts fit properly.

Here are the steps to follow for assembly:

1. **Lay one of the sides flat on the table with the dados facing up.**

2. **Put a thin layer of glue in the bottom dado.**

3. **Put a little glue on the edge of the bottom shelf and slip it into the appropriate dado groove.**

   You may need to tap the shelf in with a mallet if the joint is tight.

4. **Gently flip the side on its edge so that the front of the carcass is facing up.**

   The bottom shelf should be in its groove solidly so it will hold up the side.

5. **Run a thin film of glue in the bottom dado on the other sidepiece.**

6. **Apply glue to the edge of the bottom shelf and slip the shelf into the bottom dado groove on the other sidepiece.**

7. **Apply glue to the top dados on both sides and glue to the ends of the top board.**

8. **Place the top board into the top dados and carefully place a bar clamp across the top of the bookcase to hold the top gently in place.**

   You have about ten minutes before the glue sets, so take a deep breath and try not to get stressed.

   If your joints are really tight and you need to tap harder to get them to fit, use a scrap piece of wood (of the same species) to tap against instead of tapping directly against the side of the bookcase. Using another piece of wood as a cushion keeps you from denting the wood.

9. **Using two clamps, clamp up the front edge of the bookcase at the top and bottom.**

10. **With the front edge clamps secure, lift the bookcase slightly and slide clamps under it.**

11. **Secure the bottom clamps.**

12. **Check the bookcase for square.**

    You check for square by measuring diagonally across the bookcase. If both measurements are equal, you're square. If not, you need to make adjustments. Chapter 12 explains how to do this.

13. **Clean up.**

    Chapter 12 goes into detail about the cleanup process, so flip back there if you need to.

14. **Take a break.**

    Chances are your nerves are shot, so resist the urge to get more work done at this point. After a short break, you can get back to work (or better yet, come back to it the next day).

Let the bookcase set overnight. Then remove the clamps and admire your work. Be very careful in handling the bookcase at this stage. There is very little strength in the top dado (rabbet) joints until you get the back installed, and if you drop it or stress it unduly those joints will let go. Congratulations, you now have a bookcase carcass!

Applying the veneer edging

If you use the veneer edging that comes in a roll and attaches with hot melt adhesive, all you have to do is cut the edging to length (go a little long — you can trim it when it's attached) and iron it on.

I like to attach the shelf edging first and the side panel edging last. I follow this procedure:

1. **Cut the strips an inch longer than they need to be.**

2. **Using an iron, attach the strips to the shelves with ½ inch extending beyond the ends of the shelves.**

   Only glue down the veneer up to about 2 inches away from the edge. You want the part that you're going to trim unglued.

3. **Glue the side veneer to the edges of the carcass between each shelf. Leave the intersections with the shelves loose.**

   The veneer is slightly wider than the plywood. Make sure that the excess is on the outside of the carcass. You want the inside to be flush with the inside face of the outer panels.

4. **Take a sharp razor blade and gently trim the shelf veneer where it intersects with the side panel veneer. Remove the rimmed section from underneath the side veneer.**

   Doing so gives you clean, straight joints right at the edge of the side panel. Note that this joint won't match with the dado joint. The veneer will look like a butt joint joins the shelf to the sides.

5. **Using your iron, adhere the loose sections of the veneer and wait for it to cool completely.**

6. **Trim the excess veneer edging to make the veneer flush with the shelves and side.**

   Because the veneer is slightly wider than your plywood, it will all need to be trimmed flush. You can use a block plane (see Chapter 5) to trim it. Just make sure that you don't plane the plywood panels; otherwise, you may go through the outer ply and into the core.

Preparing and attaching the top

The top for this bookcase is made of plywood with veneer edging around it. To make this top, simply cut it to size and iron the edging onto the front and sides. You don't need to edge the back.

To attach the top to the carcass, line up the back of the top to the back of the carcass and glue in place. Use only a few dabs of glue; you don't need to put it over the entire surface. Lay a line of glue at about an inch from the edge of the entire perimeter and inside that space every few inches in a grid or cross-hatch pattern of glue lines.

If you want to use a solid wood top, don't glue it in place; you need to use screws. See the "Crafting a Craftsman Style Bookcase" section later in the chapter for details. Gluing only works with plywood to plywood because plywood is stable (it doesn't move much with humidity changes — and if the pieces do move, they will move the same ways).

Attaching the back

I always wait to cut the back piece until the carcass is fully assembled. I measure my cuts from the finished carcass to ensure that I get the exact size that's needed. I often end up with a carcass that's slightly off from the plans (I can't believe that I'm admitting this). Anyway, after you have the piece cut, just tack it in place with some ¾ to 1-inch long brads. One brad every 6 to 8 inches around the perimeter of the bookcase will hold it just fine. I avoid using glue so that the wood can expand and contract with humidity changes. (Yeah, I know it's all plywood, but it still moves a bit.)

Creating a Contemporary Style Bookcase

You can make a more contemporary-looking bookcase by adding a face frame with mitered corners on the top. Coupled with a taller stance, the face frame gives the bookcase a more dramatic look. Because this contemporary bookcase is 6½ feet tall, you don't need to put a top over the upper fixed shelf. Figure 13-8 shows this contemporary style bookcase.

I like to use biscuits (see Chapter 6) to reinforce the mitered corners of the face frame. Biscuits keep the miters from coming apart. One biscuit per corner is enough, though. And as long as you have your biscuit joiner out, you may as well put some biscuits in the bottom rail of the face frame. Follow your biscuit manufacturer's guidelines for making the cuts. Figure 13-9 shows the placement of the biscuits.

When building a face frame, I prefer to make the frame separately and then attach it to the carcass. Some people prefer to attach the frame to the carcass as they build it. I recommend my method to start with because if you mess up the face frame, you can always start over without having to redo the carcass itself.

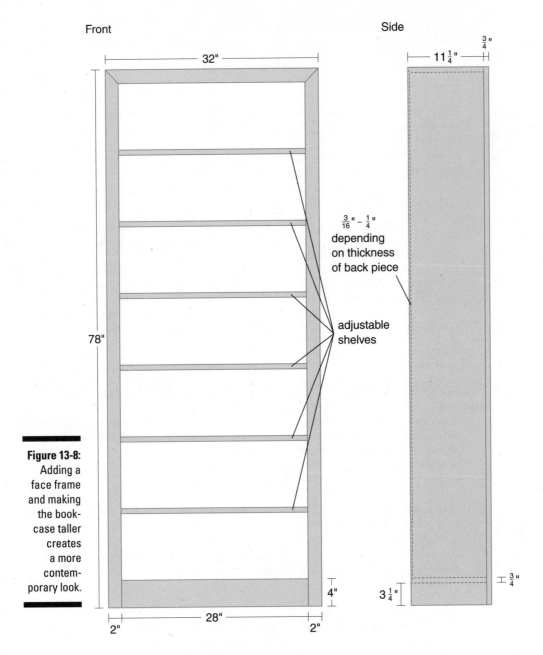

Front

Side

32"

$11\frac{1}{4}$"

$\frac{3}{4}$"

$\frac{3}{16}$" – $\frac{1}{4}$"
depending
on thickness
of back piece

adjustable
shelves

78"

Figure 13-8:
Adding a
face frame
and making
the book-
case taller
creates
a more
contem-
porary look.

4"

$3\frac{1}{4}$"

$\frac{3}{4}$"

28"

2"

2"

To make the face frame, you need the following materials (solid wood in the
same species as the veneer on your plywood):

✔ Stiles (2): ¾ x 2 x 78 inches

✔ Top rail (1): ¾ x 2 x 32 inches

✔ Bottom rail (1): ¾ x 4 x 28 inches

 = biscuits

Figure 13-9:
Biscuits in the joints of the face frame make joints much stronger.

These dimensions are approximate. The actual sizes will depend on the size of the finished carcass, so wait to cut these pieces until after you glue up the carcass. Use the finished carcass to determine your final sizes.

Because this bookcase is 6½ feet tall, you need to buy two sheets of plywood (or a half sheet if you can find one). You'll have quite a bit left over, but I'm sure you'll find a use for it. Figure 13-10 has the cut diagram for this bookcase.

For the bookcase, you need to cut the ¾-inch plywood to the following dimensions:

✔ Sides (2): ¾ x 11¼ x 78 inches

✔ Top (1): ¾ x 11¼ x 31¼ inches

✔ Bottom (1): ¾ x 11¼ x 31¼ inches

✔ Adjustable shelves (6): ¾ x 11 x 30⅜ inches

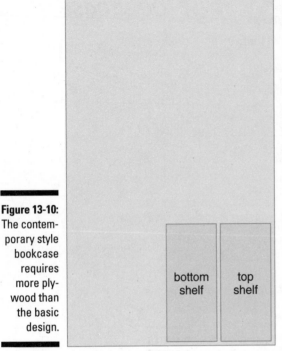
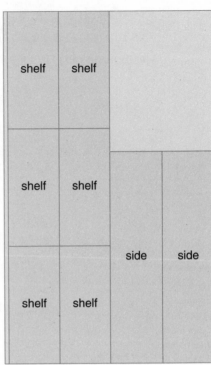

Figure 13-10:
The contemporary style bookcase requires more plywood than the basic design.

I like to make the face frame slightly larger than the carcass, by about ⅟₁₆ inch, which ensures that when I go to flush up the edge of the face frame to the carcass, I will sand the face frame rather than the carcass. Sanding through the outer veneer of today's plywood is really easy because it's so thin. You want to avoid this at all costs because the inner core is not very attractive and it will ruin the look of the wood.

To assemble this contemporary bookcase, follow the procedures to build the carcass for the basic bookcase. (See the section, "Assembling the parts" earlier in the chapter for details.) When the carcass is glued up and square, take measurements from the carcass to build the face frame. In spite of all your efforts, your carcass may not be exactly the size as the plan, so just adjust the face frame dimension to fit.

Next, build the face frame, and after it dries, attach it to the carcass by using glue and clamps or glue and small finish nails that are set below the surface, and then fill the recess holes with wood putty. Then just sand and finish. Part V has details on those procedures.

Crafting a Craftsman Style Bookcase

Craftsman or Arts and Crafts style furniture has experienced a rise in popularity over the last decade. Consisting of simple, functional design, this type of furniture blends easily with almost any other style. One of the signature design elements of this type of furniture is exposed joinery (the joints are not only structural, they are also decorative), so through tenons are common. The bookcase in this section doesn't use through tenons (or any tenons at all), but it does include decorative elements that mimic them.

For authenticity, I recommend that you use oak for this bookcase. Quarter-sawn oak is most authentic, but if you can't find or afford it, plain-sawn oak is fine.

Figure 13-11 shows a simple Craftsman style bookcase that has four adjustable shelves, through tenons, and rounded corners to give it a softer profile. Because of the rounded corners, this bookcase requires you to use solid wood for the sides, top, and bottom shelf. For more on gluing up solid wood panels, check out Chapter 14.

Table 13-2 shows the parts required for this bookcase.

Table 13-2		Craftsman Bookcase Parts and Dimensions	
Name of Part	*Number Needed*	*Dimensions*	*Material*
Sides	2	¾" x 14" x 55"	The sides consist of solid wood boards glued up to size (Chapter 14 shows you how to do this).
Fixed shelves	2	¾" x 13½" x 31¼"	Solid wood
Adjustable shelves	3	¾" x 13¼" x 30⅜"	Plywood with edging on front
Bottom rail	1	¾" x 2" x 30½"	Solid wood
Upper rail at back	1	¾" x 3" x 30½"	Solid wood
Fake through tenons	8	¾" x ½" x 2½"	Solid wood
Back	1	¼" x 31½" x 48¼"	Plywood

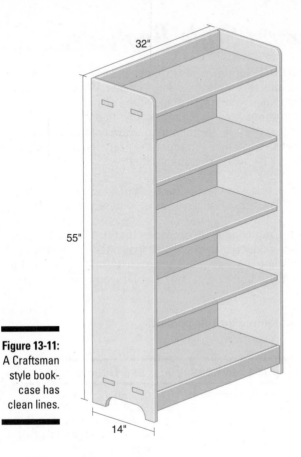

Figure 13-11:
A Craftsman
style book-
case has
clean lines.

Figure 13-12 shows the dimensions of this bookcase.

Milling the side pieces

To make the sidepieces, you most likely need to glue up some narrow boards to get you to the 14-inch width that you need: Follow the procedure for making a tabletop in Chapter 14; the process here is the same. After you have your sides at the proper size, cut the dados and rabbets on the inside of each side panel (check out the procedures for the basic bookcase in the "Assembling the parts" section earlier in this chapter).

Next, cut the 1-inch radius on the upper front corner. If you don't have a compass, measure 1 inch in from both the top and the front, and then draw an arc to connect these two marks. Figure 13-13 shows how this is done.

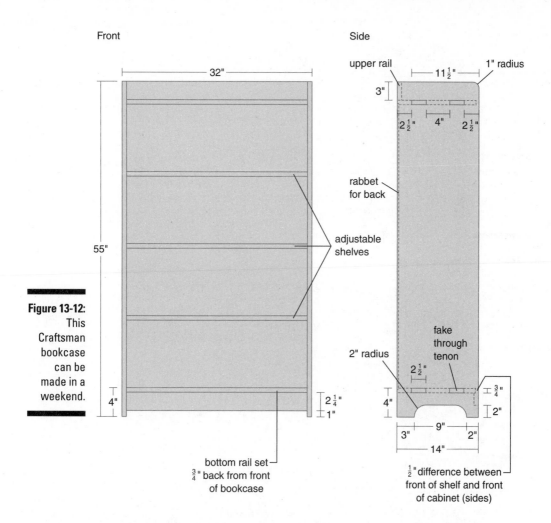

Front

Side

upper rail   1" radius

11½"

3"

2½" 4" 2½"

rabbet
for back

adjustable
shelves

32"

55"

fake
through
tenon

2" radius

2½"

¾"

2"

9"

4"   3"   2"

14"

4"   2¼"   1"

Figure 13-12:
This
Craftsman
bookcase
can be
made in a
weekend.

bottom rail set
¾" back from front
of bookcase

½" difference between
front of shelf and front
of cabinet (sides)

REMEMBER

Your radius cut doesn't have to be perfect. Just make sure that you like the
look of the arc and that both sides are the same. The easiest way to ensure
symmetry is to clamp the boards together and cut them at the same time.
Leave them clamped together while you sand them smooth as well.

Next, make the cutout for the bottom of the sides. Again, to make the arcs:

1. **Make marks 2 inches from the front and back edges along the bottom.**

2. **Make marks 2 inches up from the bottom and 4 inches in from the
   front and back edges.**

3. **Connect these marks. Figure 13-14 shows this.**

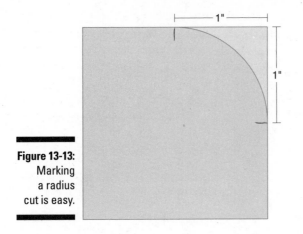

Figure 13-13:
Marking
a radius
cut is easy.

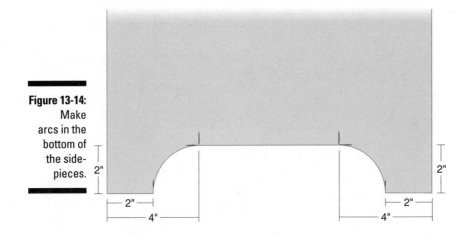

Figure 13-14:
Make
arcs in the
bottom of
the side-
pieces.

Making the "through tenons"

The heading is a little deceiving, because this bookcase doesn't really have through tenons. The joinery for the top and bottom is made with the dados and rabbets that you cut earlier in this section. The "through tenons" in this book-case are fake. Well, they're really tenons, but they don't do anything structural. These tenons consist of small pieces of wood (¾ x ½ x 2½ inches) that are put into slots cut with a router.

Start by making the tenons, as follows:

   1. **Mill a piece of wood to ¾ x 2½ x 10 inches.**

2. **The protruding part of each tenon has a chamfered (45 degree bevel) edge, so your next step is going to be chamfering over the end of the board. Follow this procedure:**

   a. **Mark your chamfer with a marking gauge set to ⅛ inch and run it along both the edge and face of the board's end.**

   Figure 13-15 shows how your board will be marked.

   b. **Plane, rout, or rasp to the marks.**

   Allow the chamfer to be a little uneven. You want a handmade look.

3. **Cut off ½ inch of the board at the end where you made the chamfer.**

4. **Follow Steps 2 and 3 until you have 8 tenons.**

Milling the "mortise"

After you've made the tenons, you need to make the mortises.

These mortises and tenons aren't structural, only decorative, but the process for making the mortises is almost the same.

Marked

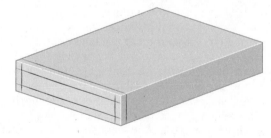

Chamfered

Figure 13-15:
Mark the chamfer on the end of the board.

I'm going to assume that you don't have a dedicated mortising machine or a mortising attachment for your drill press (if you even have a drill press). And I'm going to assume (I know, I'm just begging for trouble) that you don't want to cut the mortises by hand (not that there's anything wrong with cutting them by hand!). Given these assumptions, I can't think of a better way to make mortises than with a plunge router and, you guessed it, a jig. Don't have a jig? No problem, Figure 13-16 has an illustration of one.

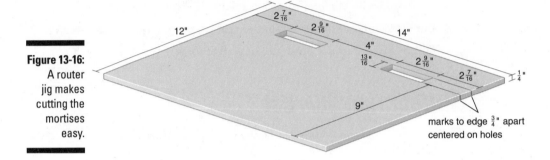

Figure 13-16:
A router jig makes cutting the mortises easy.

This jig requires you to have a straight-cutting router bit and a collar (also called a *template bushing*). In fact, the actual size of the jig depends both on what size bit you have and what size collar. This jig uses a ¼-inch bit and a collar with a ¼ inch-interior diameter (ID) and a ⁵⁄₁₆-inch outer diameter (OD). You fit the collar and the bit in your router and use the jig as a guide for the collar. Because this jig is made of ¼-inch plywood and you need to route a ¼-inch deep groove, you need to set your bit at a ½ inch depth.

This jig is sized so that you clamp it with the front edge of the jig flush up against the front edge of the carcass sides. Make sure the clamps are well out of the way of the router base when it is centered over the mortise holes. Position the jig so that the ¾-inch spaced markings center over the dado that you milled on the inside of the side panel. You want the tenons directly opposite the top and bottom shelves; otherwise, the bookcase will look funny.

With the jig in position, all you have to do is let 'er route. When you're done routing, use a chisel to square up the corners. Wait to put the tenons in the grooves until the carcass is all glued up.

Assembling the bookcase

To put this carcass together, follow the procedures for the basic bookcase earlier in the chapter (see the section, "Assembling the parts"). The top and bottom rails should be glued in after the carcass is together (I also like to wait until then to make the final cuts on those pieces just in case the carcass ends up a different size than planned). The last pieces to go on are the tenons. Just put a little glue in the mortise and then press it into place. If the fit is good, you shouldn't need to use a clamp.

Fashioning a Shaker Style Bookcase

Shaker style furniture is similar to Craftsman in that simple, functional design is the goal. The Shaker style tends to have a more refined elegance and is historically made from cherry, which has a softer appearance than the oak used in Craftsman furniture.

Figure 13-17 shows a Shaker style bookcase with one adjustable shelf. Note that it is smaller than the other bookcases in this chapter.

Table 13-3 details the parts needed for this bookcase.

Table 13-3	Shaker Bookcase Parts and Dimensions		
Name of Part	*Number Needed*	*Dimensions*	*Material*
Top	1	¾" x 42" x 14"	Can either be plywood with edging applied to front and sides or solid wood (to see how to glue up boards to make a top, check out Chapter 14)
Sides	2	¾" x 11¾" x 29¼"	¾" plywood
Fixed shelves	2	11¾" x 38¼"	¾" plywood (edge is covered by face frame)
Adjustable shelf	1	11½" x 37⅜"	¾" plywood with edging applied to front
Face frame stiles (the vertical members)	2	¾" x 2" x 29¼"	Solid wood
Face frame top rail	1	¾" x 1½" x 35"	Solid wood
Face frame bottom rail	1	¾" x 2" x 35"	Solid wood
Back	1	¼" x 38½" x 24½"	¼" plywood

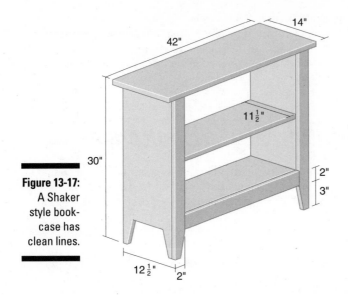

Figure 13-17:
A Shaker style book-case has clean lines.

Figure 13-18 shows the dimensions of the Shaker style bookcase.

The procedure for making this bookcase is the same as for the contemporary style bookcase described earlier in the chapter. (See the section, "Creating a Contemporary Style Bookcase.") The only real difference is that you need to cut the angles on the legs before you assemble the face frame. You can make the cuts with a handsaw, a circular saw, a jigsaw, or a band saw.

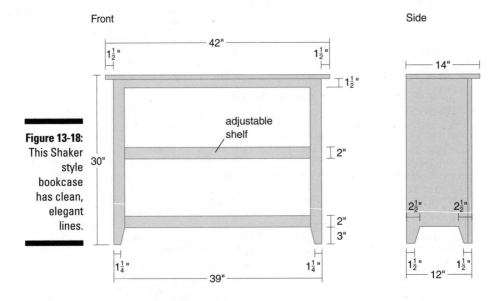

Figure 13-18:
This Shaker style bookcase has clean, elegant lines.

The top for this bookcase looks a lot better if you use solid wood glued up from well-matched narrow boards. Chapter 14 details how to glue up a tabletop. The procedure is the same for this bookcase top.

To attach the top to the bookcase, use screws through the top shelf. Don't use glue; the top will crack from the discrepancy between the movement of the solid wood top and the plywood top shelf during changes in humidity. When drilling holes through the top shelf for screws, elongate them front to back and put them in the center when you screw the top down. Placing the screws this way allows the top to expand and contract (which happens in the top's width/depth).

Making Your Mark: Designing Your Own Bookcases and Storage Units

Design style is such a personal thing. I may love the simple elegance of a Shaker bookcase, but you may find the same bookcase utterly devoid of style and interest. As you start working with wood, you'll likely want to make your design mark with your creations. Hey, who am I to stop you? (As if I could.)

If you're going to go it alone and dive headlong into uncharted territory, you may find some navigational aids useful. In this section, I try to give you some things to consider when drawing up your own plans. Most of these tips are structural considerations to keep you from making a bookcase or storage unit that doesn't perform. Others are some design conventions that can help you build something that will stand the test of time aesthetically.

When designing bookcases or storage units, keep the following things in mind:

- When using man-made sheet goods (plywood), choose lumber core instead of MDF core. Lumber core is much stronger.

- If your shelves are wider than 36 inches and you use plywood (even the lumber core), the weight of the books will cause the shelf to sag. I usually design a wide bookcase with a center divider in it to eliminate this problem. If you want to skip the divider, then consider using solid wood for the shelf or add solid wood edge bands 2 inches wide to the front of the lumbercore shelves. Even then, don't go further than 42 inches apart.

- To prevent sagging on wider bookcases, add a solid wood strip (called a *batten*) to the underside of the shelf to add strength.

✔ For tall bookcases, use either a face frame or include a fixed shelf in the center of the bookcase to support the sides. In the contemporary design earlier in this chapter, I chose to use a face frame. This adds rigidity to the side panels and keeps them from deflecting out. Also, consider attaching tall bookcases to the wall with a few screws toward the top of the bookcase (try to locate the screws in wall studs) to keep them from tipping over.

✔ If you use solid wood for the carcass and you have no face frame, use stopped dado joints instead of through (regular) dados to hide the joint.

✔ Consider using through dovetails for the top shelf. They add strength and look great (as long as you use solid wood for both the sides and top shelf).

✔ Instead of using the ultra thin veneer edging to hide the edge of plywood, consider cutting your own thicker veneer to attach to the edge. Run your edge through the jointer then cut a strip off (⅛ to ⅜ inch works well). When you attach this strip to the bookcase, put the jointed edge in for a tight fit.

✔ If you want rounded edges on your bookcase but still want to use plywood, use a thicker edging material. Just make sure you match the color and grain pattern really well. Thicker edging is more noticeable than thinner edging.

✔ If you want to hang a bookcase, consider using cleats with a beveled edge: Take a 4-inch-wide board (¾-inch thick solid wood is fine) and rip it in half at a 45-degree angle. Put one half against the wall with the angle facing up and out and the other on the bookcase with the angle facing down and in. Lift the bookcase into place and the cleats will lock together. All you have to do to remove it is empty the bookcase and lift it off again.

Chapter 14

Tackling Tables

....

In This Chapter

▶ Introducing tables

▶ Building a basic dining table

▶ Altering the plans to fit your aesthetics

▶ Designing your own coffee, end, dining, and work tables

....

1 don't know about you, but I never seem to have enough tables in my house. End tables, coffee tables, dining tables, work tables: I love tables. I hope you do too, because this chapter is all about tables.

In this chapter, you get a chance to make a few tables. I start by introducing the parts of a table and then move on to a step-by-step plan for building a basic dining/kitchen table. This chapter also features three additional table designs, so you can find one that fits your desires. You also get to choose from tabletops made of either solid wood or a combination of solid wood and plywood, so you'll definitely find a table project that fits your budget.

Introducing the Parts of a Table

Tables are pretty simple projects. They essentially consist of two basic sections: the support structure and the top.

- ✔ **The top:** Tabletops can be made of either solid wood or plywood with edging. Solid wood tabletops are glued up from narrow boards. By arranging the right narrow boards correctly, you can minimize the amount of movement and end up with a top that stays flat over time.

- ✔ **The support structure:** The support structure for a table comes from legs attached to a leg and rail (skirt) system (the vertical legs and horizontal boards that are under the tabletop). Leg and rail systems are generally built using mortise-and-tenon joinery (see Chapter 10), which is the strongest joint you can use for this purpose.

Some tables will have a shelf or drawer in them as well. (For more on shelves, check out Chapter 13, and for more on drawers, go to Chapter 15.) The tables in this chapter don't include shelves or drawers, however.

Likewise, some tables add a stretcher to the lower part of the legs to lend support. A *stretcher* consists of a board or boards (called *rails*) that connect front and back legs and another board (called the *stretcher board*) that connects the rails together. This stretcher board is generally located toward the center of the two rails. A stretcher board adds quite a bit of strength to the legs, but it can sometimes get in the way of a chair.

Digging In to Building a Dining Table

One of the easiest and most functional tables you can make is the dining table. A basic dining table (see Figure 14-1) has very few parts: the top, the legs, and the *rails,* which attach to the legs and hold up the top.

Going over the basics

The dining table shown in Figure 14-1 uses solid wood and can be built in a weekend. It could be done in a day if you have enough clamps and make the leg assembly first, but I recommend taking the whole weekend to do this project.

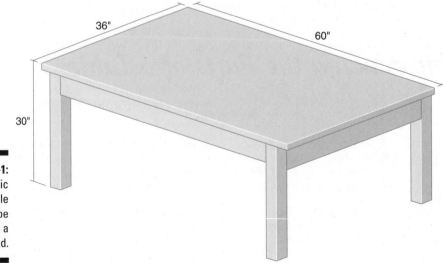

Figure 14-1:
This basic dining table can be made in a weekend.

Tooling up

To make this table you need some basic tools, including

- ✔ A table saw or circular saw with a guide to cut the wood to size
- ✔ A jointer to square up the edges of the boards
- ✔ A planer to make the boards the correct thickness
- ✔ A bunch of bar clamps (at least four, but six is better) and some wood glue (Chapter 8)
- ✔ The necessary finishing supplies, such as sanders and sandpaper

Knowing what techniques to use

You'll use edge-to-edge gluing (see Chapter 10) for the tabletop, and mortise-and-tenon joinery for the frame. To attach the top to the table, you use screws. For the details on the joinery, check out Chapter 10. Also, because this project is made from solid wood, you need to be able to pre-mill the boards before you can use them. Chapter 12 has more on this procedure.

Assembling a materials list

This table calls for 1-inch-thick wood. Because you need to pre-mill the wood to get it flat and smooth, I suggest buying 5/4 wood (wood that is 5/4 inches thick, for more about this, check out Chapter 2). This wood is generally around 1⅛-inches thick, which gives you some room to work with. Unfortunately, you can't find 5/4 wood at the local home center, so you need to take a trip to the lumberyard. (Chapter 2 has more on finding a lumberyard and choosing wood.)

Almost any good-looking wood will do for this table. Because of its simple design, I like to use pine if I want a rustic look or maple for a more contemporary appearance. This table requires the following wood (Chapter 2 details the board feet and wood sizing guidelines):

- ✔ **For the top and legs:** Twenty-five board feet of 5/4 wood. This gives you a little extra so that you can choose nicely matching pieces for the top.
- ✔ **For the rails:** Five board feet of 4/4 wood. Make sure that you get boards that are at least 5 feet long and in multiples of 3 inches wide.

The actual number of board feet of wood that you need depends on the dimensions of the boards and the quality of the grain patterns. When you choose your wood, map out where the cuts are going to be and check off the parts on your list as you find boards for them.

Managing your cut list

Table 14-1 lays out the pieces you need for this project. Figure 14-2 shows illustrations of this table.

Table 14-1		Cut List for Dining Table	
Name of Part	*Number Needed*	*Dimensions*	*Material*
Tabletop	1	1" x 36" x 60"	Solid wood glued up from narrow boards
Legs	4	2" x 2" x 29"	Solid wood glued up from two 1" thick boards
Long rails	2	¾" x 3" x 55⅜" (including tenon)	Solid wood including 1¹¹⁄₁₆" tenons on each end
Short rails	2	¾" x 3" x 31 ⅜" (including tenon)	Solid wood including 1¹¹⁄₁₆" tenons on each end

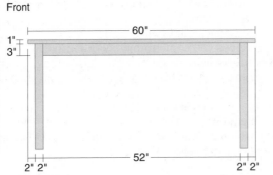
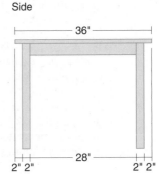

Figure 14-2: This 36-x-60-inch table is a comfortable size and has only nine parts.

Tackling the tabletop

Because this tabletop is made of solid wood and is 36 inches wide, you need to glue up several boards. This gluing is critical, because the right boards in the best configuration give you not only a beautiful top but also a stable one that will last for generations. I can tell you from firsthand experience that spending a ton of time, energy, and money building a tabletop only to have it warp or crack after just a few years (or even months) is no fun. So, I highly recommend that you take your time getting the tabletop just right before gluing it up.

Okay, I'll step off my soapbox now. Here are the steps I take to glue up a tabletop (by the way, this process works for any project where you need to edge glue two or more boards):

1. **Select the boards you want to use based upon grain patterns and coloring.**

   This process starts at the lumberyard. Remember: Your tabletop will only be as beautiful as the wood you choose.

2. **Pre-mill the boards to get them flat and straight.**

   You need to let the wood sit after pre-milling so it can "relax." Only then can you mill it down to approximate size. (For more on this subject, see Chapter 12.)

   To ensure stability, *rip* (cut along the grain) any boards more than about 6 inches wide down to 3 or 4 inches wide, joint them, and glue them back together with the growth rings alternating, as shown in Figure 14-3. The new glued-up board will be more stable and flatter than the original.

3. **Run all your boards through the jointer to make sure that the edges are perfectly straight and square to their faces.**

   If you don't have a jointer, get one (just kidding, although it does make things a lot easier). You can plane the edges of the boards with a plane; choose the one with the longest bed. (Chapter 4 has more on hand planes.) Using a hand plane takes time, but it can be done.

   The cleaner the edges of the boards, the easier it is to glue them up.

4. **Lay out the boards with the growth rings alternating, if possible.**

   Doing so increases the stability of the final board (see Figure 14-3).

5. **Mark all the boards every 8 inches or so for biscuit slots and use a pencil to draw a triangle across the entire field of boards so that you know the order to put them back together again.**

   Refer to Figure 14-3 to see how to do this.

6. **Cut the biscuit slots according to the procedures in your biscuit joiner's owner's manual.**

   If you don't have a biscuit joiner, you can use dowels, a spline joint (see Chapter 11), or a tongue-and-groove joint (see Chapter 10). I'm not a fan of edge-to-edge butt joints without some sort of reinforcement, such as biscuits or dowels. However, many people are fine with edge-to-edge butt joints without reinforcement; if you're one of those people, skip the steps about marking and cutting biscuit joints.

7. **Put your bar clamps on your worktable with the jaws facing up.**

   Set them to be about an inch or two wider than the total number of boards you're gluing up.

   When gluing up four or more boards, consider gluing them into subassemblies of two or three boards each. Glue the subassemblies into the larger field after the glue is cured. Doing so makes it easier to line the boards up properly.

8. **Arrange your boards on the clamps and tighten the clamps to see how your boards line up.**

   If you can see gaps along the edges of the boards after applying moderate pressure to the clamps, run them through your jointer again. If you're hand planing, you'll need to spend a few more minutes *truing up the edges* (getting them straight and square to the faces of the boards).

9. **After your edges line up properly, tilt them up one at a time to apply glue along the edges and in the biscuit slots (if you're using biscuits).**

10. **Insert the biscuits.**

11. **Line up the boards and gently tighten the clamps until they're pulled together.**

   Be careful not to apply too much pressure. If you do, the boards will either pop out of the clamps or rise up from them. You need to exert only enough pressure to pull the boards together. If parts of the boards pull together but you see gaps along parts of the edge, your edges aren't jointed properly. Resist the temptation to pull them together with the clamps. Chances are you'll squeeze all the glue out or pull the boards out of flatness.

   Putting a clamp across the top of the glued-up boards can help keep them from riding up from the clamp pressure. One clamp across the center is enough for this purpose.

12. **Wipe off any excess glue with a damp rag.**

13. **Let the boards sit in the clamps overnight.**

   If you're gluing subassemblies, wait four to six hours before you remove the clamps and attach the two assemblies.

14. **Wipe the sweat off your brow and take a break; you've earned it.**

Making the table frame

Making the structure for the top to sit on is pretty straightforward. All you have to do is cut the parts to size (including the tenon on the rails), cut the joints (mortises in the legs and tenons on the rails), and glue them up. This section details the process.

Creating the legs

The legs are 2 inches thick and need to be made by gluing up two boards, because 2-inch-thick wood is more expensive, and two boards glued up are more stable than one thick piece. The best way to make the legs is to find a board at least twice as wide as the width of the legs. Cut the two pieces that will make the leg from the board and turn the boards into each other so that the grain at the cuts forms one of the outer sides of the legs. Figure 14-4 shows this process.

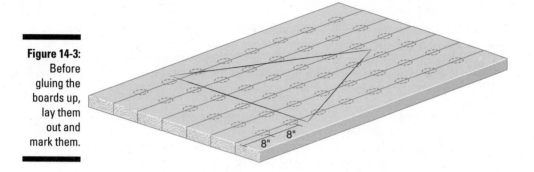

Figure 14-3:
Before gluing the boards up, lay them out and mark them.

8" 8"

Make the legs oversized by ⅛ inch in overall width and ½ inch in length to give you some room to run the board through a jointer and/or planer and crosscut to finished length after they're glued up: The boards may shift slightly when you clamp them. If they do shift, run one edge through the jointer until you have a flush surface. Next, run that board through a planer with the freshly jointed edge against the planer bed. Then square one end at the table saw and crosscut to finished length.

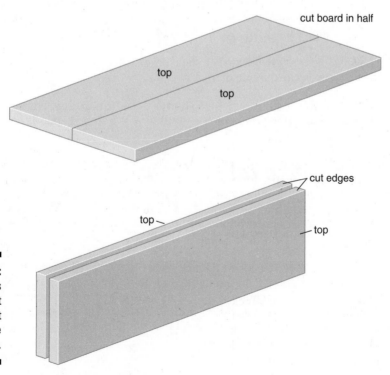

cut board in half

top

top

cut edges

top

top

Figure 14-4:
Table legs look best when cut from the same board.

Making mortises

You can cut the mortises in several different ways: with a chisel, a drill press and chisel, or a dedicated mortising machine. (Chapter 10 details these options.) For this basic table, you want the mortises to be ½ x 2¼ x 1¾ inches. The mortise should go ½ inch down from the top of the leg and ¼ inch from the outer edge. Figure 14-5 shows the positioning of the mortise.

In this project, the two mortises on the leg will meet, so you'll end up with a hollowed-out section in the leg. But this isn't always the case. If the leg were wider, the two mortises might not meet, but because it's only 2 inches wide and the joint will be under a tremendous amount of stress, I choose to have them meet so that the tenon is as long as possible. Some other designers might be happy with a mortise that's only 1¼ inches deep to keep them from meeting inside the leg.

Taming tenons

After you cut your mortises (see previous section for instructions), you want to measure the final dimensions of the mortise and make your tenons to fit. Assuming your mortises are the size they're supposed to be (you'd be surprised how often they aren't), your tenons will be ½ x 2¼ x 1¹¹⁄₁₆ inches. Figure 14-6 shows how the tenon should be cut. Notice how the tenon has a 45-degree angle on the end. This is because the tenons will meet in the middle of the leg. If the mortises didn't meet, you would need to cut this angle.

The angle on the tenons needs to face inward. In other words, the long side of the angle is on the outside of the rail.

Notice how the tenons are ¹⁄₁₆ inch shorter than the mortises. The shorter tenon gives some breathing room on the mortise as the wood expands and contracts with humidity changes.

If you don't want to cut a 45-degree angle on the end of each tenon, you can just make them 1³⁄₁₆ inches long instead. If you do this, I highly recommend that you install pegs into the joints (use ³⁄₈-inch dowels) after they're glued up. Installing pegs adds strength to the joint. (Check out the section, "Creating a Craftsman Style Table" later in this chapter for details on adding pegs to mortise and tenon joints.)

You probably need to adjust the size of the tenons to fit well in the mortises. You want them to be tight enough to not be sloppy but loose enough to push together by hand, because when you add the glue it will be harder to get them together. Work on trimming the tenons until they all fit well using a chisel, rasp, or coarse sandpaper. Be very careful that you don't damage the shoulder of the tenon when you trim it.

top

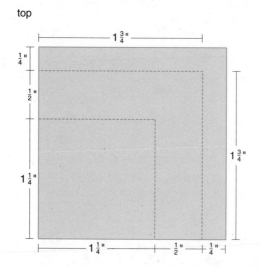

side

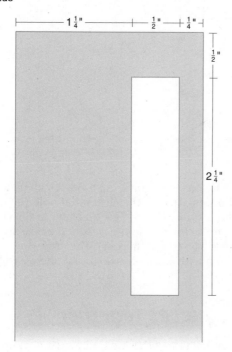

Figure 14-5:
The mortises
in the legs
are cut
to these
dimensions.

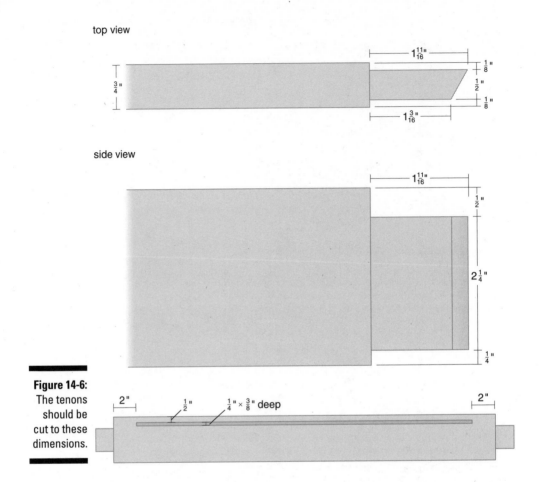

top view

side view

Figure 14-6:
The tenons
should be
cut to these
dimensions.

After you finish milling the tenons in the rails, cut a ¼-x-⅜-inch dado in the inside of the rail ½ inch from the top for the cleats that hold the top to the support structure (See the "Adding the top" section later in the chapter for more about cleats.). Don't go all the way to the ends of the board. Stop about 2 inches short (refer to Figure 14-5 to see this cut). The easiest way to cut this groove is with a router fitted with a ¼-inch straight bit and an edge guide.

Putting all the pieces together

When you've created joints that fit together well, all you have to do to assemble them is apply a little glue to both the mortise and tenon and pull them together. You want to assemble the rails and legs in two stages: attach the short rails to the legs, then the long rails. Doing so keeps your stress down and improves the chances that you'll end up with a square table that doesn't rock.

Timetable for a dining table

A basic dining table can be made in a weekend. But if you're feeling a bit time-challenged, here's a quick look at how I'd divide the weekend when tackling this project.

Saturday

1. **Select and pre-mill the wood.**

   You should really do this the weekend before you make the table so that the wood has a chance to stabilize. See Chapter 12 for more on this process.

2. **Dimension and glue the tabletop.**

   This will likely take most of your bar clamps, so do it in the morning to free up your clamps for later.

3. **Dimension the rails and legs.**

4. **Glue up the short rails and the legs.**

Hopefully you have two clamps left over to do this. If you don't, you need to use a couple of clamps from the tabletop assembly. If you need to raid any clamps from your tabletop, I recommend that you wait until early the next morning to do so to give your tabletop enough time to dry.

Sunday

1. **Glue up the rest of the leg assembly.**

2. **Plane and sand the tabletop.**

3. **Make the cleats that hold the top to the leg assembly.**

The final sanding and assembly of the top to the legs must wait until the glue on the leg assembly has had time to sufficiently cure. I like to wait a day before I remove the clamps. After the clamps are removed, you can sand and finish the project. This will take another weekend.

The procedure for gluing up the legs and rails is as follows:

1. **Test your joints by doing a *dry fit* (fit the joint without glue first) of the entire assembly.**

   If everything fits properly, take it apart and set the long rails aside.

2. **Apply a thin layer of glue on the tenons and in the mortises for the short rails.**

3. **Slide the tenons into the mortises.**

   You may need to tap them in with a rubber mallet. Do one joint at a time and get the tenon all the way into the mortise before moving to the next joint. This means the shoulders of the tenons should be snug with the legs.

   If the joint won't go together with a light tap of the mallet, put both tenons together partway by hand, then use a bar clamp to pull them together. Work quickly and don't let a joint sit halfway assembled for more than a couple of minutes, because the glue may start to set. If this happens, your joint will lock at this halfway point.

4. **When both joints are done, clamp a bar clamp across the legs at the rails and tighten the clamps until some glue oozes out of the joint.**

5. **Check the legs for square by running a tape measure diagonally from the bottom of one leg to the top of the other.**

   If these measurements are the same, you're square. If not, follow the procedure in Chapter 12 for details on how to correct this. Follow this procedure for both legs.

6. **Exhale and wipe any excess glue from the wood with a damp cloth (see Chapter 12 for cleanup details). This includes glue that oozed inside the open mortises.**

   Set this assembly aside and do the other leg/short rail assembly following the same procedures.

Let both leg assemblies sit overnight and then glue the long rails to the short rail assemblies. The procedures are the same as those in the previous list, except that you need to do an extra squaring-up check when you're done. This check involves not only verifying the leg bottom/leg top diagonals, but also the diagonals from leg bottom to leg bottom across the entire assembly.

You'll be assembling two sets of joints and be working on a much larger assembly. Take your time getting used to the steps by performing a couple of dry fit run-throughs before adding any glue.

Adding the top

The tabletop can't be glued to the rails, or else it will crack. The top expands and contracts with changes in moisture at a different rate than the rails, so you need to allow for these differences while also making sure that the top is secured to the rails.

You can secure the top to the rails in several ways; one of the best that I know of is to make *cleats* that you slide into a groove in the rails and attach to the underside of the top. (See the "Taming tenons" section earlier in this chapter for instructions on how to make the dado in the rails for the cleats.) Figure 14-7 shows the cleat.

You can use any scrap hardwood to make the cleat; just make sure that the rabbet is cut on the end of the board and not from the side. Also, make sure that the rabbet runs horizontally to the growth rings. This will give you the strongest cleat. When you have the cleat cut to size, drill an elongated hole in it so that the screw can move with the top (Figure 14-7). A 1¼-inch wood screw (#6 or #8 is fine — see Chapter 11 for more about screws) gets screwed into the underside of the top. Apply eight cleats to the top: One on each end and three along the sides.

The easiest way to attach the top to the leg assembly is to put the top upside down on a blanket on your bench and place the leg assembly on that. Center the leg assembly on the top and pre-drill holes for the screws (make sure that you don't drill through the top).

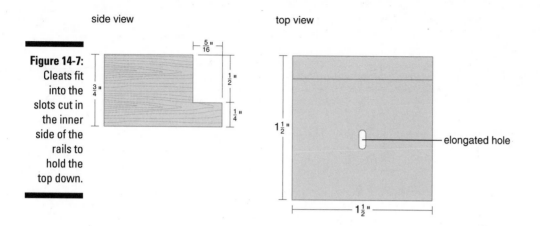

Figure 14-7: Cleats fit into the slots cut in the inner side of the rails to hold the top down.

Crafting a Shaker Style Table

The Shaker style table (see Figure 14-8) is a lot like the basic table with the exception of being slightly larger, with a thinner top and tapered legs.

To make this table you need the following wood:

- ✔ **For the legs:** 5 board feet 5/4 cherry wood.
- ✔ **For the rails and top:** 22 board feet 4/4 cherry wood.

Table 14-2 shows how to cut the wood.

Table 14-2	Cut List for Shaker Style Table		
Name of Part	*Number Needed*	*Dimensions*	*Material*
Top	1	¾" x 38" x 68"	Solid wood glued up from narrow strips
Legs	4	2" x 2" x 29¼"	Solid wood glued up from thinner boards then tapered to 1" at bottom
Long rails	2	¾" x 3" x 59⅜"	Solid wood including 1¹¹⁄₁₆" tenons on each end
Short rails	2	¾" x 3" x 33⅜"	Solid wood including 1¹¹⁄₁₆" tenons on each end

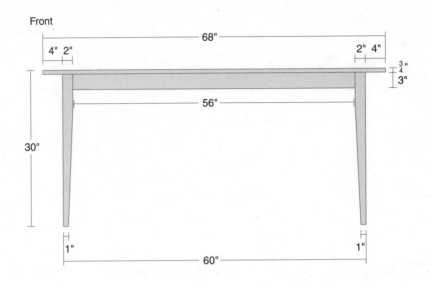

Front

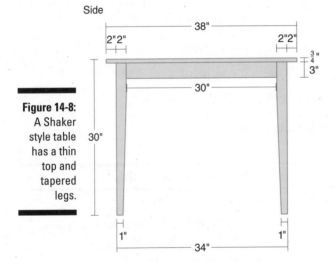

Side

Figure 14-8:
A Shaker style table has a thin top and tapered legs.

The procedures for making a Shaker table are the same as the ones for making a basic table (see the "Digging In to Building a Dining Table" section earlier in this chapter). Start with the tabletop, and then glue up the boards to make the thickness of the legs. From there, you can cut the mortises for either the legs or the tapers first.

Either way, when you get to the tapering phase, you need to taper the leg from 2 inches to 1 inch starting 5 inches from the top of the leg. Each leg gets two tapers, which run along the inside of the legs. So when you cut these, make sure that the tapers are on the same faces of the leg as the mortises. (Be sure to double-check this. I've made the mistake of putting the taper on the wrong side. It's not pretty.) Figure 14-9 shows the proper placement of the taper.

The simplest way to make a tapered leg is by using — yep, you guessed it — a tapering jig. To make this jig, you need two pieces of ¾-inch-thick wood cut to 6 x 30 inches and one piece of ¾-inch-thick wood cut to 1 x 8 inches.

For hardware, you need a hinge with ⅝-inch screws, a curved lid support, a ¼-inch bolt 5 inches long, and a ¼-inch wing nut with a washer. (You can find the curved lid support at your local home center).

If you'd rather not hassle with making your own tapering jig, you can buy one from any of the woodworking tool suppliers for about $20.

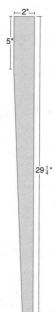

Figure 14-9:
The legs for the Shaker table taper.

Making this jig is easy (see Figure 14-10). Just follow these steps:

1. **Attach the two long boards together with the hinge at one end.**

2. **Attach the 1-x-8-inch piece to the opposite end on one board.**

3. **Attach the curved lid support to the board with the end support.**

4. **Drill a ¼-inch hole through the second board where the lid support crosses it.**

5. **Drill a ⅜-inch hole, ½ inch deep from the bottom side of the board where the ¼-inch hole comes through.**

6. **Feed the bolt through the hole with the head in the ⅜-inch section of the hole.**

7. **Put the washer over the bolt and the wing nut over that. Tighten.**

Because the tapering jig can cut a variety of tapers, you need to adjust the angle of the jig before you cut your table leg. Follow these steps (see Figure 14-11):

1. **Put the jig against the table saw fence.**

2. **Place a table leg against the outer long board tight against the end support with the top end closest to the hinge.**

3. **Move the outer board of the jig out about 2 inches from the other board.**

4. **Measure the distance at a point on the outer side of the table leg 5 inches down from the top of the leg (from the hinged end of the jig) to the fence.**

5. **Measure the distance from the fence to a point that is 1 inch across the width at the bottom of the leg.**

6. **Adjust the jig until both the measurements from Steps 4 and 5 are the same ("A" in Figure 14-11).**

7. **Tighten the wing nut.**

With the tapering jig set to the correct angle, you can cut the tapers in the legs. Follow these procedures to cut the legs:

1. **Move the table saw's fence over until the blade touches the leg 5 inches from the top end of the leg. Make sure the bottom of the leg is in contact with the 1-x-8-inch stop board at the end of the jig.**

2. **Adjust the height of the blade to slightly over 2 inches and back off the leg.**

3. **Turn the saw on and gently push the jig and leg forward.**

   Keep your hands away from the blade.

To make the tenons and assemble the table, follow the steps in the "Taming tenons" and "Putting all the pieces together" sections earlier in the chapter.

After you have all the assemblies glued up and sanded, you can attach the top to the legs. Follow the procedures in the "Adding the top" section earlier in this chapter.

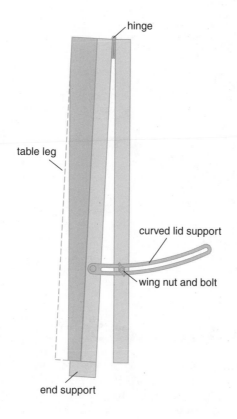

hinge

table leg

curved lid support

wing nut and bolt

end support

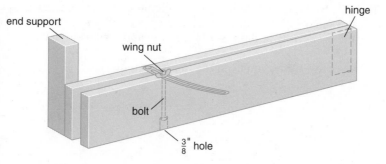

Figure 14-10:
A tapering jig makes quick work of cutting tapered table legs.

end support

wing nut

hinge

bolt

$\frac{3}{8}$" hole

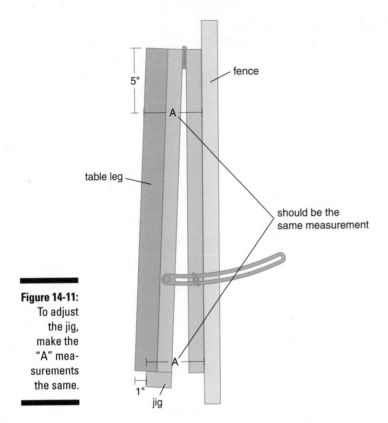

fence

5"

A

table leg

should be the
same measurement

Figure 14-11:
To adjust
the jig,
make the
"A" mea-
surements
the same.

A

1"

jig

Creating a Craftsman Style Table

Craftsman style furniture has become very popular. Two of the reasons for its popularity are that it has a timeless simplicity and that it's relatively easy to make. Craftsman style furniture doesn't involve any complex curves or curved details like some furniture styles from the earlier Victorian era.

Figure 14-12 shows drawings of this table. The legs and top are slightly thicker than the basic table described in this chapter, but the construction techniques are the same with the addition of some pegs at the mortise-and-tenon joints on the legs. These additions add stability and visual appeal.

To make this table, you need the following materials:

- ✔ **For the legs:** 5 board feet of 6/4 wood
- ✔ **For the top:** 7 board feet of 5/4 solid wood and 3 x 5 feet of ¾-inch hardwood plywood of the same species (oak, for example)
- ✔ **For the rails:** 5 board feet of 4/4 wood

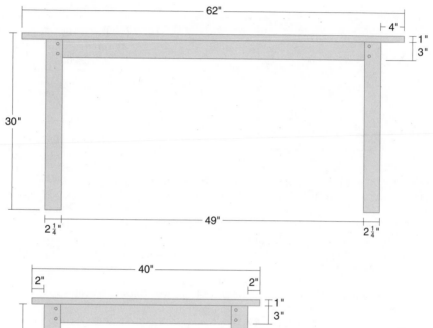

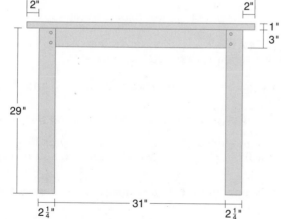

Figure 14-12: A Craftsman style table has thicker dimensions for a more substantial look.

Table 14-3 shows the parts for this project and how to cut the wood.

Table 14-3		Cut List for Craftsman Style Table	
Name of Part	*Number Needed*	*Dimensions*	*Material*
Top	1	1" x 40" x 62"	Consists of ¾" x 32" x 52" plywood with (2) 1" x 4¼" x 52" applied edge bands, and (2) 1" x 6" x 40" breadboard ends
Legs	4	2¼" x 2¼" x 29"	Two 6/4 boards glued up (or three 4/4 boards if you can't find 6/4 thick wood)
Long rails	2	¾" x 3" x 52⅜"	Solid wood including 1¹¹⁄₁₆" tenons on each end.
Short rails	2	¾" x 3" x 34⅜"	Solid wood including 1¹¹⁄₁₆" tenons on each end.

The Craftsman style table features a top with a *breadboard end,* a board on each end that runs perpendicular to the field of wood. The breadboard end hides the end grain of the tabletop and gives a more sophisticated look. Another advantage to having a breadboard edge is that you can use plywood in the top and save yourself some money. Of course, you don't have to use plywood in the center of the tabletop, but it does make building the top easier and less expensive.

Figure 14-13 shows the layout of the wood for the tabletop.

To make the top, follow these steps (be sure to have some wood glue and a bunch of bar clamps at your workbench before you start):

1. **Cut the boards to the sizes described in Table 14-3 and the previous paragraphs.**

2. **Cut ¼-x-¼-inch grooves in the edge of the plywood board.**

   Use a table saw and follow the procedures in Chapter 10. If you center the groove, it will be ¼ inch from both the top and bottom of the ¾-inch plywood.

3. **Cut ¼-x-¼-inch tongues on the edge boards ¼ inch from the top of the board.**

   Chapter 10 details how to mill this tongue. Because the plywood is only ¾ inch thick and the edge board is 1 inch thick, the top of the boards will be flush, but the bottom will not (the bottom board will extend ¼ inch from the plywood).

4. **Attach the edge boards to the plywood.**

   Because the solid wood moves more than the plywood does in response to changes in humidity, I like to *spot glue* the board (put spots of glue along the joint every 6 inches or so) instead of gluing it along the entire joint.

This gives some breathing room. Some people leave the joint loose, but I find that there is little movement along the length of the board compared to the plywood, so adding spot glue doesn't seem to cause any problems.

5. **Clamp this assembly up and set aside to cure.**

6. **While the edge/plywood assembly is curing, cut the mortise in the end boards.**

   Figure 14-14 shows the mortise-and-tenon detail. The mortise is ¼ x 1 inch deep. It should be centered in the width of the board with ⅜ inch on both sides. The mortise should stop 1 inch from the ends of the board.

   I find that a plunge router in a router table with a straight bit does the best job of cutting this mortise.

7. **After the edge/plywood assembly has set up, cut the tenons to fit in the end board mortise.**

   Chapter 10 details how to cut tenons on your table saw. The tenons should be ¼ x 1 inch. They should extend to 1⅛ inches from the edge of the board. Make sure that you center the tenons on the edge boards and not the plywood of the tabletop.

8. **Dry fit the end boards to the plywood assembly.**

   The joints should fit snugly, and the tops of all the parts should be flush. In fact, because there won't be any glue in the joint, you want a fairly tight joint that requires the use of light tapping with a mallet to get together.

9. **Tap the joint in place.**

10. **Turn the top over and drill ⅜-inch holes through the end boards 2 inches from the edges and 5½ inches from the ends.**

    This will put the hole ½ inch from the inner edge of the end board.

    Don't drill all the way through the top; only drill ¾ inch deep. You only want the drill through the tenon inside the joint.

11. **Drop some glue in the hole and tap a ¹³⁄₁₆-inch-long ⅜-inch diameter dowel in the hole.**

    It will stick out ¹⁄₁₆ inch. You can sand this off after the glue dries.

If you want a more classic look, mill a shallow (¹⁄₁₆-inch-deep) v-groove, or *chamfer,* at the junction of the edge boards/plywood and the end boards/plywood/edge boards (Figure 14-13 shows where these grooves go). Use a router with a v-groove bit (see Chapter 6) and a guide set to run the bit at the junction of the boards. The v-groove will hide any movement in the wood as the humidity changes.

To make the structural assembly for this table, follow the procedures in the section, "Digging In to Building a Dining Table" earlier in this chapter. After you have the leg/rail assemblies together, you can drill ⅜-inch diameter holes 1 inch deep and ½ inch in from the inside edge of the leg and ¾ inch from the upper and lower edges of the rails. This puts the holes 1½ inches apart, centered on the rail, and ½ inch from the end of the rails.

Drop a little glue in the hole and tap $^{13}/_{16}$-inch dowels into the holes. Sand them flush after the glue dries.

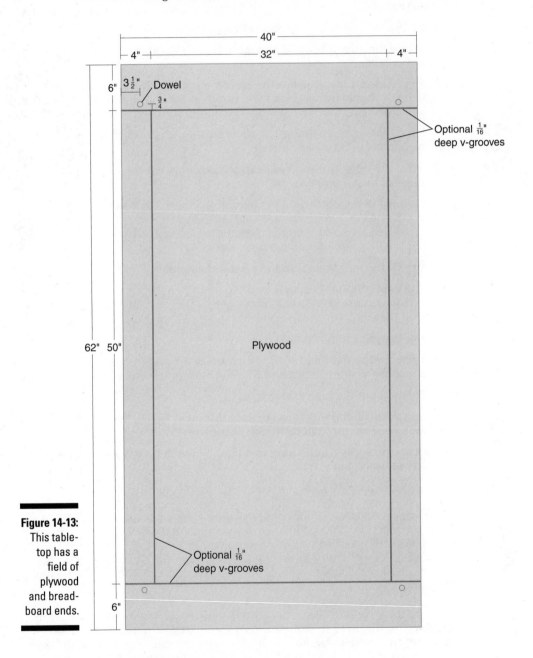

Figure 14-13:
This table-top has a field of plywood and bread-board ends.

To finish this table, follow the procedures in Part V.

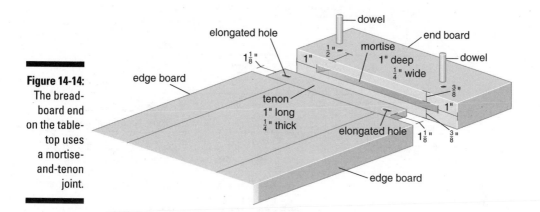

Figure 14-14:
The bread-
board end
on the table-
top uses
a mortise-
and-tenon
joint.

Tackling a Trestle Table

Feeling ambitious? Well, I have a table for you. A trestle table (see Figure 14-15) has a ton of mortise-and-tenon joints and some curved cuts. This project will take you more time than the others in this chapter, but I think the end results are worth it.

The one drawback to this table (aside from the amount of work it takes to make) is that it uses a lot of wood, so it can be expensive to build. But, again, I think it's worth it.

You need the following materials to make this table:

✔ **For the top:** 32 board feet 6/4 wood

The top really needs to be between 1⅛ and 1¼ inches thick in order to provide the correct balance between the top and the trestle, so resist the temptation to save some money by making it thinner.

✔ **For the trestle structure:** 10 board feet 5/4 wood

I recommend using cherry, quarter-sawn oak, or a good quality pine (you won't find this at your local home center). Plain-sawn oak will do in a pinch, but it doesn't look as nice. If you can afford it, I think you'll find that the extra expense for the good stuff is worth it.

Table 14-4 shows you how the wood should be milled.

Table 14-4		Cut List for Trestle Table	
Name of Part	*Number Needed*	*Dimensions*	*Material*
Top	1	1¼" x 40" x 72"	Solid wood glued up from narrow boards
Legs	4	2" x 2" x 28¾"	Solid wood glued up from 1" thick boards
Rails	2	1" x 3" x 43⅜"	Solid wood including 1¹¹⁄₁₆" tenons on each end
Top leg supports	2	2" wide x 3" high x 28"	Solid wood glued up from 1" thick boards
Bottom leg supports	2	3" wide x 4" high x 30"	Solid wood glued up from 1" thick boards

After you have the wood and have matched the boards so that you have a beautiful top, you can prepare and glue it up according to the directions in the "Digging In to Building a Dining Table" section earlier in this chapter.

The trestle assembly will take some work. You have to glue up quite a few boards to get the thickness you need. You also need to make some curved cuts. These curved cuts are best done on a band saw. I strongly suggest that you not try to build this table without a band saw unless you can handle a tremendous amount of frustration. You need to cut curves in 3- and 4-inch-thick wood. A jigsaw can't handle cutting wood this thick.

Cutting the parts down to size

The first step in making the trestle assembly is to get the parts to the right size. For this assembly, you need to cut the pieces and glue up the boards for the legs and the top and bottom support pieces. The legs and top supports require two boards to get to the 2-inch thickness needed, and the bottom support takes three boards. Try to cut these pieces from the same board and lay them out so that the grain patterns match as closely as possible. I describe this process in more detail in the "Creating the legs" section earlier in the chapter.

Make all these parts slightly oversized (by ⅛ inch each in width and thickness) so that you have some room to joint and plane the glued-up parts to size.

After you have the raw size, you can cut the joints in the top supports and top of the legs as shown in Figure 14-16. Start by cutting the mortise in the top of the leg and then making the tenons in the top support to fit. You want a snug fit. The easiest way to cut these joints is with a table saw fitted with a dado blade.

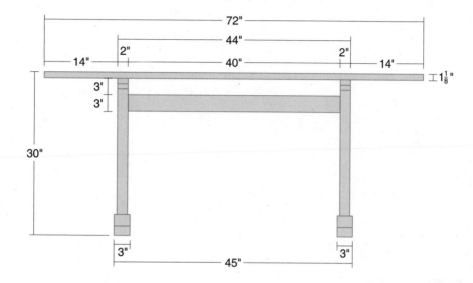

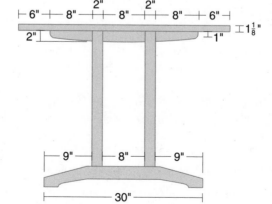

Figure 14-15: A trestle table is a challenge but worth the work.

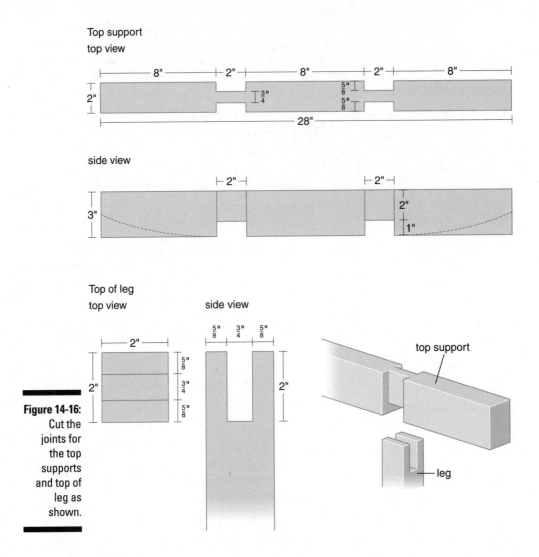

Figure 14-16: Cut the joints for the top supports and top of leg as shown.

Cutting the mortise in the top of the leg

To cut the mortise in the top of the leg, follow these steps:

1. **Install a dado blade set at ¾ inch width in your table saw.**

2. **Position the fence ⅝ inch from the inside edge of the blade.**

3. **Set the blade height to 2 inches.**

4. **With the top end of the table leg on the table and one side against the fence, position a scrap piece of wood behind the leg to support it as you feed it through the saw.**

For this size leg, I recommend gluing up three ¾-inch pieces of plywood cut to 6 inch squares. Place this piece behind the leg with the three pieces parallel to the fence. This will give you a support that is 3 x 6 x 6 inches for the legs.

5. **Clamp the support piece to the leg at the top of the support block.**

6. **With one hand holding the leg and the other pushing the support block from behind, feed the leg into the saw until the blade clears the leg and the support block.**

7. **Repeat Steps 5 and 6 with the other three legs.**

Cutting the tenon in the top support

To cut the tenon in the top support, follow these steps:

1. **Place your miter gauge in the miter slot to the left of the blade and use the same dado blade as you did for the mortise in the top of the leg.**

2. **Place a scrap piece of wood (called a gauge block) against the fence of the saw ending about 1 inch in front of the leading edge of the blade.**

3. **Set the fence so that the distance from the outer face of the scrap piece is 8 inches from the inner (closest to the rip fence) edge of the blade.**

4. **Set the depth of cut to ⅝ inch.**

   This depth has to be finagled a bit until the tenon fits the mortise properly. Start with a 2-inch-thick piece of scrap and run it through the blade once on each side, adjusting the depth of cut as necessary to give you a tenon that fits snugly in the leg's mortise.

5. **Place the top support board on its 3-inch-wide face against the miter gauge and slide it up to the scrap piece of wood (gauge block) attached to the fence.**

6. **Run the top support board through the saw.**

7. **Flip the board over and make the same cut on the other 3-inch face.**

8. **Rotate the board end for end, and make the same cut on the other end of the board.**

9. **Flip it again, and cut the other 3-inch face from this end of the board.**

10. **Repeat Steps 5 through 9 on the other top support board.**

11. **Move the fence over until the outer (farthest from the rip fence) edge of the blade is 10 inches from the scrap piece of wood attached to the fence.**

12. **Repeat Steps 5 through 10 for the second top support board.**

13. Cut out the remaining wood from the tenon.

This will give you a ½-inch section in the middle of this tenon that has to be cut out. Adjust the rip fence so that the blade will cut this section out and follow Steps 5 through 10 on both boards.

14. Cut the notch in the bottom of the support piece.

To make the notch in the 2-inch face of the support, adjust the depth of cut to 1 inch and follow Steps 5 through 10, omitting Step 7. Run the board through the saw on the bottom 2-inch face.

Making the mortise in the bottom support

To cut the mortise you can use a mortise chisel and mallet and a drill press with a 1-inch forstner drill bit, and you can square up the corners with a chisel or a dedicated mortising machine. Cut this mortise like you would any other mortise. Chapter 10 has more specific details on this procedure. Figure 14-17 shows the placement of the mortise in the bottom support.

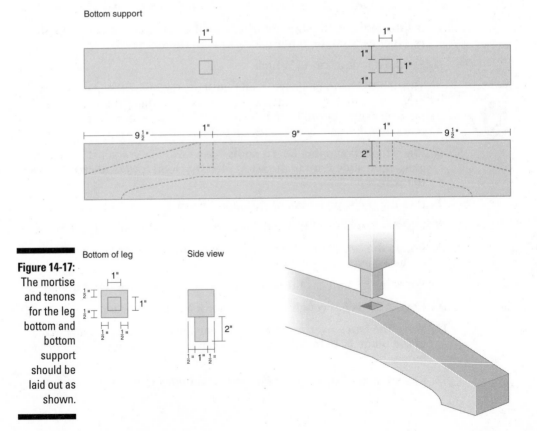

Figure 14-17:
The mortise and tenons for the leg bottom and bottom support should be laid out as shown.

Cutting the tenon in the leg bottom

This tenon can be cut with the same basic procedure as the tenons on the top support. You need to adjust the fence first to 2 inches from the inner edge of the blade and then closer to cut the entire length of the tenon. Set the blade at a depth of ½ inch. Figure 14-17 shows how the tenon should look.

Be sure to use scrap to start with and make adjustments as necessary in order to get the tenon just the right size. Better yet, make it snug and loosen it up with a file or rasp or coarse sandpaper.

Milling the mortise for the rail in the leg

For the rail in the leg, cut the ½-x-2-x-1¾-inch mortise 3½ inches from the top of the leg and ¾ inch from the edges. Figure 14-18 shows this placement.

Tackling the tenons in the rails

The tenons for the rails should be ½ x 2 x 1¹¹⁄₁₆ inches set ¼ inch from the edges and ½ inch from the top of the rail (see Figure 14-18). Follow the standard tenon-making procedures to make the cuts (Chapter 10). Also, be sure to test the tenon using scrap wood to ensure a snug fit.

Cutting the curved supports

After you've cut all the joints for the trestle assembly, you can cut the top and bottom supports to their final profiles. These are shown in Figure 14-19.

The cutouts on the top support and the top of the bottom support can be either straight or curved. If you choose to make them straight, simply mark the boards as shown and draw a straight line between them. If you want a curved part, use a large piece of poster board and draw a full-size picture of the support with a pencil, erasing and redrawing as necessary until you get the look you want. Cut out that drawing and use it as a template. Transfer the curve to the board by tracing the edge of the poster board onto the board using a pencil.

Make these cuts on the boards and cut them on your band saw, leaving the line as you cut. Sand off the line with either a belt sander followed by a random orbit sander or an oscillating spindle sander if you have one.

Assembling the trestle structure

To put this thing together, follow the procedure described in the "Putting all the pieces together" section earlier in the chapter.

You should assemble this table in two stages: first the end units, consisting of top and bottom support and legs, then the rails should be attached to those two assemblies. Then attach the top using screws through the top leg supports that have slotted holes to allow for expansion/contraction of the tabletop across its width. Drill these holes in the top leg supports before you assemble the trestle assemblies, because it will be a lot easier to do before assembly.

Rail

Top of leg

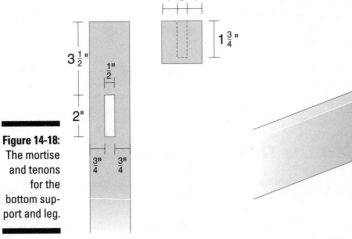

Figure 14-18:
The mortise and tenons for the bottom support and leg.

Top support

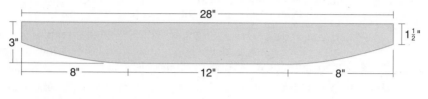

Bottom support

Side

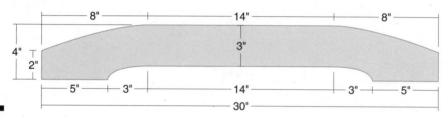

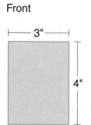

Figure 14-19:
The support
pieces
should have
cutouts
according
to these
drawings.

Front

When You Want to Get Creative: Designing Your Own Tables

Tables come in an almost unlimited variety of shapes and sizes, and following
some basic guidelines ensures that your own table designs are usable.

✔ Dining tables are almost always between 29 and 31 inches tall, which is a comfortable height for most people. If you're especially tall or short, you may find that a different height works better for you.

✔ End tables are often either 24 or 30 inches tall. End tables 24 inches tall work well for many bedside applications, and those that are 30 inches tall are good next to sofas or chairs.

✔ Coffee tables tend to be 15 to 18 inches tall. I usually set the height to the same as the seat on the sofa. This often puts the table 16 inches high.

✔ Worktables or display tables are best at a height of 36 to 38 inches tall.

✔ Don't be afraid to go into furniture showrooms or antique shops with a tape measure. I often start by measuring a table that I like and then design mine from there.

Chapter 15

Creating Cabinets

. . . .

In This Chapter

▶ Introducing cabinets, dressers, and cupboards

▶ Building a storage cabinet with drawers and doors

▶ Making a dresser

▶ Constructing an entertainment center

▶ Designing your own cabinets

. . . .

*I*f you want to build a dresser, a cupboard, an entertainment center, a kitchen island, or a rolling work/storage cabinet, be aware that they all use the cabinet as their basic form. Cabinets have either doors or drawers — or both — to help you store and organize your stuff. Cabinets come in many varieties, for many different uses.

In this chapter, I introduce you to the core elements of the cabinet and help you build a basic work cabinet. I also include directions on how to make a classic four-drawer dresser with turned legs (no turning necessary; you can buy them already done). If that's not enough, you can also try your hand at building an entertainment center based on a Shaker style armoire. To top it off, this chapter offers some design ideas that can help you come up with your own cabinet creations.

Introducing the Parts of a Cabinet

Cabinets, including dressers and cupboards, consist of several parts: the carcass, the face frame, the drawers, and the doors. Take a closer look at each part:

✔ **The carcass:** The carcass is the main structural component of dressers and cupboards. A carcass can be made of either sheet goods (plywood) or solid wood panels. If you use plywood products, you need to cover the edges of the wood to hide the inner core. You can do this with veneer edging or by including a face frame in the design.

✔ **The face frame:** The face frame is an aesthetic consideration, and although it adds some rigidity to the carcass, that's not its purpose. Carcasses can be made with or without face frames — it all depends on the design. All the projects in this chapter have face frames.

Face frames are made out of solid wood and are built before they're attached to the carcass. I always make them slightly larger than they're supposed to be and then sand or plane them flush with the carcass.

✔ **The drawers:** You can tell the skill of a craftsperson by the quality of her drawers. The most important part in making drawers is in how you attach the fronts to the sidepieces. I know of two acceptable ways to do this: with sliding dovetails or classic dovetails. I explain both of these approaches in this chapter.

✔ **The doors:** Doors allow you to have access to large storage spaces while keeping them hidden from view (and from dust). Doors come in many varieties, from simple solid doors to paneled doors with an almost infinite variety of decorative profiles. In this chapter, I show you how to make the simple solid door and the classic rail and stile paneled doors. With these two core approaches under your belt, you can tackle any door project that comes your way.

Making Your Own Storage/Work Cabinet

When you have a workshop in which to build things, you'll probably discover that you don't have enough places on which to do your work. The basic storage/work cabinet (see Figure 15-1) that I talk about in this section will provide you with a solid table to work on as well as some much-needed storage space for your tools and supplies. This unusual design has an open shelf right underneath the top for tool storage.

Going over the basics

The overall dimensions of the cabinet shown in Figure 15-1 are 40 inches wide by 30 inches deep by 32½ inches high (with the casters it should be the same height as your table saw). The top in the plan is designed for woodworking, so it's larger than the cabinet itself so that you have room to clamp your work down on the top.

Tooling up

If all you have is a table saw, you can still build this project; however, I find a miter saw helpful for cutting the miters on the top edging and the crosscuts for the face frame.

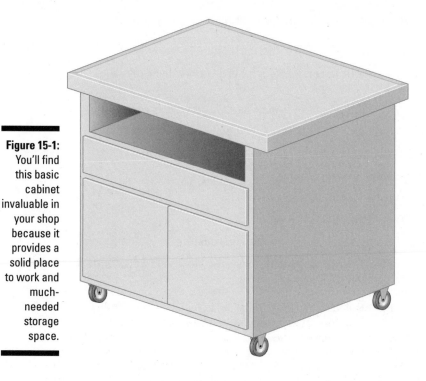

Figure 15-1:
You'll find
this basic
cabinet
invaluable in
your shop
because it
provides a
solid place
to work and
much-
needed
storage
space.

Knowing what techniques to use

If you've built any of the projects in Chapter 13, you're well on your way to being able to handle this project. If you haven't, then you'll get a chance to cut dados and rabbets to build the carcass. The face frame is simple butt joinery unless you have a pocket hole jig, in which case it becomes even easier (if that's possible).

The drawers use dado, rabbet, and sliding dovetail joints. The doors and applied drawer front are simply plywood panels wrapped with edging strips (iron-on wooden edge band tape). In the case of the top, the edging is 1½ inches wide x ¾ inch thick solid wood edge banding with mitered corners. The doors have thin edging like those found in the basic bookcase described in Chapter 13.

Assembling a materials list

This project uses plywood and some solid wood for the face frame and edging around the top. I recommend oak or birch. These woods will keep your costs down because neither solid oak nor birch is very expensive. If you want to paint the cabinet, consider using poplar for the face frame and top edging (poplar is a great, inexpensive wood that takes paint well).

You need the following materials to build the storage/work cabinet:

- ✔ (1) 4-x-8-foot sheet of ¾-inch melamine
- ✔ (2) 4-x-8-foot sheets of ¾-inch hardwood veneer plywood, such as oak or birch
- ✔ (1) 4-x-4-foot sheet of ¼-inch hardwood veneer plywood
- ✔ (1) 5-x-5-foot sheet of Baltic birch plywood
- ✔ 5 board feet of 4/4 hardwood, such as oak or birch
- ✔ 18 feet of veneer edging
- ✔ (2) pairs ¾-inch face frame overlay
- ✔ (1) set 20-inch drawer slides
- ✔ (4) 2½- to 3-inch heavy duty swivel casters
- ✔ (16) ¼-x-1¼-inch bolts with nuts and washers, to attach the casters to the carcass

If you want this cabinet to function as an in-feed/out-feed table for your table saw, plan to make the cabinet match the height of your table saw before you start this project. Measure the height of your saw, and if it's less than 36¼ inches high, you either need to buy smaller casters than those that I recommend or reduce the overall height of the cabinet. I suggest that you get smaller casters, because altering the plans increases the likelihood of mistakes.

Managing your cut list

Table 15-1 runs down the different parts for the storage/work cabinet and Figure 15-2 shows the dimensions of the project.

Table 15-1		Cut List for Storage/Work Cabinet	
Name of Part	**Number Needed**	**Dimensions**	**Material**
Top	1	1 ½" x 30" x 40"	Consists of (1) ¾" x 28½" x 38½" piece of melamine or other plastic laminate sheet stock. (1) ¾" x 28½" x 38½" piece of MDF which will be attached to the underside of the melamine board. (2) ¾" x 1½" x 30" solid hardwood, and (2) ¾" x 1½" x 40" solid hardwood. These are the edging strips.
Top cleats	2	¾" x ¾" x 22⅜"	Solid wood

Name of Part	Number Needed	Dimensions	Material
Carcass sides	2	¾" x 23¼" x 31"	Plywood
Carcass back	1	¾" x 26" x 31¼"	Plywood
Top shelf	1	¾" x 23¼" x 31¼"	Plywood
Bottom shelf	1	¾" x 23¼" x 31¼"	Plywood
Face frame rails	3	¾" x 1½" x 29"	Solid wood
Face frame stiles	2	¾" x 1½" x 31"	Solid wood
Doors	2	¾" x 15" x 18½"	Plywood with veneer edging
Drawer face front	1	¾" x 5½" x 30"	Plywood with veneer edging
Drawer sides	2	½" x 4¼" x 22¼"	Baltic birch plywood or solid wood
Drawer front	1	½" x 4¼" x 28"	Baltic birch plywood or solid wood
Drawer back	1	½" x 3¾" x 27½"	Plywood or solid wood
Drawer bottom	1	¼" x 21½" x 27¾"	Plywood
Drawer slide	2	¾" x 1½" x 4"	Solid wood or plywood support blocks

Creating the carcass

The carcass requires quite a few dado and rabbet cuts in the sides and some rabbets in the top and bottom pieces. Start by cutting the plywood panels for the sides, top, bottom, interior shelf, and back to the dimensions listed in Table 15-1. Then add the appropriate dado or rabbet joints to the pieces. (For details on how to cut these joints check out Chapters 10 and 13.)

Dadoing the sidepieces

All the dados should be ¾ inch wide (or the thickness of your plywood) x ⅜ inch deep. They are positioned at the following locations (Figure 15-3 shows these cuts):

- 4½ inches from the top
- ¾ inch from the bottom

Front

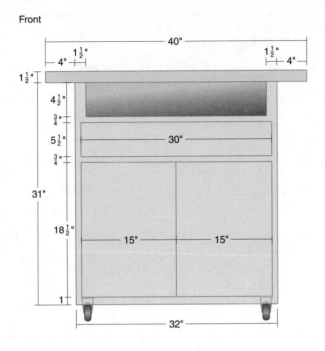

Side

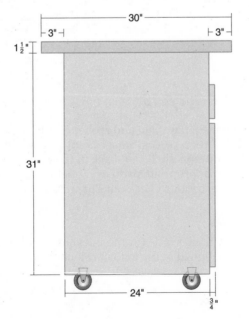

Figure 15-2:
This storage/ work cabinet takes a couple of weekends to make.

dados

$\frac{3}{8}$" $\frac{3}{8}$"

$4\frac{1}{2}$"

31"

Figure 15-3:
The dados
cut in the
side panels
are placed
in these
positions.

$\frac{3}{4}$"

$\frac{3}{4}$"

Rabbeting the side, top, and bottom pieces

A ½-inch-deep x ¾-inch-wide (or the thickness of your plywood) rabbet gets cut into the back edge of the side, top, and bottom pieces. These rabbets hold the back in place.

Putting it together

The next step is to assemble the carcass. To do this, you need to have a couple of bar clamps, some wood glue, a rubber mallet, and a damp rag near your worktable. The easiest way to assemble the carcass is to follow the procedure in the upcoming list.

Before you add any glue to the joints, do a *dry fit* of the carcass by following the assembly steps without the glue. Doing so gives you a chance to rehearse your moves and ensures that all the parts fit properly.

1. **Lay one of the sides flat on the table with the dados facing up.**

2. **Put a thin layer of glue in the top and bottom dados.**

3. **Put a little glue on the edge of the top shelf and slip it into the appropriate dado groove.**

   You may need to tap it in with a mallet if the joint is tight.

4. **Repeat Step 3 with the bottom shelf.**

5. **Gently flip the side on its edge so that the front of the carcass is facing up.**

   The top and bottom shelves should be solidly in their grooves and will hold up the side.

6. **Run a thin film of glue in all the grooves on the other sidepiece.**

7. **Apply glue to the edges of the shelves.**

8. **Work quickly to align all the shelves to the grooves and put the sidepiece on.**

   This is much easier said than done. You have about ten minutes before the glue sets, so work quickly, but effectively.

   I've found the best way to get all the joints lined up and attached is to start by tipping the sidepiece up at an angle and aligning the shelves to the bottom part of the grooves. After you have the top and bottom pieces partway in the grooves (it's generally just an inch or so at this point), attach two clamps to the sides at the top and bottom shelves to keep the side from popping out when you tilt it up further.

9. **Tilt the side up further and tap it into place with a mallet.**

   As long as your joints aren't too tight, this step shouldn't be that difficult. If your joints are really tight and you need to tap harder to get the joints to fit, use a scrap piece of wood of the same species to tap against instead of tapping directly against the side of the carcass. Doing so keeps you from denting the wood.

10. **Using two clamps, clamp up the front edge of the carcass at the shelves.**

11. **With the front edge clamps secure, slightly lift the carcass and slide clamps under it.**

12. **Secure the bottom clamps.**

13. **Check the carcass for square.**

    You do this by measuring diagonally across the carcass. If both measurements are equal, you're square. If not, you need to make adjustments. See Chapter 12 for details on how to do this.

14. **Clean up.**

    Chapter 12 goes into detail about the process.

15. **Take a break.**

    You've just completed a major task, so resist the urge to get more work done at this point. After a short break you can get back at it (or better yet, come back the next day).

16. **Let the carcass set overnight.**

After you have the carcass together, glue and nail the back in right away. This will help you square the unit.

Building the top

The top consists of two ¾-inch-thick pieces of melamine glued together and then wrapped with ¾-inch solid wood to hide the edges. I chose melamine for this project because it's easy to find at your local home center and you don't have to apply a plastic laminate over the top of the MDF core. But there's no reason that you can't use MDF and buy plastic laminate to put over it if you can't find melamine or if you want a different color laminate (melamine only comes with a white laminate attached).

The only problem with this method is that you can't use regular glue to attach melamine to melamine. Get a tube of construction adhesive or use white melamine glue if you can find it. To glue up the melamine pieces, spread the adhesive on one surface, press the other piece over it, and use some screws (1¼-inch #8 wood screws will work fine) fastened though the underside piece.

Cut the melamine panels slightly larger than their final dimension (about 1 inch in each direction) and trim them to size after they're glued together, to ensure that the edges are perfectly flush.

After you get the two pieces of MDF together and trimmed to size, you can apply the edge banding by following these steps:

Because these pieces are mitered at the corners, the measurement from the tabletop represents the short measurement on the edging piece's miter.

1. **Measure and cut one side, and then temporarily tape it in place.**

2. **Measure the next edge using the existing piece as a guide.**

3. **Repeat this procedure for the remaining two sides.**

You may have to do some fine-tuning on the cuts to make sure that the miters are tight. After all the pieces are cut, apply some glue to both the edging and the edge of the tabletop and clamp them in place with several clamps for each side.

Place one set of clamps running along the top of the tabletop and the other set along the bottom. This way the clamps won't cross and get in each other's way.

Finagling the face frame

You have to build the face frame before attaching it to the carcass. Because your carcass is already together (see the "Creating the carcass" section earlier in this chapter for details), measure the outer dimensions of the front of the carcass to make sure that it turned out the size you intended it to. Then cut the parts for the face frame based on those measurements.

Figure 15-4 shows the layout of the face frame.

Cut the *rails* (the horizontal pieces) for the face frame 1/16 inch longer than necessary so that the face frame is slightly larger than the carcass.

The easiest way to make a face frame is to use a *pocket hole jig* (see Figure 15-5) and screw the face frame together. One pocket hole and screw per joint is plenty for this face frame. Just drill the hole with the jig, apply a little glue to the joint, and screw it together. You get an instant joint that's as solid as a rock.

face frame

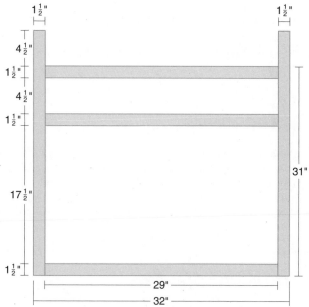

$1\frac{1}{2}$" $1\frac{1}{2}$"

$4\frac{1}{2}$"

$1\frac{1}{2}$"

$4\frac{1}{2}$"

$1\frac{1}{2}$"

31"

$17\frac{1}{2}$"

$1\frac{1}{2}$"

29"

32"

Figure 15-4:
The face
frame for
this project
has five
parts.

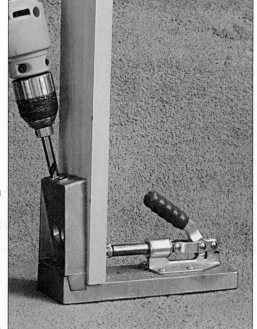

Figure 15-5:
A pocket
hole jig
makes quick
and easy
work of
making face
frames.

After the face frame is made, you can just attach it to the front of the carcass with some glue and clamps. If you want to get hardcore, I recommend that you use some biscuits every 8 to 10 inches around the perimeter. Your biscuit joiner's manual describes how to mark and cut the slots.

Plane, scrape, or sand the edges of the face frames flush with the sides of the carcass after the glue is set.

Detailing the doors

The doors for the storage/work cabinet are simply pieces of plywood cut to size with a thin edging strip around the outside. If you use the thin iron-on veneer edging (available at most woodworking supply stores), you don't need to make adjustments in the size of the door. But if you make your own edging by cutting ⅛- or ¼-inch strips of solid wood, you need to adjust the door size accordingly.

Digging into the drawer

The drawer for this storage/work cabinet is constructed of ½-inch *Baltic birch* plywood. This type of plywood has more plies to it than regular hardwood plywood and has no voids, so you can leave the edges uncovered. The drawback to this wood is that you can't find it at your local home center (a good lumberyard will have some, though) and it costs more than the regular stuff.

You can use regular hardwood plywood in a pinch. It just won't look as nice, but for a storage cabinet it probably doesn't matter.

The drawer for this cabinet consists of a five-sided box with dado and dovetail joints and a face front attached to it. Figure 15-6 shows the drawer construction.

Making this drawer is straightforward. Just follow these steps:

1. **Cut the parts to the sizes listed in the cut list (Table 15-1) earlier in the chapter.**

   This consists of the front, back, bottom, and sidepieces.

2. **Cut ¼-inch-deep dados in the sidepieces and front pieces as shown in Figure 15-7.**

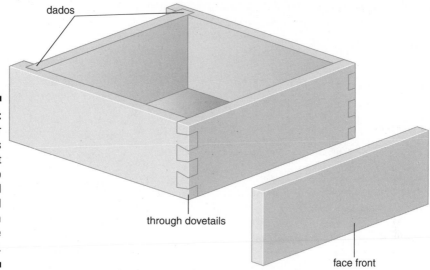

dados

through dovetails

face front

Figure 15-6:
The drawer for this cabinet uses dado and dovetail joints and has a separate face front.

3. **Cut dovetails in the front pieces and sidepieces.**

   Follow the directions in your dovetail jig manual for through dovetails.

   Use scrap wood to test the settings and the fit before you start cutting your actual drawer parts. It will take some time to get the adjustments just right. You want a tight-fitting joint that goes together without much force (light tapping with a mallet should be sufficient).

4. **Dry fit the drawer to make sure everything fits properly.**

5. **Take the drawer apart and apply glue to the joints.**

   Start with the dovetail joints, followed by the back piece.

6. **Clamp the drawer together.**

7. **Slide the bottom piece in the dados cut in the sidepieces.**

   Don't use glue. This piece will be attached with two nails into the back piece.

8. **Test the drawer for square.**

   Measure diagonally across the drawer in both directions. If these measurements are the same, you're square. If not, you need to make some adjustments. Chapter 12 provides details about the squaring-up process.

9. **Turn the drawer over and tap two nails through the bottom piece into the back.**

   ⅝-inch brads work well for this procedure.

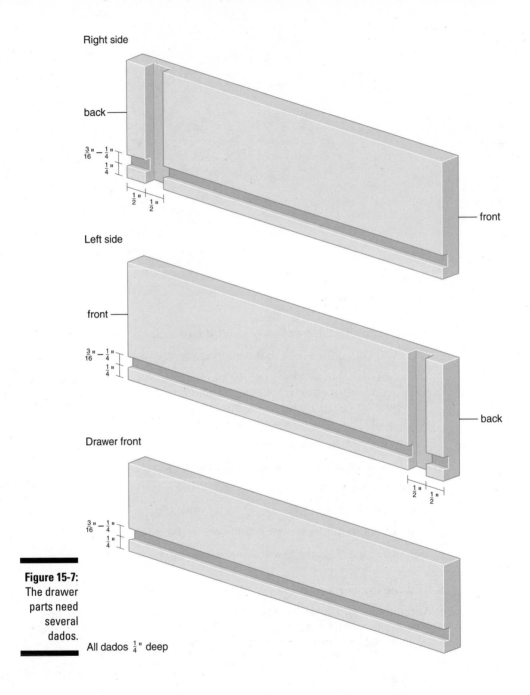

Right side

back

$\frac{3}{16}$" — $\frac{1}{4}$"
$\frac{1}{4}$"

$\frac{1}{2}$" $\frac{1}{2}$"

front

Left side

front

$\frac{3}{16}$" — $\frac{1}{4}$"
$\frac{1}{4}$"

back

Drawer front

$\frac{1}{2}$" $\frac{1}{2}$"

$\frac{3}{16}$" — $\frac{1}{4}$"
$\frac{1}{4}$"

Figure 15-7:
The drawer
parts need
several
dados.

All dados $\frac{1}{4}$" deep

Adding the drawer and doors to the carcass

To attach the doors and drawer to the carcass, you need some hardware. This hardware includes two sets of hinges and a set of drawer slides. These items are listed in the "Assembling a materials list" section earlier in the chapter.

Before you attach the doors and drawer, sand and finish the project. Part V walks you through the process of sanding and finishing.

Attaching the doors

Attach the door to the face frame according to the hinge manufacturer's instructions.

Attaching the drawer

To attach the drawer slides to the carcass, screw the ¾-x-1½-x-4-inch drawer slider blocks (support block) to the back of the side panels of the carcass. To do this, follow these steps:

1. **Place one of your drawer slide pieces in position with the front at the edge of the face frame.**

2. **Mark the place where the rear screw holes in the sliding mechanism sit at the carcass.**

   This is where you want your support block.

3. **Remove the sliding mechanism.**

4. **Apply some glue to the support block and screw the block in place.**

5. **Repeat this procedure for the other drawer slide.**

6. **Attach the drawer slides to the drawer and carcass according to the instructions included with the slides.**

7. **Slide the drawer in place.**

To attach the applied drawer (face) front onto the drawer, follow these steps:

1. **Place three short pieces of double-sided tape on the front of the drawer.**

2. **Position the drawer face front in relation to the doors and face frame.**

   The drawer should be even with the doors on the sides and should be equidistant between the open shelf and the top of the doors.

3. Press the face front onto the tape.

4. Open one of the doors and gently push the drawer open from underneath.

5. Mark the position of the face front on the drawer (use a pencil and draw a line along the bottom and sides).

6. Remove the face front and tape from the drawer.

7. Put the face front back in place and clamp it.

8. Screw two screws from the inside of the drawer front into the face front.

9. Close the drawer and admire your work.

Attaching the top

The top is attached to the cabinet with cleats that get screwed into both the underside of the top and the side of the carcass. Use 1¼-inch #8 screws (you need eight screws total).

The following steps describe the procedure:

1. Measure 4¾ inches in from the long sides and 3¹¹⁄₁₆ inches in from the short sides of the top.

   Mark the bottom side of the top piece.

2. Using two screws, screw the cleats to the underside of the top where the lines intersect.

3. Lay the top onto the cabinet with the cleats positioned between the sidepieces and just behind the face frame.

4. Screw two screws through each side and into the cleat.

Attaching the casters

The last step in making the storage/work cabinet is to attach the casters. Ideally, you want the height of the top even with your table saw. If your table saw is the same height as mine (36¼ inches), you should be able to bolt the casters to the bottom shelf and be done. But if your table saw is taller, you need to add some wood to the bottom of the shelf to raise up the cabinet.

If your saw is shorter than 36¼ inches, you either need smaller casters than those I recommend in the "Assembling your materials list" section earlier in the chapter or you need to go back to the beginning of the project and start over (just kidding — get the smaller casters).

Building a Four-Drawer Dresser

If you want to get good at making drawers, I can't think of a better way to do it than making a dresser. To keep you from getting overwhelmed, this project has only 4 drawers, instead of 10 or 12 like some dressers. This four-drawer dresser (see Figure 15-8) is one I made for my daughter before she was born. (I finished it and brought it into the house just 4 hours before my wife went into labor. How's that for timing?)

Going over the basics

This dresser is a simple design with decorative feet and dovetailed drawers. It has a face frame and the drawers are *inset* (the fronts of the drawers are flush with the front of the face frame). The only tricky part of making this dresser is that you have to make the drawers just the right size in order for them to look good. Fortunately, I can help you with that.

Figure 15-8:
This dresser features inset drawers and clean lines.

Tooling up

This project requires a table saw, a thickness planer, a jointer, a router with dovetail and roundover bits, and a dovetailing jig. I also find that a miter saw for crosscutting the face frame boards and a pocket hole jig for assembling the face frame are very helpful.

Knowing what techniques to use

This project involves building a carcass, which uses dado, rabbet, and tongue-and-groove joints. The drawers use half-blind dovetails and all solid wood, so you need to be able to pre-mill, joint, and thickness plane your boards (see Chapter 12 for details). The top requires edge-to-edge gluing (see Chapter 10) as well as the pre-milling steps you use on the wood for the drawers.

Assembling a materials list

This dresser is constructed with hardwood plywood for the carcass and solid wood for the face frame, top, and drawers. Because this is a painted dresser, I recommend using birch plywood for the carcass and either birch or poplar for the solid wood top, drawers, and face frame. If you don't want to paint this dresser, choose woods such as oak, maple, or cherry, depending on your taste in wood. Be sure to choose the same wood species for both the plywood and solid wood. You need the following materials to build this dresser:

- (1) 4-x-8-foot sheet of ¾-inch birch veneer plywood
- (1) 4-x-8-foot sheet of 1/4 birch veneer plywood
- 15 board feet of 4/4 birch or poplar
- 15 board feet of 3/4 birch or poplar
- (6) drawer slides

   For this dresser I like to use classic wood slides
- (4) feet such as the French bun feet on my dresser
- (6) drawer knobs

   I used sunflower shaped ones that I found at my local home center.

Managing your cut list

Table 15-2 shows the different parts you need for this project. (Figure 15-9 illustrates those parts.)

Table 15-2		**Cut List for Four-Drawer Dresser**	
Name of Part	*Number Needed*	*Dimensions*	*Material*
Top	1	¾" x 18" x 36"	Solid wood glued up from narrower boards

Name of Part	Number Needed	Dimensions	Material
Sides	2	¾" x 16½" x 36¾"	Plywood
Bottom	1	¾" x 16¼" x 33¾"	Plywood
Carcass frames	4	¾" x 16¼" x 33¾"	Plywood. Consists of 3" wide pieces made into a frame consisting of (2) ¾" x 3" x 10¾" (including ¼" tongues on each end) and (2) ¾" x 3" x 33¾". (8) of each are needed to make (4) frames
Face frame stiles	2	¾" x 1½" x 31"	Solid wood
Face frame bottom rail	1	¾" 2¼" x 31½"	Solid wood
Face frame center rails	2	¾" x 1" x 31½"	Solid wood
Face frame top rail	1	¾" 1¾" x 31½"	Solid wood
Face frame top drawer stile	1	¾" x 1¼" x 7"	Solid wood
Top drawer fronts	2	¾" x 6⅞" x 15"	Solid wood
Top drawer sides	4	½" x ⅞" x 16½"	Solid wood
Top drawer backs	2	½" x 6⅜" x 14½"	Solid wood
Top drawer bottoms	2	¼" x 14½" x 16¼"	Plywood
Middle drawer front	1	¾" x 8⅜" x 31⅜"	Solid wood
Middle drawer sides	2	½" x 8⅜" x 16½"	Solid wood
Middle drawer back	1	½" x 7⅞" x 30⅞"	Solid wood
Middle drawer bottom	1	¼" x 16¼" x 30⅞"	Solid wood
Bottom drawer front	1	¾" x 9⅜" x 31⅜"	Solid wood
Bottom drawer sides	2	½" x 9⅜" x 16½"	Solid wood
Bottom drawer back	1	½" x 8⅞" x 30⅞"	Solid wood
Bottom drawer bottom	1	¼" x 16¼" x 30⅞"	Plywood

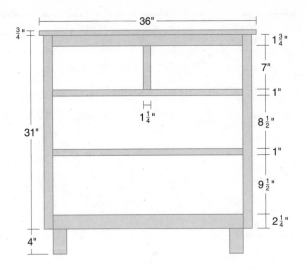

Figure 15-9:
This dresser is made from plywood with a solid wood face frame and top.

Putting the carcass together

To make the carcass, you need to cut all the parts to the sizes listed in Table 15-2, mill the dados and rabbets in the sidepieces, and make the carcass frames.

Milling the dados

All the dados in the carcass are ⅜ inch deep. They're positioned according to the measurements in Figure 15-10.

All the measurements are based on the plywood being ¾ inch thick. If it's thinner than that, make sure you make your cuts by measuring down from the top of the piece. These measurements need to be exact; otherwise, the face frame and drawers won't fit properly. (Chapters 10 and 13 detail how to cut dados and rabbets.)

front

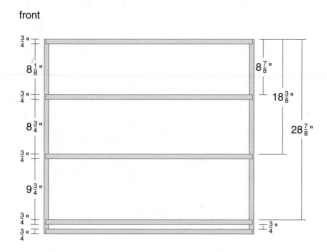

Figure 15-10:
The carcass for this dresser has many dados and a carcass frame made from plywood.

carcass frame

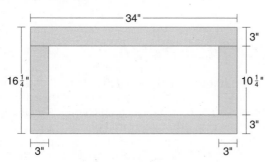

Fashioning the carcass frame

Instead of using shelf panels for the interior dividers in the carcass, this dresser uses frames made out of plywood cut in 3-inch-wide strips. These frames provide the same stiffening that a complete panel does, but they weigh much less. When you have three interior dividers like this dresser does, the frame makes quite a bit of difference in the final weight of the project.

To make these panels, cut a ¼-inch-thick and ¼-inch-long tongue centered on the short pieces and a ¼-inch-wide by ¼-inch-deep groove centered on the long pieces (Figure 15-10 shows the frame layout). Chapter 10 details how to make tongue-and-groove joints. After you have the tonguing and grooving done, all you have to do is glue the frame up.

When gluing up the frames, don't put too much pressure on the joints with your clamps. If the frame is bent at all, it won't fit in the dado in the side-piece. Use just enough pressure to pull the joint together.

Assembling the carcass parts

Putting this carcass together is similar to the procedure I describe for the carcass in the "Making Your Own Storage/Work Cabinet" section earlier in the chapter. You can just follow the steps listed in that section for this project as well. One word of caution, however: This carcass will be a bit trickier to put together because you have three dados and two rabbets to fit.

I recommend that you fit the dados for the interior frames first and then add the top and bottom boards to their rabbet joints.

Because of the number of parts in this carcass, I highly recommend that you perform a dry fit run-through or two to get used to the process. You won't have a lot of time to fit the joints, and working with five pieces at a time can be challenging. The more prepared you are for the process, the easier it'll be.

Producing the face frame

Because the fit of the face frame is critical to getting drawers that work well, I recommend that you hold off on cutting the parts until the carcass is complete. If your carcass frames are off from the plans, you need to alter the placement of the face frame rails (the horizontal pieces) to match. The tops of these rails need to be exactly ⅛ inch higher than the tops of the carcass frames. This gives you the proper clearance for the drawer slides.

Assuming that your carcass frames are where the design says they should be, the face frame should be put together according to the drawing in Figure 15-11.

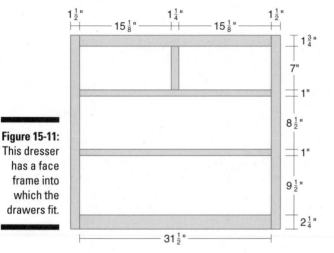

Figure 15-11:
This dresser has a face frame into which the drawers fit.

The layout for the face frame in relation to the carcass frames is based on the drawer slides that I recommend in the materials list (see the "Assembling your materials list" section earlier in the chapter). These slides have a ³⁄₁₆-inch *clearance* (the height of the bottom piece of the slider where the groove is cut). If your slides have a different clearance, adjust the difference between the top of the carcass frame and face frame rails so that the slide is ¹⁄₁₆ inch up from the face frame rail.

To give you some wiggle room, make the *stiles* (outer vertical pieces) ¹⁄₃₂ inch wider than shown in the plan. They will extend over the edge of the carcass by that ¹⁄₃₂ inch. You can sand them flush and end up with a nice clean edge.

This is the kind of face frame where a pocket hole jig comes in really handy. With the narrow rails, you don't have enough room to use biscuits, and with the placement of the rails being so critical, gluing up butt joints is less than ideal (things tend to move when you clamp them).

If you use a pocket hole jig, the parts tend to move a little when you drive the screw in. To remedy this, line up your joint and clamp a couple of blocks on either side of the joining board to keep it from shifting when you screw. Figure 15-12 shows how to do this.

After the face frame is glued up and the glue is set, you can attach it to the carcass. Either glue it straight on or use biscuits.

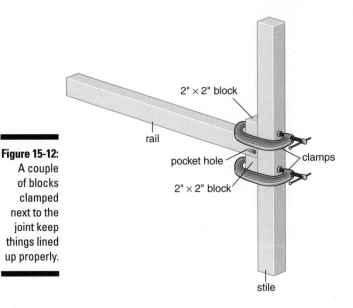

2" × 2" block

rail

pocket hole

clamps

2" × 2" block

stile

Figure 15-12:
A couple
of blocks
clamped
next to the
joint keep
things lined
up properly.

Crafting the drawers

Making the drawers for this dresser is very similar to making the drawer for
the storage/work cabinet that I describe earlier in the chapter. Do consider
these differences:

✔ These drawers are made from ½-inch solid wood instead of ½-inch Baltic
birch plywood.

✔ These drawers are inset in the face frame, whereas the drawer in the
storage/work cabinet was overlaid. Making an overlaid drawer is much
easier than the inset version. In order to look right, the inset drawer has
to have a ¹⁄₁₆-inch space around all four sides. Getting this gap perfect
takes some skill. (You'll be able to handle it with a little patience.)

The best way to make the drawers for this dresser is to measure each of the
openings in the face frame and cut the drawer front to fit. It may take you
some time and you may have to make a few drawer fronts more than once to
get them right, but you will figure out how to measure and cut accurately by
doing this task.

If your face frame matches the one in Figure 15-11, your drawer parts should
be the same as those listed in Table 15-2 earlier in this section. But if your
drawer fronts vary from the ones listed in Table 15-2, you need to make
adjustments to the other pieces of the drawers. For example, if your drawer
front is ¹⁄₁₆ inch narrower than the plans call for, then your back piece needs
to be ¹⁄₁₆ inch narrower too. Likewise, if your drawer front is ¹⁄₁₆ inch taller

than called for, adjust your sidepieces by that same amount. If your pieces are exactly the same as those in the plans, congratulations!

Making and assembling the drawers involves the same steps as the storage/work cabinet, shown earlier in this chapter. (See the section titled "Digging into the drawer" for specific details.) The only difference here is that you use half-blind dovetails to attach the sides to the front of the drawer. Your dovetailing jig will detail how to make those joints. The layout for the dados is the same as those shown in Figure 15-7.

Fitting the drawers

If all went well with your drawer-making, putting the drawers in should be comparatively easy. The top drawers get one slide set in the center of the drawer. The bottom two drawers each get two slides. The slides should be positioned 7 inches from the inside edge of the cabinet.

Follow these steps to fit the drawers:

1. **Mark the position of the slide on the carcass frame at both the front and back of the cabinet.**

   The slides need to be exactly perpendicular to the front of the cabinet; otherwise, the drawer will bind when it's opened and closed.

2. **Attach the cabinet part of the slide first (the part with the groove in it).**

3. **Slide the mating part of the drawer slide into the cabinet piece.**

4. **Slide the drawer into the cabinet.**

   Center the drawer in the opening.

5. **Go around to the back of the cabinet and mark where the slide is on the underside of the drawer.**

6. **From behind, gently open the drawer a few inches by pushing on the slide (not the drawer).**

7. **Go around to the front of the cabinet and mark the position of the slide on the underside of the drawer.**

8. **Remove the drawer and moving slide piece.**

9. **Turn the drawer over and attach the slide piece with some screws.**

   Be sure to sink the screw heads in far enough so that they don't hinder the sliding action.

10. **Apply some paste wax to both pieces of the slides.**

11. **Slide the drawer into its home.**

12. **Repeat Steps 1 through 11 for the rest of the drawers.**

13. **Take a break; you've earned it.**

Tackling the top

The top for this dresser is made of solid wood. Follow the procedures listed in Chapter 14 for making a solid wood tabletop.

After you have the top glued up and cut to its final size, you can put the rounded edge on it. You do this with a router fitted with a ¼-inch roundover bit and collar. The collar rolls along the edge of the top, while the bit routes a rounded edge. Only route the front and the sides; don't route the back edge. Depending on the wood you used, you may need to route the rounded edge in two passes, taking a little bit at a time to reduce the risk of splitting the wood with the spinning bit (tear-out).

To attach the top to the carcass, drill elongated holes through the top carcass frame and screw a 1¼-inch #8 screw into the underside of the top through the frame. A washer between the head of the screw and the carcass frame keeps the screw from popping through the hole. One screw at each corner and one in the middle on the front and back is sufficient.

All that's left to do is sand (see Chapter 16) and paint (see Chapter 17) the dresser.

Crafting a Shaker Entertainment Center

As far as I'm concerned, nothing is as unsightly as a TV or stereo with a bunch of CDs or DVDs sitting randomly on top. An entertainment center helps hide the clutter and adds a bit of elegance to the home. In addition, nothing beats a big project to make you feel like a true woodworker. (Big projects also help justify the money you spent on those big, expensive machines sitting in your shop.)

Going over the basics

This entertainment center is based on a Shaker style armoire. It will easily fit a TV or stereo and all the stuff that goes with them. You can put it in a living room, family room, or bedroom (maybe you should make more than one). Figure 15-13 shows the dimensions of the project.

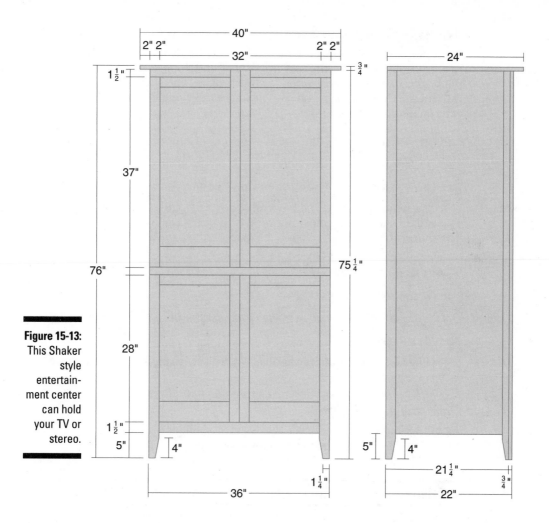

Figure 15-13:
This Shaker
style
entertain-
ment center
can hold
your TV or
stereo.

Tooling up

This project requires a table saw, a thickness planer, and a jointer. I also find
that a miter saw (for crosscutting the face frame boards) and a pocket hole
jig (for assembling the face frame) are very beneficial.

Knowing what techniques to use

This project involves building a carcass, which requires cutting dado and
rabbet joints (see Chapter 10). The doors require tongue-and-groove joints
(also in Chapter 10). The rails and stiles use solid wood, so you need to be
able to pre-mill, joint, and thickness plane (see Chapter 12) your boards. The
top requires edge-to-edge gluing (see Chapter 10) as well as the pre-milling
steps you use on the wood for the door parts.

Assembling a materials list

This entertainment center is constructed with hardwood plywood for the carcass and solid wood for the face frame, top, and doors. Call me a snob, but I think you must use cherry wood for this project. The sleek lines work great with the soft look of the wood. You need the following materials to build this entertainment center:

✔ (2) 4-x-8-foot sheets of 3/4 cherry veneer plywood

✔ (1) 4-x-8-foot sheet 1/4 cherry veneer plywood

✔ (1) 4-x-8-foot sheet ⅛-inch cherry plywood

The ⅛-inch plywood will have one good side and is actually ⅛ inch. This is unusual because most plywood is thinner than marked. You'll be putting two pieces back to back to make the panels for the doors. You can find this plywood (also called a *door skin*) at a decent lumberyard.

✔ 24 board feet 4/4 cherry

✔ (8) hinges

You want classic mortise hinges for inset doors.

✔ (4) knobs

I like Shaker style cherry knobs. Any woodworking store should have some.

Managing your cut list

Table 15-3 shows you the parts of this entertainment center. Refer to Figure 15-13 to see the dimensions for this project.

Table 15-3	Cut List for Shaker Entertainment Center		
Name of Part	**Number Needed**	**Dimensions**	**Material**
Top	1	¾" x 24" x 40"	Solid wood glued up from narrower pieces
Sides	2	¾" x 21¼" x 75¼"	Plywood and solid wood. The sides are made from an 18" x 70¼" plywood piece edged with a 2" x 75¼" piece attached to the back and a 1¼" x 75¼" piece attached to the front. The top of the plywood is flush with the top of the edging pieces. The plywood stops 5" short of the edging at the bottom.

Name of Part	Number Needed	Dimensions	Material
Carcass top	1	¾″ x 21″ x 35¼″	Plywood
Center shelf	1	¾″ x 21″ x 35¼″	Plywood
Bottom	1	¾″ x 21″ x 35¼″	Plywood
Face frame stiles	2	¾″ x 2″ x 75¼″	Solid wood
Face frame top rail	1	¾″ x 1½″ x 32″	Solid wood
Face frame center rail	1	¾″ x 1½″ x 32″	Solid wood
Face frame bottom rail	1	¾″ x 2″ x 32″	Solid wood
Top door outer stiles	2	¾″ x 2″ x 37″	Solid wood
Top door inner stiles	2	¾″ x 2¼″ x 37″	Solid wood
Top door center piece	1	⅝″ x ¾″ x 37″	Solid wood
Top door rails	2	¾″ x 2″ x 12⅜″	Solid wood. Length includes ⅜″ tongue on each end.
Top door bottom rails	2	¾″ x 4″ x 12⅜″	Solid wood. Length includes ⅜″ tongue on each end.
Top door panels	2	¼″ x 12⅜″ x 31¾″	Plywood. Consists of 2 pieces of ⅛″ plywood glued back to back.
Bottom door inner stiles	2	¾″ x 2¼″ x 28″	Solid wood
Bottom door outer stiles	2	¾″ x 2″ x 28″	Solid wood
Bottom door center piece	1	⅝″ x ¾″ x 28″	Solid wood
Bottom door top rails	2	¾″ x 2″ x 12⅜″	Solid wood. Length includes ⅜″ tongue on each end.
Bottom door bottom rails	2	¾″ x 5″ x 12⅜″	Solid wood. Length includes ⅜″ tongue on each end.
Bottom door panels	2	¼″ x 12⅜″ x 21¾″	Plywood. Consists of 2 pieces of ⅛″ plywood glued back to back.

Forming the carcass

The carcass consists of the two side panels made from plywood and solid wood. The parts for the sides need to be glued up before you do any other work. For best results, I recommend that you use biscuits (see Chapter 7) and space them about 8 to 10 inches apart along the joint.

Figure 15-14 shows the layout of the side parts.

When your side panels are glued up, you can cut the dados and rabbets in the sides. They should be positioned as shown in Figure 15-15. The dados are ⅜ inch and ¾ inch (or whatever the thickness of your plywood is) wide. The tops of the shelf pieces are positioned as follows:

✔ Flush with the top

✔ 38½ inches from the top

✔ 7 inches from the bottom

The rabbet is ¼ inch deep by ½ inch wide, cut along the back edge.

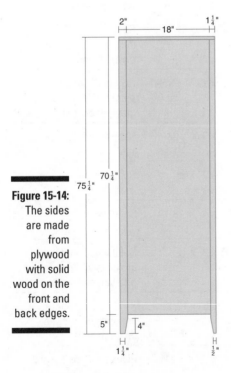

Figure 15-14:
The sides
are made
from
plywood
with solid
wood on the
front and
back edges.

$\frac{3}{8}$" deep $\frac{3}{4}$" wide dados

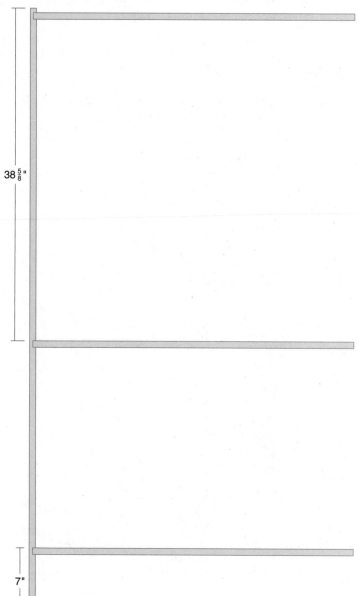

$38\frac{5}{8}$"

7"

Figure 15-15:
Cut dados
in the
sidepieces
at these
locations.

When you want to assemble the carcass, follow the same instructions that I give for the storage/work cabinet at the beginning of this chapter. See the section called "Creating the carcass" for details.

Making the doors

The doors for this cabinet are classic rail and stile doors with flat panels. Figure 15-16 shows the details of the doors.

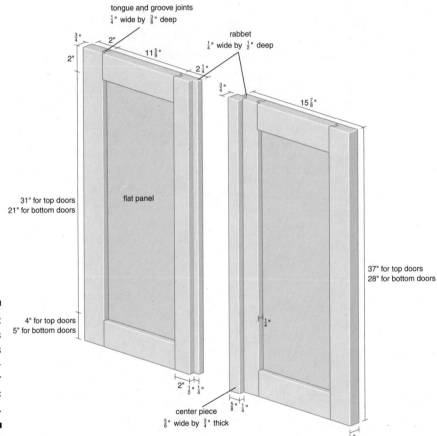

Figure 15-16: The doors for this entertainment center have classic flat panels.

The doors for this project are inset. This means that you have little room for error when making them. Before you start cutting the parts for the doors, measure your finished carcass to make sure it's the same size as the plans. If so, continue on with the dimensions listed in Table 15-3. If your carcass is slightly larger or smaller, you need to increase or decrease the size of the doors to fit. There should be slightly more than a $\frac{1}{16}$-inch gap around and between the doors.

Tonguing and grooving

To make the doors for this project, cut the rails and stiles to size and then cut a $\frac{1}{4}$-inch-wide by $\frac{3}{8}$-inch-deep groove in the inside edges of the *stiles* (vertical piece) and a $\frac{1}{4}$-inch-thick by $\frac{3}{8}$-inch-long tongue on the rails. (Chapter 10 details the tongue-and-groove-making process.)

You also need to put a groove in the inside edge of the rails for the panel to rest. This groove is also $\frac{1}{4}$-inch wide by $\frac{3}{8}$-inch deep.

Rabbeting

The fronts of the doors each have a $\frac{1}{4}$-inch-wide by $\frac{1}{2}$-inch-deep rabbet where they meet in the center. Two of the doors get a $\frac{5}{8}$-inch-wide-x-$\frac{3}{4}$-inch-thick piece of wood in the rabbet, and the other is left as is. When the doors close, the extra piece on one door fits into the rabbet on the other.

Preparing the panels

To make the panels for the doors, just cut the plywood $\frac{1}{2}$ inch oversized in both length and width and glue two pieces back to back with the good sides facing out. After the glue has dried, trim the panels to their finished size.

Choose the wood for the panels carefully so that the front of the doors has the best grain patterns. Also, try to get the panels for the top doors to match each other and the panels for the bottom doors to match each other. This will make the doors look better than if you use unmatched panels.

Gluing the panels

Apply glue to both surfaces and sandwich them between some leftover $\frac{3}{4}$-inch plywood, melamine, or MDF. Then clamp the panels tight and let them sit overnight.

Assembling the doors

Follow these procedures to assemble the doors:

Do a dry fit run-through before you use any glue, so skip Steps 1 and 2 the first time through to get used to the procedure involved in putting these pieces together.

1. **Apply glue to left side of the bottom rail and the bottom portion of the groove on the left stile.**

2. **Apply glue to left side of the top rail and the top portion of the groove on the left stile.**

3. **Slide the panel into the groove with the best side facing toward the front.**

   The panel doesn't need glue — it will float to allow for expansion and contraction with humidity changes, although some people use glue since the panel is plywood and it won't expand or contract very much. Still, I prefer to be safe and just dab a little glue in the joint rather than glue the entire thing.

4. **Apply glue to both the rails and the top and bottom portions of the right stile.**

5. **Attach the joint and clamp it up.**

   Make sure that the outside edges of the rails are flush with the ends of the stiles.

   One clamp at each rail is sufficient.

6. **Repeat Steps 1 through 5 with the other three doors.**

7. **Glue the center piece on the right-hand doors.**

   Put it in with the ⅝-inch edge facing out. The center piece will protrude ¼ inch from the front of the door and ⅜ inch to the side.

Fitting the doors

The doors for this project are inset, and that ordinarily means that you need to fit them perfectly in their openings. But because this cabinet has doors with a center strip and rabbets in them, you have some room for error.

Attaching the doors is as simple as mortising (see Chapter 10 for more on mortising) the face frame and outer doors' edges for the hinges. The easiest way to do this is to mark the outlines of the hinge and use a chisel to carve out the mortise, although some people prefer to use a plunge router and an edge guide.

The hinges should be positioned 4 inches from the top and bottom of the doors — two per door. If the center gets in the way of the doors' closing, just plane it down until the doors close smoothly.

Fashioning the top

The top is made from solid wood and needs to be made from narrow boards that are edge glued. Check out the "Tackling the tabletop" section in Chapter 14 for details on how to make a tabletop from solid wood.

The top will be attached to the carcass with screws through the top shelf. Elongate the hole through the top shelf and use washers to keep the screws from popping through the shelf holes. A 1¼-inch #8 screw works fine, although you can use a #6 if that's all you have handy.

Bucking Tradition: Designing Your Own Cabinets

The possible designs for cabinets are limited only by your imagination. If you're not sure where to start, this section may give you a few ideas, but you can also find plenty of other good resources — check out Chapter 21 for a few to get you going. In the meantime, here are a few things to consider when designing your own cabinets:

- ✔ For a simple, classic cabinet design, use a face frame and inset the door and drawers. Both Shaker and Craftsman style cabinets follow this principle.

- ✔ For a contemporary-looking cabinet, skip the face frame and use over-laid doors and drawer fronts. This gives you a clean line. Also, many contemporary style cabinets use sheet stock such as plywood and MDF, so the edges of the wood are sharp and crisp.

- ✔ The use of molding around the base or top adds weight to the look of the project. You don't need a shaper or a router table with a ton of bits to add moldings. You can often find quite a few styles of molding pre-made at either the lumberyard or home center. You may be limited in the species of woods available, though.

- ✔ Head to your local high-end furniture store with a tape measure. If you see a piece you like, take some basic measurements to get a sense of the scale of the piece. Don't be afraid to measure the entire thing if you really like it.

- ✔ If you want to make a kitchen worktable with a butcher-block top, consider buying the top already made. It's often less expensive than doing it yourself. And it's a lot less work.

Part V
The Grand Finale: Sanding and Finishing Your Masterpiece

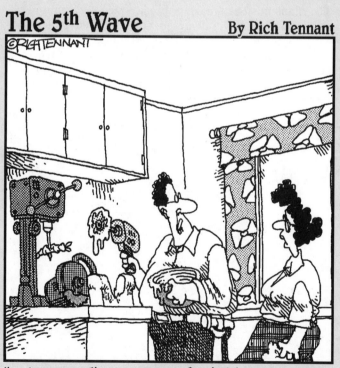

The 5th Wave   By Rich Tennant

"...because I'm more comfortable using my own tools. Now—how much longer do you want me to sand the cake batter?"

In this part . . .

The final finish can make or break a piece of furniture. Although most woodworkers consider their project nearly complete after they glue up all the parts, the reality is that as much time needs to be put into sanding and finishing the piece as was put into cutting and assembling it. Part V explores the process of sanding, staining, and topcoating a piece of furniture.

Chapter 16

Smoothin' It Out by Sanding and Filling

- -

In This Chapter

▶ Dealing with imperfections

▶ Making wood smooth

- -

I don't know about you, but after I get the project I'm working on assembled, I'm ready to move it into my house. The last thing I want to do is sand and finish the thing. And I don't know too many other woodworkers who like to deal with the sanding process, because sanding often takes as much time as building. However, if you're one of those woodworkers who likes to sand and finish — congratulations. Oh, and could you come over to my place? I have a few projects you can work on!

If you're not a lover of sanding, don't lose heart. This chapter can help you to get the best final finish with the least amount of hassle (and effort). You discover typical ways to fill holes or cracks as well as how to use sandpaper and scrapers to eliminate minor surface imperfections.

Filling Holes and Cracks

Even though you may have tried to use wood without any cracks, splits, holes, or gouges, sometimes you end up with imperfections you didn't notice or couldn't avoid. Or sometimes these imperfections are the result of a misplaced chisel or other accidents when you made the piece. For most types of furniture, you want to get rid of any of the problems before you do the final sanding. This section shows you how to fill both small and large defects as well as raise dents without hassle.

Fixing small imperfections

Cracks, scratches, or even slightly mismatched joints can be filled with several different products, including wood putty, wax sticks, and shellac sticks. Each of these items has its strengths and weaknesses, as I explain in the following list:

- **Wood putty:** You can find this common wood filler at hardware stores or your local home centers. Wood putties, like "plastic wood," come as a thick paste that you spread into the hole (crack or split) with a putty knife (a thin, flat, flexible-bladed tool) and then let dry and sand flush. Wood putties are available in a variety of colors, so one is sure to match the wood you're working with. If you can't find one that matches, you can either add some stain to the putty when it's still soft (before you apply it) or paint on some artist's paint to match the wood's surface after you've sanded it down.

- **Wax sticks:** Wax sticks are sticks of wax (makes sense, huh?) that are like crayons, only harder. They come in various colors to match different woods. There are essentially two ways to use a wax stick: before you apply the final finish and afterward. If you use one before the final finish is applied, you need to first seal the wood with shellac. This step isn't necessary when you use one after the final finish because the finish seals the wood.

  To apply a wax stick, simply draw it on by pressing it into the defect with the tip of the wax stick, a putty knife, or your finger and then remove the excess with either a putty knife or a piece of plastic like a credit card.

  I don't use wax sticks unless I put a wax finish on the piece, which I don't do very often. You can find out why in Chapter 18.

- **Shellac sticks:** I like shellac sticks. They come in tons of colors, look good, and are easy to apply. Shellac is a natural, low-toxic product made from beetle excretions (see Chapter 18, if you really want to know more about that particular piece of information) that you melt with a soldering iron and let drip into the surface imperfection. You then press it in with a putty knife or chisel and wait for it to harden. After the shellac is hard, you can scrape it flush with a chisel or thin cabinet scraper and then sand it lightly with fine sandpaper. (For more about different grades of sandpaper, check out the "Sanding" section later in this chapter.)

- **Glue and sawdust:** On occasion, I've been known to use a mixture of wood glue and sawdust to fill a hole or crack in my project. This allows me to exactly match the wood I'm working with, because I use sawdust that I created while milling the boards for the project. This is a low-tech solution that requires just the right amount of glue and sawdust to get a filler that is both durable and will stain well (not hard to do — it just takes some experimentation).

Dealing with big holes

If you have some big holes — from using recycled wood or from a loose knot, for instance — you can fill them with another piece of wood, called a *dutchman*. This technique has been around as long as people have been working with wood. Some purists cringe at the thought of using wood that has a blemish large enough to require a dutchman, but in the Southwest (my neck of the woods) where using recycled wood raises the value of the furniture, dutchmans are common. Heck, here many people don't even bother to fill cracks or holes.

Whether you like the rustic look or not, you should know how to make a dutchman. The procedure is pretty simple, and it's made even simpler with a plunge router, a ⅛-inch straight-cutting bit, and two collars: one ⁵⁄₁₆-inch and the other ⁹⁄₁₆-inch. In fact, you can buy kits that contain these parts at most woodworking tool suppliers. They're called *inlay kits* or *inlay bushing bit with removable collar*. The procedure with this setup is as follows:

1. **Make a template of the dutchman out of ¼-inch plywood or Masonite.**

   Measure the size of the defect in your project and add a little extra around it (about ½ inch or so on all sides). Cut out a hole in the template material to this size. Be sure to use a large enough piece of wood so that you can clamp this piece to the wood you want to work with and have enough room for the plunge router to move freely in the template. I recommend a piece at least 12 inches square.

2. **Attach the ⁵⁄₁₆-inch collar to the base of your plunge router followed by the ⁹⁄₁₆-inch collar.**

3. **Insert the bit into the plunge router.**

4. **Set the depth of cut to ⅛ inch.**

5. **Clamp the template onto the board with the defect, making sure that the hole in the template is over the defect.**

6. **Run your plunge router clockwise along the inside edge of the template.**

7. **Carefully route or chisel out the remaining material in the center of the template.**

8. **Remove the outer collar (the ⁹⁄₁₆-inch one).**

9. **Lower the depth of cut to ³⁄₁₆ inch.**

10. **Select a piece of wood that has a similar color and grain pattern to the wood where the defect was and clamp the template onto it.**

11. **Route around the edge of the template in a clockwise direction.**

    Be sure to keep tight to the edge of the template; otherwise, you cut into the dutchman itself.

12. **Remove the dutchman from the scrap wood by setting your table saw to cut ⅛ inch into the board.**

    If you use ¾-inch stock, set the rip fence ¹⁹⁄₃₂ inch from the side of the blade farthest from the rip fence (if your blade has a kerf of ⅛ inch, the rip fence is ¹⁵⁄₃₂ inch from the side of the blade closest to the rip fence).

13. **Set the depth of cut in the table saw so that it is higher than the dutchman on the board.**

14. **With the dutchman facing out, run the board through the saw.**

    The dutchman will fall out of the board as you run it through.

15. **Apply glue to the underside of the dutchman and a little to the receiving groove and then press it into place.**

    You may need to tap it lightly with a mallet. Use a scrap piece of wood of the same species to tap against. This will keep from damaging the wood. The dutchman will stick up ¹⁄₃₂ inch from the surface of the wood.

16. **Sand the dutchman flush after the glue dries.**

Raising dents

If your wood has a dent, you don't need to fill it with putty or anything else. All you have to do is place a damp cloth over the dent and cover it with a hot iron for a few seconds. The steam from the cloth will seep into the pores of the wood and lift the surface of the wood. Then all you have to do is sand the surface smooth. Pretty simple, huh?

Smoothing Out Your Wood

After you have your major defects out of the wood (see the "Filling Holes and Cracks" section for instructions), you need to smooth out the fillers and get rid of the minor scratches and milling marks. Then it's time to make the surface smooth enough for the finish you want to apply. This part of the process involves using sandpaper or a scraper. I cover both of these approaches in this section.

Sanding

Nearly all woodworkers sand to smooth the surfaces of their projects before finishing. This process isn't rocket science — all it takes is some simple steps and a ton of patience. The only times I've gotten a finish that I didn't like, I simply didn't spend enough time sanding. Try not to make this mistake yourself.

The process of sanding wood involves making progressively finer scratches in the surface. These scratches remove imperfections in the wood, such as visible scratches or uneven surfaces. Moving from one grit to the next finer one will reduce the size of the scratches until they are so small that the wood seems smooth. Never skip a grit of paper when sanding, because doing so makes it difficult to remove scratches that the previous grade of sandpaper would've removed easily. You'll spend a lot more time trying to get a smooth finish.

Understanding different types of sandpaper

Sandpaper comes in a variety of types, including glass, garnet, aluminum oxide, and silicon carbide. Each type has its benefits, which I detail in the following list:

✔ **Glass paper.** You find this cheapie paper at the local hardware store. Glass paper is yellow in color and breaks down quickly. I don't recommend it for your woodworking projects, because even though it's inexpensive, it'll end up costing you more in time and money than other papers. Resist the urge to buy glass paper.

✔ **Garnet paper.** Garnet sandpaper is made from small, sharp pieces of garnet (a type of mineral) that are fairly brittle, so they break down as you sand the wood. Garnet paper is a good balance between cost and quality for softwoods and some hardwood applications. Garnet paper has a reddish tint to it and can be found in most stores that carry sandpaper. Even though it's easy to find and is inexpensive, I generally don't use it in my shop because it's not as durable as aluminum oxide paper and it doesn't work very well for some of the harder woods.

✔ **Aluminum oxide.** Aluminum oxide sandpaper is harder than garnet sandpaper and is excellent for almost all woodworking tasks. This is the stuff I use. It lasts a relatively long time and is able to effectively sand all types of wood. I use it for everything but metal and wet sanding.

I recommend that you stock up on aluminum oxide paper in a variety of grits. You can find this type of paper in sheets for hand sanding and sized for most power sanders.

✔ **Silicon carbide.** Silicon carbide paper is the black stuff you see at your sandpaper store (home center or wherever). Silicon carbide is harder even than aluminum oxide, so it can handle sanding metal. But because you're a woodworker, you probably won't be sanding much metal; otherwise you'd be a metal worker.

Anyway, I use wet-dry silicon carbide paper for wet-sanding an oil finish (see Chapter 18), so I recommend that you have some fine grit paper on hand (the "Getting into grits" section has more on sandpaper grits).

Getting into grits

Sandpaper comes in differing levels of abrasiveness, called the *grit*. The grit refers to the number and size of the particles in the sandpaper. The fewer and larger the particles, the rougher the paper. Grits range from 40 to 600 — the lower numbers are for rougher papers. For the most part, I use 80- to 320-grit papers unless I'm doing wet-dry work with silicon carbide paper. In this case, I may go up to 600-grit for oil finishes.

Aside from the number rating of sandpaper grits, you have general categories such as:

- **Very coarse:** This category consists of 40- and 60-grit papers.

- **Coarse:** Coarse refers to 80- and 100-grit papers. This paper will get rid of scratches and other surface imperfections.

- **Medium:** Medium is where you do most of your sanding. This category consists of 120-, 150-, and 180-grit papers.

- **Fine:** For final sanding, fine refers to papers from 220- to 280-grit.

- **Very fine:** Very fine papers go from 320- to 600-grit and are only used occasionally.

Trying your hand at sanding

My regular sanding procedure consists of removal of major surface defects with a belt sander, followed by smoothing with a random orbit sander, and then finishing off with a final hand sanding. I cover the basics of using belt and random orbit sanders in Chapter 6, so you can flip back there for details. Stick around here for some information on hand sanding, though.

Be sure to sand thoroughly with each grit of paper before moving on to the next finer grit. It can be kind of hard to determine when you've done enough sanding on one grit until you gain some experience, so my recommendation is to sand a few minutes longer than you think you need to with each grit of paper.

Follow these suggestions for a better and easier job hand sanding:

- **Wrap the paper around a block of wood to provide a flat, solid backing.** If you just hold the paper in your hand and press with your fingers you won't get a flat, even surface, and your hand will get tired much faster.

- **When sanding irregular shaped surfaces such as moldings, use a contoured block in the same shape as the surface you're sanding.** You can make the block yourself by using a round dowel, for instance, on rounded sections, or you can buy sanding blocks in a variety of shapes and sizes.

✔ **Tear the full sheets of sandpaper into halves or quarters to make working with it easier.**

✔ **Clean the sandpaper when it gets clogged. Simply tapping the paper with your hand will remove some of the accumulated dust.** Blowing on the paper or spraying it with some compressed air will also do the trick.

✔ **Replace the paper when you can no longer clean it well.** If the paper remains clogged after you try to clean it, don't hesitate to get a new sheet. Sanding with dull or clogged paper is a recipe for frustration.

✔ **Follow the sanding guidelines for the type of finish you intend to apply.** Some finishes such as oils work best with a finely sanded finish (320-grit, for example), but others, such as polyurethanes, can handle a rougher finish (150-grit). Different finishes require slightly different surface preparation to work best. Do your homework (Chapter 18 helps you out here) and decide what type of finish you want to use before doing any final sanding.

Scraping

Some woodworkers prefer a scraper to sandpaper. A *scraper* is simply a piece of metal with an edge on it that you scrape along the surface of the wood to smooth it out. When I use a scraper, I do the rough sanding work with a belt sander (if necessary) and random orbit sander up to about a 120-grit paper. From there, I use the scraper to smooth the wood.

Others prefer to use the scraper instead of the sanders. If you choose this route and your wood has major defects, you'll either need to use a hand plane or a thick cabinet scraper (heavy-duty scraper) to remove the defects before you move on to a regular (lighter-duty) scraper. A scraper is a good choice for projects with oil finishes, because it opens the pores of the wood and lets the oils penetrate deeper. This gives the illusion of more depth to the final finish. A scraper is not a good choice for finishes that are designed to sit on the top of the wood, such as polyurethanes.

Chapter 17

Adding Color: Stains and Paints

In This Chapter
▶ Choosing and using stains
▶ Selecting and working with paints

Most people think wood looks better after it develops a patina. *Patinas* develop through a process called oxidation, and they create a color that's darker than the raw, freshly sanded wood that your project has right after you finish building it. Stains are often used to give the effect of an aged patina right from the start. And stains are also used to give a less expensive wood the look of a more expensive one. Sometimes, they're used to even out the color differences in some wood. Paints, on the other hand, are used to give color to a less-than-beautiful wood.

In this chapter, I go over the ins and outs of adding color to your creations. From stains to paints, dyes to oxidizers, you find out how to choose the best approach for the type of wood you're working with. This chapter also shows you how to apply these different products for the best results.

Adding coloring agents such as stains, dyes, or paints requires you to sand the wood smooth (Chapter 16 covers this in detail) and know in advance the type of topcoat you intend to use (Chapter 18 has more on topcoats).

Understanding Types of Stains

Wood stains come in several configurations, including pigments, dyes, and combinations of pigments and dyes. Likewise, you can find stains with an oil base, water base, or lacquer base. In this section, I lay out all the options for you.

Pinpointing pigment stains

Pigment stains use minerals to create their color. Pigment stains don't actually change the color of the wood; they simply add a color by distributing these minerals into the pores of the wood. The minerals are suspended in mineral spirits, water, or lacquer thinner (called *carriers*) and are sealed into the pores by a component, called the *binder.*

Pigment stains are good for wood that has consistent pores, such as oak or ash, where you want to accentuate the grain patterns. Pigment stains aren't the best choice for wood where you want to even out color changes, such as the contrast between the heartwood (the darker colored wood stuff) and sapwood (the lighter colored wood) in cherry. I also wouldn't use pigment stains on a figured wood such as curly maple because it tends to look blotchy. Take a look at the color section to see a pigment stain applied to cherry wood.

Because of this tendency to look blotchy, many pigment stains also have some dyes in them to even out the distribution of the color and reduce the blotchiness. This makes them useful for more types of woods.

Choosing pigment stains

Pigment stains come in a large variety of colors, so you're sure to find one that fills your needs. After you pick the color, you need to decide what delivery medium to use: water, oil, or gel.

- ✔ **Water:** I really like water-based stains because they're non-toxic (you can work with them all day and not feel sick afterward), easy to clean up, and can be layered to get just the right amount of color on your wood.

  The only real disadvantage to water-based stains is that they tend to raise the grain (meaning, the grain swells slightly from the water and creates a rough texture). This means that you need to lightly sand the stained wood after the first coat. No biggie: Just make sure not to sand too much. All you want to do is take the hairs off the wood.

  Water-based stains are also compatible with a variety of topcoats and can be used safely on children's toys and eating surfaces (after they're dry, anyway).

- ✔ **Oil:** The days of oil-based stains are nearing their end. Oil-based stains were the old standby, but because of their toxicity and the improvements in water-based products, oil-based stains are really taking a back seat these days. An oil-based stain has only one advantage over a water-based one: Because oil-based stains have a longer dry time, you have more time to work with the stain, which can be helpful for beginners. However, the longer dry time is a minor factor and one that offers no advantage after you get comfortable staining wood.

I don't recommend oil-based stains unless you're restoring furniture and you need to match an existing oil-based finish.

✔ **Gel:** Okay, a gel stain is really an oil-based stain, but it acts so differently than a regular oil stain that I think it merits its own category. Gel stains are handy for non-horizontal surfaces and for tricky parts like turned legs, because they're thicker than other stains. This thickness reduces the amount of dripping. Gel stains also tend to lessen the blotchy appearance of some woods, because they don't soak into the wood.

Gel stains are relatively new on the market, and their main drawback is that they're still somewhat expensive and you won't find quite as many color choices as you do with other more popular stains. They are oil-based, so they're smelly and messy compared to the water-based varieties. Still, these stains are a good choice especially for blotch-prone wood like birch.

Applying stains

You can apply stain with a brush, but I prefer to use a rag. A rag allows for better control of drips, and you get to feel the wood as you work (this helps me better control the coverage). I always wear latex gloves when I use the rag approach because it can get pretty messy. Also, solvent- (oil-) based stains are toxic and can cause health problems, so it's important to protect your skin from contact with these finishes.

Before you put on a stain, be sure to seal the wood with a wood sealer or a diluted version of your topcoat. This keeps the stain from creating a blotchy appearance on the wood. Flip to the color section to see the difference between a stain on a piece of cherry (a blotch-prone wood) with and without the sealer. Stain applied to wood without the sealer looks blotchier and goes on unevenly. Choose a sealer based upon the stain and topcoat (see Chapter 18) that you intend to use. The label on the stain will provide the manufacturer's recommendations.

Putting the stain on is pretty easy: Just wipe it on in the direction of the grain (going across the grain produces an uneven finish), wait a few minutes, and wipe the excess off. For a darker color, you may need to apply additional coats (I find that two coats are generally adequate). If you do use more than one coat, be sure that you wait until each coat is dry before you add another. The length of time for drying depends on humidity, temperature, and the type of stain that you use. Check the instructions on your stain container to see what's recommended for your stain.

Age, fast and easy

I usually don't mention a product by name, but I know of one stain product that is so unusual, effective, and easy to use I just can't help myself. (No, I'm not in any way affiliated with this company.) Let me first say that I like getting an antiqued look on my furniture and often like to use recycled wood when I can find (and afford) it. If I can't use old wood, I use a product called "Old Growth," a two-part wood coloring product that speeds up the oxidizing effects on wood. The wood gets noticeably darker really fast. All you have to do is apply the activator solution, wait for it to dry, and then wipe on the catalyst solution. If the result is too dark for your tastes, just dilute the activator solution before you apply it.

This product is made by Old Growth Ltd., P.O. Box 1371, Santa Fe, NM 87504; phone 888-301-9663.

Cleaning up

Your cleanup procedures will obviously vary depending on the type of stain you use. Here's a look at the main differences:

- Water-based stains clean up with, you guessed it, water. Easy cleanup is the main reason I prefer this type of stains. Just toss the rag you used to apply the stain in your wastebasket, wash your hands with soap and water, and wipe up any spills with a wet rag or towel. That's all you need to do.

- Oil-based stains require more work to clean up. You need to use mineral spirits (found at your local hardware store or home center) to remove drips or spills from your shop and any stain that got on your hands (unless you follow my recommendation and use gloves). You need to dispose of the used rag carefully so it doesn't become a fire hazard. I usually lay it out to dry on a brick or cement floor and then put it in a covered metal wastebasket after that.

Digging into dyes

Dyes actually change the color of the wood. One of the nice things about dyes is that they go on more evenly than pigments. I really like to use dyes for cherry if I end up having to use a board with some sapwood (lighter colored wood) in it because the dye evens out the difference in color between the darker heartwood and lighter sapwood. Look at the color section to see what red dye looks like on a piece of cherry wood.

Dyes stain whatever they touch — much like wine or blood. Whatever the dye touches will stain. Soap and water don't remove dye — only time does. So, I highly recommend that you use latex gloves whenever you work with this stuff. Oh, and wear clothes that you don't mind ruining. Also, some dye colors are toxic in powder or dissolved form. Read the labels on the product to determine what precautions you need to take.

Deciding among dye stains

Even though dyes are available that dissolve in oil, lacquer thinner, and alcohol, I'm a big fan of water-soluble dyes for woodworking. The dyes are generally sold as a powder that you simply mix with hot water and stir until it dissolves. This process takes just a minute or so. Dyes come in a staggering variety of colors and can be mixed as desired to get just the right color for your project. You won't find powdered dyes at your local home center; you need to get them from a specialty woodworking store.

Putting on the dye

You apply dyes with a rag, but unlike pigment stains you don't need to wipe off the excess. Just wipe the dye on, being careful to make sure that you put it on evenly with the grain and keep a wet edge (don't apply the wet dye over a portion that has dried already).

Dye stains benefit from having a sanding sealer applied to the wood first. Flip to the color section to see a picture of the difference between the dye with and without a sanding sealer. The wood with the sanding sealer takes the dye more evenly and looks much better.

Tidying up

Rags can be disposed of right in the trash, and you don't have to worry about any toxic smells or flammability issues. If you use a dye that dissolves in mineral spirits, lacquer thinner, or alcohol, you'll need to take the precautions needed for any of these products. See the "Pinpointing pigment stains" section earlier in this chapter.

You can find quite a few products at your local home center that use a combination of pigments and dyes. These stains are relatively easy to get a decent finish on. For your first projects, you may want to try these out and see whether you like them.

Picking Up on Paints

Painting is a good choice if you want to hide a less-than-beautiful wood or if you want the look of a solid color.

Picking the right paints

Paints come in several varieties: oil-based, water-based, and spray-on lacquers. I detail each type in the following list.

- **Oil-based:** For a long time, oil-based paints were the professional's choice. They went on smooth and flattened out well. Their main problem is that they're toxic, but most professionals overlooked that because of the results. This toxicity has become more a problem over the years due to environmental regulations, and oil-based paints are becoming less and less common.

  Because of the vast improvement of water-based paints in the last few decades, I don't use oil-based paints any longer and I don't know of anyone else who does either.

- **Water-based (Latex):** For brushed-on paint, this is my choice. Water-based latex paint goes on almost as well as an oil-based paint and it's not toxic. Water-based paints are the way of the future. Before long, you won't even be able to find an oil-based paint. Because of this, you can find an almost unlimited array of latex paints on the market. You won't have any problem finding a color to work for you.

- **Lacquers:** If you want that professional look, you can't go wrong with a lacquer. Lacquers need to be sprayed on in thin coats, and they dry so fast that you have no time to get dust on the finish. And you can often spray the next coat as soon as you're done with the first.

  The main drawback to painting with lacquer is that you need special equipment, such as an air compressor and spray gun, and you'll need some time to get the feel of spraying the paint. After you have the stuff and figure out how to spray well, I'm willing to bet that you won't touch another paintbrush again (at least for putting on paint).

Putting paint on

The number one thing to remember when applying paint is that you need a primer coat in order to get professional-looking results. Some people think that they'll skip the primer and just put on two coats of paint. Resist this temptation. Paint primers are special formulations that seal the wood and increase the bonding power of the paint. You get a much better finish if you use primer. Make sure you choose one compatible with your paint. I usually choose primer from the same company that makes the paint I'm using.

After you have a good (and dry) primer coat on your wood, you can brush the paint on. If you use a water-based primer, you need to lightly sand the wood with 320-grit paper to smooth the grain. When brushing, use long, smooth strokes and don't put too much paint on the brush at a time.

For sprayed paints, the key is to keep the sprayer moving parallel to the wood's surface and apply several thin coats rather than one thick one. This reduces running and dripping.

Cleaning up

Paint cleanup follows the same guidelines as any other finish material. Oil-based products need mineral spirits, lacquers need lacquer thinner, and water-based products clean with water.

Brushes and sprayers need a good cleaning with the proper solvent followed by a soap and water wash to keep them in good condition. Make sure you dispose of your rags properly. Oil-based products need to go into metal containers after they're left out to dry in a safe, non-flammable place.

Cleanup time is when you really start to appreciate a good water-based product!

Chapter 18

Protecting Your Work with Topcoats

After all your hard work milling the wood, assembling the parts, filling defects, smoothing the wood, and getting the color you want, you're finally ready to put on the protective layer: the topcoat. A topcoat is essential to maintain the beauty and structure of the piece. It protects your work, not only from spills, but also from natural moisture changes that cause the wood to expand and contract seasonally. Without the protection of the topcoat, your wood constantly expands and contracts and is more susceptible to warping and cracking. Topcoats also improve the look of the wood by adding depth and color.

In this chapter, I go over the most common topcoat options and weigh the pros and cons of each to help you make an informed choice about what to put on your work. I also walk you through the process of preparing your wood, applying the topcoat, and cleaning up the mess when you're done.

The Good, the Bad, and the Ugly about Various Topcoats

Many types of topcoats are available to woodworkers, and each offers different levels of protection and beauty. Table 18-1 shows you the most common types and clues you in to their pros and cons.

Table 18-1	Comparison of Common Top Coats	
Type	*Pros*	*Cons*
Shellac	Natural, nontoxic, renewable, and beautiful	Not water-resistant
Oil	Easy to apply and renew, beautiful	Not water-resistant, lacks polished look
Wax	Easy to apply, low-toxicity, develops nice polished look	Not very durable, scratches easily
Varnish	Very durable, waterproof	Solvent based/toxic, dries slowly, hard to clean up
Water-based finishes	Nontoxic, waterproof	Raises wood grain, lacks richness (looks like plastic)

Shining It Up with Shellac

Shellac is one of the oldest and most loved topcoats. It gives wood a rich, deep finish, is easy to apply and repair, and is nontoxic. Shellac is a natural product made from — get this — beetles. Yep, you read correctly. Shellac is the product of beetle secretions. Okay, before you get grossed out, I have to tell you that you've probably encountered shellac many times before. In fact, I'm sure you've probably even eaten it before. Shellac is used to coat pills and vegetables, among other things. I say this to let you know just how safe this stuff can be. Shellac is my preferred finish for child toys, for example.

In order to use shellac on furniture, though, you need to add it to alcohol. Most times you mix it with denatured alcohol, which can be found at most home centers and hardware stores.

The main drawback to shellac is that it doesn't hold up to liquids, heat, or scratches very well. (Some people consider these serious shortfalls.) This can be minimized, however, by using a dewaxed shellac and by putting a layer of varnish or wax over the top (of course this reduces your ability to easily repair the shellac surface).

You can buy shellac as flakes or premixed with the alcohol. The premixed varieties have a shelf life of about 6 months maximum (one company claims to make a premixed shellac that lasts years), but the flakes, for the most part, last almost indefinitely.

I recommend that if you choose to finish with shellac, you buy the flakes and mix it yourself. This gives you not only a longer shelf life, but also the ability to make the shellac the consistency that you want.

Shellac comes in many varieties: blond, white, garnet, lemon, buttonlac, and orange, to name a few. Each of these has a different color, so you can often skip the stain when using shellac. Take a look at the color section to see some of the colors shellac can add to wood. Pictured is birch wood with blond, orange, and garnet shellac.

Preparing shellac

If you buy shellac already mixed, you don't have to do anything to prepare to use it. If you buy shellac as flakes, you need to mix it with denatured alcohol. I can't give you a set ratio; you can choose from many mixes. The ratio of shellac to alcohol is called the *cut* and refers to how many pounds of flakes are mixed with gallons of alcohol. For most topcoats, a 2-pound mix is good (2 pounds of shellac flakes to one gallon of alcohol). For sealing the wood, a ½-pound to 1-pound mix is good (I prefer the ½-pound mix, because it goes on easily).

To prepare the wood surface for shellac, you need to really sand the project well, going all the way up to a 320-grit paper. Shellac sits on the surface of the wood and doesn't hide sanding scratches (in fact, it seems to accentuate them!).

If you take your time sanding and do a good job, you'll absolutely love the look you get from a few coats of shellac. If you skimp on the sanding, however, you're likely to be disappointed with your final finish. After you finish sanding, remove all the dust from the surface by wiping with a cotton cloth dampened with *mineral spirits* (also called paint thinner; you can find this at hardware stores and home centers) and then wipe the surface again with a lint-free rag dampened with alcohol.

Applying shellac

Shellac can be applied in numerous ways: You can spray it on or apply it with a cloth, a brush, or with a rubbing pad made up of a wad of wool wrapped in a linen cloth.

Shellac is somewhat tricky to apply, because it dries so quickly. If you're new to using shellac, then mix it in a 1½-pound cut (1½ pounds shellac flakes to

1 gallon alcohol). This makes the shellac easier to brush on and reduces brush marks. If your shellac dries too fast, you can just add some shellac retardant to slow the drying process (shellac retardants are available where you get the shellac flakes).

To apply shellac with a brush (a common and easy way to apply shellac), you need the finest brush you can find. Use a natural bristle brush called a *fitch brush,* which is made with polecat or skunk hair.

Apply the finish using the following steps:

1. **Dip the brush halfway into the shellac and lightly press it into the side of the container to remove excess finish.**

2. **Start about an inch or two from the edge of the wood and lightly drag the brush to the edge, reverse directions, and go all the way to the other edge, gently lifting your brush as you reach the edge.**

3. **Do another stroke next to this one with a small overlap of about ¼ inch.**

4. **Repeat until you cover the entire surface.**

5. **Next shellac the edges, repeating Steps 1 through 3.**

6. **Let it dry for at least an hour, then lightly sand it with 320-grit paper.**

    Make sure that you clean or change the paper when it gets clogged. This will happen fairly quickly.

7. **Rub the finish with #0000 steel wool.**

8. **Wipe the surface clean with a lint-free rag.**

9. **Apply a second coat of shellac and let it dry overnight.**

10. **Start the next day by sanding this coat with 320-grit paper and follow it with the #0000 steel wool.**

11. **Wipe it clean with a lint-free rag.**

12. **Repeat Steps 9 through 11 until your piece has four or five coats.**

13. **Rub it out with #0000 steel wool to get the sheen you want.**

Cleaning up

One of the great things about shellac is ease of cleanup. Alcohol dissolves the shellac again, so if you have any misplaced shellac, use denatured alcohol on a rag to remove it. For cleaning brushes, I've found that regular household ammonia works well. I like to put some ammonia in a small container and swish my brush around in it until it's clean. Afterward, I simply wash the brush with mild soap and water.

Opting for Oil

For a while, I used nothing but oil to finish my projects. Oil finishes, such as tung oil, Danish oil, teak oil, salad bowl oil, and linseed oil, are fast and easy to apply but take time (and a lot of coats) to look really good. With the exception of Danish oil, which has some hardeners and varnishes in it, they don't protect very well against moisture.

Oils penetrate into the pores of the wood, and because of this, oils don't give you the polished look that you can achieve with shellac or varnish. Also, oil finishes need to be *refreshed* as the finish wears — you need to add additional coats. Oils do impart a rich, almost antiqued look to wood, though, which is why many people use oils.

Preparing for oils

Because oils don't build up on the surface of the wood, the wood itself needs to be perfect in order for oils to really look great. This means that you need to sand meticulously with up to 320-grit sandpaper. You almost want the wood to shine on its own before the oil goes on. After you get the surface perfectly smooth (or as close as you can), wipe it down with a rag dampened with mineral spirits. Doing so removes the dust and sanding residue from the wood.

Applying oils

Here's the easy part of oil finishes: the application. Follow these simple steps:

1. **Put on a pair of latex gloves to protect your hands.**

2. **Using a lint-free cloth, generously wipe the oil onto the wood.**

3. **Let stand 5 or 10 minutes.**

4. **Lightly sand it with 600-grit wet/dry sandpaper.**

   This step isn't necessary for some oils, such as salad bowl oil. It only needs to be done on the first one or two coats.

5. **Wipe off the excess.**

6. **Let it dry for 24 hours.**

7. **Buff it with a soft cloth.**

8. **Repeat this procedure until you have four or five coats, skipping Step 4 after the second coat.**

9. **Buff the final coat with a soft cloth until you get the gloss you want.**

When using oil, watch the wood for *weeping* (releasing from the pores of the wood). Some woods, such as cherry, will ooze out oil for a while, and if you don't wipe it from the surface before it dries, you need to sand it off before adding another coat. This is a real pain. (Trust me on this one. I have a dining table that took me hours and hours to fix because I wasn't vigilant about wiping the oil off.) You may need to wipe this oozing oil a few times, so don't go anywhere after applying the first coat of oil until the wood is done weeping.

Cleaning up

The cleanup after using oil is as simple as disposing of the used rags and washing your hands. Use mineral spirits to get the oil off your hands (that is, if you didn't use gloves). Follow it up with some mild soap and water and hand lotion (the mineral spirits will dry your hands). If you spill or drip any oil, use mineral spirits to clean it up. To dispose of the rags, lay them out flat until they dry completely and then put them in a metal container.

Oil-soaked rags are flammable — *very* flammable. In fact, they're so flammable that they have been known to spontaneously combust. Don't put them in a wastebasket with other stuff until they are completely dry. I usually lay my rags flat on the brick patio outside of my shop to dry them out.

The only other way to deal with oil-soaked rags is to put them in a metal container filled with water until you can dispose of them properly.

Working with Wax

Wax is another easy-to-use, age-old finish. Wax, like shellac and varnish, lies on top of the wood and can be built up by applying several thin layers. Wax adds a nice patina (the natural oxidation process of wood that produces a darker, rich color) to wood and can be purchased with coloring agents to add more color to the piece.

I'm going to be completely honest: I don't like to use wax as a primary finish; instead, I'll add it to varnished or shellacked wood. Wax is too delicate for me — just put a glass of water on it and you get an instant ring. To me, the beauty of wax is as a final topcoat buffed to a nice gloss.

Don't let my lack of enthusiasm for wax deter you from using it, though. You have many good wax products to choose from. Check out your local wood-working store and I'm sure you'll find a product that will provide the results you're looking for. Most waxes are a blend of beeswax and carnuba wax. The more carnuba wax present, the more durable the finish, only it takes more effort to get it to buff up.

Preparing for wax

Because wax is supposed to sit on the surface of the wood, I prefer to seal the wood first. Doing so protects the wood when the wax gets damaged and keeps any oils in the wax from penetrating the wood, which would make removing the wax very difficult. The wood surface under the wax doesn't need as diligent a sanding as wood you prepare for either shellac or oil, but you do need to create a nice smooth surface. You really only need to sand to 220-grit to use wax successfully.

After the wood is sanded and cleaned with a rag dampened in mineral spirits, I recommend that you seal it with a ½-pound cut of shellac. Heck, I'd even apply two coats of the shellac first. You'll get a better finish, and applying two coats doesn't take that long.

Applying wax

Applying wax is very easy. It's the same as waxing your car with paste wax. Here are the steps:

1. **Put a liberal amount of wax on a cloth.**

2. **Wipe it on the wood using overlapping circular motions until the entire surface is covered.**

3. **Let the wax dry until a whitish film appears.**

4. **Using a clean, dry cloth, buff the wax until the film disappears and a glossy shine replaces it.**

   Replace the cloth with a clean one as it gets dirty.

5. **Get yet another clean cloth and keep buffing.**

6. **Keep buffing until you have a hard, shiny surface (you can't buff too much).**

   If you use a power buffer, make sure that you keep the polishing pad moving, or you may melt the wax.

7. **Let the wax dry for 24 hours.**

8. **Repeat these steps at least two times (for three coats minimum).**

Cleaning up

Wax is easy to clean up. Just a little soap and water will get it off your hands and rags. If you use old cotton cloths to apply and buff wax, just throwing them away is easier than cleaning them.

Employing Varnish and Oil-Based Polyurethane

Varnish is a common finish and comes in many varieties. Traditional varnishes are made using pine resins, but modern varnishes use a variety of solutions that produce a hard, durable surface. The most common type of varnish is polyurethane.

Varnish is the best topcoat for a project that will take a ton of abuse. However, varnish is toxic and hard to clean up and it can take a while to dry, so you may end up with dust in your finish. However, these problems are becoming less of an issue as new formulas are developed. Always wear gloves and a respirator when using an oil-based varnish.

Preparing for varnish and polyurethanes

Sanding to 150- to 220-grit works well for most varnishes. You don't need to go any smoother. Just make sure you've done the best job you can, getting all the imperfections out of the wood. Varnish works best with a sealer coat applied to the wood first. I don't recommend that you use a special wood sealer; instead, just thin the varnish down 10 or 20 percent with mineral spirits and apply it as you would a regular coat (see next section).

The surface should be clear of sanding residue and dust. Clean the surface by wiping a rag dampened with mineral spirits over all the surfaces to be varnished.

Applying varnish and polyurethanes

Varnish goes on just like paint, so if you've done any painting, you can handle varnishing without any problems. Here are the basic steps:

1. **For the first coat, thin the varnish out by adding 10 to 20 percent mineral spirits.**

2. **Dip the brush into the varnish about $\frac{1}{3}$ of the way.**

3. **Press the brush gently against the side of the container to remove excess finish.**

4. **Brush a thin layer on the surface.**

5. **Brush out any lap marks (overlapping brush strokes) and drips by going over the finish with your slightly dampened brush.**

   Don't worry about getting rid of all the brush marks, only the big ones. The small brush marks will settle before the finish dries.

6. **Let the piece dry for 24 hours.**

7. **Sand it out with 400-grit wet/dry sandpaper.**

   You can use mineral spirits as a lubricant to make the process easier and keep from clogging the paper as quickly.

8. **Repeat Steps 2 through 7 until you have four or five coats.**

9. **After the final coat, you can rub it out with #0000 steel wool to give it the gloss you want.**

Cleaning up

Because varnish is solvent-based, you need to use mineral spirits to clean up when you're done. I keep a bucket of mineral spirits around to dip my brushes in. Swishing the brush around in the bucket removes the finish. I usually follow up with a mild soap and water rinse and wrap the brush in plastic until I need it again. Some people skip the soap and water and let the brush dry.

For washing hands, mineral spirits are the only way to go. To avoid the mess, I use disposable gloves and throw them away after I'm finished. Use a metal container with a lid on it to reduce the smell.

Using Water-Based Polyurethane

If you like the idea of varnish but don't want to put up with the smell and mess of a solvent-based product, a water-based polyurethane might be the solution for you. Water-based finishes are becoming very common and give you the best attributes of varnishes with the ease and low-toxicity of water-based products. However, these finishes over varnish look less-than-sexy. (Okay, I'll admit it — they look like plastic to me. I feel much better now.) They also raise the grain of the wood, so you have to add an extra step when using them.

Water-based polyurethanes are a relatively new product and they aren't all without problems. For example, most aren't as durable as the oil-based varieties.

Preparing for water-based topcoat

Preparation for water-based polyurethanes is the same as for oil-based versions. Sand the surface well with 220-grit paper and wipe it clean. You can use a water-dampened rag to wipe off the sanding dust, but remember it will raise the grain, which means you have to sand it lightly again. This leaves some sanding dust, which leads to you wanting to wipe again, and so on. I usually just wipe the final sanding with a tack cloth.

Because the grain is going to rise no matter what, I apply a sanding sealer and, after it dries, I go over the surface with a 320-grit sandpaper to knock the grain down again. Then I wipe the surface with a dry cloth.

Applying water-based polyurethanes

Apply water-based polyurethanes following the same procedure as oil-based preparations. (See the section "Applying varnish and polyurethanes" earlier in this chapter.) The only difference is that some water-based products dry pretty quickly, so you need to stop messing with the finish before it starts getting tacky. Also, I usually don't sand after the first grain-raising coat unless I need to get rid of some brush marks or dust specks that may have gotten in the finish. After the final coat (three or four is usually enough), you can either leave it alone or give a rub down with #0000 steel wool wetted with water if you want less gloss.

Cleaning up

Because this product is water-based, cleanup is easy. Just use soap and water.

Part VI
The Part of Tens

The 5th Wave   By Rich Tennant

"To preserve the beauty and durability of the dental molding, we put fluoride in the trim paint."

In this part . . .

A staple of every *For Dummies* book, the Part of Tens in *Woodworking For Dummies* contains some information that the amateur woodworker is likely to use almost every day. From ten useful woodworking tips, to ten common woodworking pitfalls to avoid, to ten resources to help you improve your woodworking skills, this Part of Tens has it all (well, almost).

Chapter 19

Ten Great Habits to Get Into

In This Chapter

▶ Making your woodworking more efficient

▶ Working safer

*W*onder what's the most important thing you can do to make sure you have a successful woodworking experience? Stay consciously aware of your surroundings and everything you do while you work. I regularly do a few specific things to reduce my chances of an accident. In this chapter, I share these pointers with you.

Slowing Down

Go slow. Take your time when cutting or sanding anything. If you're in a hurry, you're more likely to make mistakes, and mistakes cause injuries. You also get much better results with your tools if you work slowly, because the blades and cutter heads are able to more easily cut through the wood.

Standing Guard

Never remove the guards from your power tools. The guards are placed on tools to make them safer, and some tools are downright dangerous without them. Yeah, the guards can sometimes make it hard to see what you're doing, but their benefits more than make up for this deficit. If you really don't like the guards that come with your tools (on your table saw, for example), you can find aftermarket guards that may work better than the ones that came with your tool.

Wearing Protection

Always wear your eye, ear, and lung protection. Yes, it can be a pain to put all that stuff on every time you want to cut, sand, or finish something, but making it a habit and a nonnegotiable part of woodworking increases the likelihood that you'll be wearing protection when it truly matters.

Likewise, wear the appropriate clothes for woodworking. This means no loose-fitting shirts or pants. I like to wear short-sleeved shirts or roll the sleeves up on long-sleeved shirts to keep my forearms clear, because they get close to the machines all day. Long hair should be tied up. Also, you should take off any dangling jewelry or any jewelry that goes on your hands or wrists, such as rings and watches.

Staying Fresh

Don't work when you're tired. I understand the temptation to make just one more cut before ending the day, but try to resist. When you're tired, you're less able to pay attention and more likely be in a hurry. Leave that last cut until the morning and you reduce the chances of an accident (not to mention your chances of messing up the cut and wasting your valuable wood).

Being Prepared

Have a first-aid kit and emergency numbers handy just in case something goes wrong. Also, let someone know when you're going to be in your shop, and make sure someone is nearby to help you if necessary.

Checking Up on Key Equipment

You should routinely check several pieces of equipment to make sure they work properly. These include:

- ✔ **Fire extinguishers.** They lose pressure after time and need to be recharged. All fire extinguishers have a gauge on them that indicates their status. Check these gauges every few months and recharge or replace your fire extinguishers as needed.

- ✔ **Power cords.** Make sure that they aren't frayed or cut and replace any that are defective.

- ✔ **Blade guards.** Guards tend to loosen up as the machine vibrates. Double-check them every time you use the tool and tighten any parts that come loose.

Staying Sober

This one almost goes without saying: Make sure that you're fully able to focus on the task at hand. Any deficit in mental capacity can cause irreparable harm. Stay away from any alcohol or drugs when you work with wood. Even over-the-counter flu medications can cause you to lose your ability to focus. Heck, even too much caffeine has caused some people to miss a step and do something they wish they hadn't.

Stay aware and alert and stay away from any substance that lessens your ability to do so.

Lighting Up

Make sure that you have adequate lighting in the shop. Try to have as much natural light as possible, because it gives you the truest representation of wood color and maximum visibility of hand and power tool operations. If you have fluorescent lighting in the shop, you can mix cool and warm white tubes to get better color balance.

Keeping Clear

Keep a clear workspace. Tidy up things such as

- ✔ **Sawdust, wood chips, and liquid spills:** Sawdust and liquids are extremely slippery on a cement floor, so keep your floor as clean as possible. You may feel like you're sweeping all day long, but if you sweep throughout the day, end-of-the-day cleanup takes you no time at all.

- ✔ **Obstacles, such as cords and hoses:** To run most of your tools, you need power. Unfortunately, most of your power tools are attached to cord and dust collection hoses as you work. Be sure that you plan your moves with each tool to eliminate any awkward cord and hose placement. Routers, circular saws, and sanders are the worst culprits, because they need to be moved around a lot while you use them.

✔ **Tools:** Give yourself enough room to move freely and safely around each tool. I'm a firm believer in rolling stands for all tools. If all your tools are on wheels, you can easily move them out of the way when you're done using them.

Staying Sharp

Periodically sharpen your tools to keep them cutting their best. Sharp tools are both easier to use and much safer because you won't need to use as much pressure to get them to cut. You can sharpen your chisels and planes yourself (Chapter 4 shows how to do this), but with saw blades you're better off taking them to a professional.

Before you send your saw blades out to be sharpened, give them a good cleaning (see Chapter 7), because a dirty blade cuts like a dull one. If after you clean the blade it still cuts poorly, take it in for a sharpening.

Chapter 20

Ten Common Woodworking Pitfalls and How to Avoid Them

In This Chapter

▶ Preventing common mistakes

▶ Working faster but still accurately

▶ Making the woodworking process easier

1 have yet to meet a woodworker who hasn't had some unexpected thing ruin his project (or at least something that forced him to do a ton of work to fix it). This chapter presents ten of the most common pitfalls and ways to either fix them or avoid them in the first place.

Going Too Fast

I've mentioned this a few times in this book, but this point is so important that it bears repeating. In my experience, going too fast is the most common pitfall that woodworkers fall into. You get in a hurry and you want to finish a task as soon as possible. Don't do it. I can't tell you the number of times I've really messed up a project because I was in a hurry. And I've been lucky. Hurrying is the number one cause of workshop injuries.

If you find yourself wanting to hurry things along, take a break and remind yourself that hurrying isn't safe and that it could end up costing you more time in the long run if you have to fix a mistake or, worse yet, take a trip to the emergency room.

A Blotchy Finish

Sometimes you get blotchy finishes from using an oil finish, such as Danish oil, or a stain. The finish turns out blotchy because the pores in some woods, such as cherry, take in differing amounts of the oil and have an uneven appearance.

You can't correct this after the damage has been done, so you need to make sure that you plan for it before you start finishing. You can avoid this problem two ways:

- Use a sanding sealer or other pore-filling product to fill the pores of the wood before you apply the final finish.
- Use a finish that sits on top of the wood rather than absorbing into it. Varnish and shellac are two examples.

Drawers/Doors Don't Fit

I've watched people finish working on a cabinet and then try to slide the drawer in, only to find out that the drawer's too big to fit the opening. These folks often stand there baffled as to why this happened. After all, they followed the plans.

The problem is that they followed the plans. Let me explain. When you build the carcass of a cabinet, your measurements may be off by $\frac{1}{32}$ inch here and there, for example. When you try to put the carcass together, very small discrepancies can add up to enough of a difference in overall size to make your drawer not fit right.

The solution is simple: Wait to make the drawers or doors until after your carcass in completely done. Then disregard the dimensions on the plan and work from the carcass itself. This ensures that your drawer or door dimensions match those of the carcass.

A Table Rocks

More often than not, when I'm done making a table, it wobbles. (I can't believe I'm admitting this).

To avoid this problem, make sure that you cut all the legs to the exact same length. I usually put them on a panel-cutting jig and run them all through the table saw at the same time. You also need to make sure that you get the table perfectly square when you glue it up. Assemble the table leg/rail system in two stages: First, glue the short rails to the legs and then, after they've had a chance to dry completely, glue these two assemblies to the long rails. Check for square in both directions — across the top of the assembly and from leg bottom to opposite leg top.

Try as you might to get everything perfectly square from the start, some problems may occur. To fix a wobbly table after glue-up, adjust the length of the legs until you get them even. To do this, put the table on a flat bench and rock it to see which leg is the longest. Next, move the table until this long leg is off the bench. Push the leg tight against the edge of the bench and level the table. If this is the long leg, it will extend slightly down from the tabletop. Using a utility knife, score the point where the top of the bench crosses the table leg. Use a sander or plane to shorten the leg to this mark.

Stain Doesn't Take

The most common reasons that a stain doesn't take are that you used a non-staining wood filler or you have some glue that you didn't completely wipe off after assembling the piece.

Both problems are easy to prevent but not as easy to correct. So make sure you use a wood filler that can take stain, and be sure to wipe off all the glue that oozes out of a joint when you assemble it.

If you do end up with an unstained spot on your project, apply some colored *glaze* (semi-transparent solution similar to thinned-out paints or stains) to the unstained area, adjusting the color and coverage until you get a match to the stained wood. Let it dry and then topcoat it.

Sanding Makes the Wood Fuzzy

Some woods, such as birch, get fuzzy when you sand them too much. The fibers of the wood tear and create hairlike fuzz on the surface of the wood. You don't want to stain or topcoat wood in that condition.

If your wood does get fuzzy, go down a grit or two with the sandpaper (120-grit is a good place to start) and sand out the little furs. The way to avoid fuzzy wood is to make sure you don't sand with a paper finer than 150 grit. And don't use a scraper (see Chapter 16) either.

Joints Don't Fit Together

You've taken great care to get joints that are tight, but when you put the glue on and try to pull the joint together, it doesn't go. Either you have joints that are too tight, or you pulled the joint together only partway and are experiencing "lock-up."

To avoid overly tight joints, always dry fit first. If you have to pound (or even moderately tap) the joint together with a mallet, you need to loosen the joint before you add glue to it. If your joint is a mortise-and-tenon, shave down the tenon slightly until you're able to pull the joint together by hand or with minimal tapping.

If the joint locks up on you when you're assembling it, you need to do some serious mallet tapping and clamping to get it to move again. Depending on how long the joint's been locked, you may not be able to get it to budge. Just avoid a locked joint in the first place, which is as simple as pulling the joint fully together when you first try to assemble it. Resist the temptation to partially attach the joint. Always attach a joint completely before moving to another one.

Tabletops Aren't Flat

After all your effort in choosing, milling, and assembling board for a tabletop, you remove the clamps — only to find out that the tabletop isn't flat. Assuming your wood wasn't warped, cupped, or twisted, you have two possible reasons for your problem. Either the edges of the board weren't perfectly straight and square, or you applied too much clamp pressure when gluing the boards together.

To avoid these problems, make sure that you use a jointer that is adjusted properly to make perfectly square edges on a board. Don't apply so much pressure to the clamps that the board starts to deflect up from the clamps. A clamp or two positioned on top of the boards can help this too.

To flatten an uneven tabletop, you need to plane and sand it flat. You will lose thickness in the board, so you may not want to go this route. Your best option is to cut the top apart at the joints and start over again. Trust me, it's not as bad as it sounds, and it is far easier than trying to flatten with a plane and sander.

After the boards are separated again, joint them until they have square edges, dry clamp the edge joints and check for flat, then re-glue them using just enough pressure to bring the boards together.

Wood Splits When Cutting

Running a piece of wood through a saw sometimes causes *tear-out,* which is the result of the spinning blade grabbing the unsupported edge of the wood as the board leaves the saw. Tear-out occurs on the back edge of boards when you cut across the grain.

The way to avoid tear-out is to put a backing board against the back edge of the wood when you cut. The backing board acts as a sacrificial board for tear-out. Also, if you have a board that needs both rip cuts and crosscuts, do the crosscuts first and the rip cut second. Because the blade is unlikely to cause tear-out on a rip cut, you don't have to worry about using a backing board.

Joints Too Loose

Sometimes a joint fits too loosely. If you're working with mortise-and-tenon joints, loose fit is a particular problem, because their strength depends on a tight fit between mortise and tenon.

So what do you do if the tenon is too loose in the mortise? Well, aside from cutting a new tenon, I find that using a glue that fills gaps works well for me. Regular carpenter's wood glue won't work. You need an epoxy resin glue — a two-part glue that often expands as it cures to fill gaps in the wood. Check out Chapter 9 for details about this type of adhesive.

Your other option is to glue a thin piece of wood to the tenon to make it bigger and then trim the newly sized tenon to fit the mortise.

Chapter 21

Ten Great Woodworking Resources

In This Chapter

▶ Finding ways to improve your skills

▶ Working faster

▶ Making the woodworking process easier

*O*ne of the great things about being a woodworker is that you're among a large group of people who enjoy this pastime. As a result, you can easily find quality information, top-notch project plans, and people to commiserate with about all the details of woodworking. This chapter offers you ten ways — including everything from online forums and magazines to woodworking guilds to conventions — to increase your woodworking skills, knowledge, and enthusiasm.

Online Forums

Thanks to the Internet, you can talk to people all over the world about woodworking without so much as leaving your home. Online forums are one of the best ways to communicate with fellow woodworkers. These forums come and go, but some of the most active are:

✔ www.forums.woodnet.net/ubbthreads/ubbthreads.php

✔ woodworking.about.com/mpboards.htm

You can start here or do a search using **woodworking forums** as your keyword.

Magazines

People often ask me where I find out about all the latest gear or where I get ideas (and plans) for making some of my furniture. I tell them magazines. You can find dozens of woodworking magazines, and all of them are worth their subscription prices for all the knowledge, ideas, and plans they offer. The most popular are

- *American Woodworker,* Subscriber Dept., P.O. Box 2134, Harlan, IA 51593-0323; phone 800-666-3111; Web site www.americanwoodworker.com. Published seven times a year.

- *Better Homes and Gardens Wood Magazine,* P.O. Box 37439, Boone, IA 50037-0439; phone 800-374-9663; Web site www.woodmagazine.com. Published nine times a year.

- *Fine Woodworking,* Taunton Press, 63 S. Main St., P.O. Box 5506, Newton, CT 06470-5506; phone 800-888-8286; Web site www.taunton.com/finewoodworking/index.asp. Published seven times a year.

- *Popular Woodworking,* P.O. Box 5369, Harlan, IA 51593; phone 515-280-1721; Web site www.popularwoodworking.com. Published six times a year.

- *Woodworker's Journal,* P.O. Box 56585, Boulder, CO 80322-6585; phone 800-765-4119; Web site www.woodworkersjournal.com. Published six times a year.

Woodworking Guilds

Most larger cities have *woodworking guilds* or associations — member organizations that help woodworkers network. Guilds can be as simple as a group of woodworkers who get together once a month or so and talk about woodworking or as active as an association that promotes woodworking throughout the region by offering shows, classes, and more. Check out your local lumberyard, woodworker's supply store, or call a local woodworker to find out whether your area has a guild or association.

Community Colleges/University Extension

Most community colleges or universities have noncredit classes on a whole host of subjects — woodworking among them. Call your local community college or university extension program to find out whether they offer woodworking classes. Often, the community's best woodworkers teach in these programs, and other people with all levels of skill take them. Classes are definitely worthwhile to meet face to face with other woodworkers.

Books and Videos

You can find plenty of great books and videos on woodworking (as I'm sure you already found out when choosing this book). The only drawback to this is trying to find the right book for you when most books cover only one area of woodworking, such as routers or jigs.

Hopefully, after reading this book you have a pretty good idea of the areas you want to explore further. Just pick an interest — for instance **mortise-and-tenon joints** — and use that as a keyword in your search (Amazon.com is a good place to look for titles that may interest you) or head on down to your local bookstore. Also, any decent woodworking store will have a library of books that you won't find in your local chain bookstore, so don't forget to check them out when you feel the urge to add to your library.

Online Instruction

Like everything else on the Internet, woodworking is covered by countless sites. You can find anything from a site where Joe Hobbiest built his own shrine to woodworking to full-blown online courses offered by top-notch schools. The easiest way to find these sites is to do a search using **woodworking tips** as your keyword. Here are a couple of great sites to get you started:

✔ www.woodworkingtips.com/woodtips/
✔ www.wood-worker.com/tips.htm

Plans

The magazines listed in the "Magazines" section earlier in this chapter are great places to find woodworking plans. The only real drawback to these magazines is that you can't necessarily find a plan for a particular piece of furniture (unless you get lucky). If you're looking for a plan for an early American chest of drawers, for instance, you may not find one in the magazine you subscribe to. For this, your best bet is to do an online search (using the style of furniture as your keyword) or simply use **woodworking plans** as your keyword.

The best places for plans on the Internet are the Web sites of the major woodworking magazines. These plans are of high quality and are usually free. Visit the sites I list in the "Magazines" section of this chapter for a list of the most popular magazines. In addition, you can find good books with plans at your local woodworking store, in mail-order catalogs, or in the classified ads in the back of any of the magazines listed in this chapter.

Local Woodworkers

People love to share information, especially people who are passionate about a given subject. Woodworkers fall into this category. I've yet to meet a woodworker, professional or amateur, who wouldn't offer a few tidbits of info to a novice.

The easiest place to find other woodworkers in your area is to visit your local woodworking store or lumberyard. If this doesn't work, you can always look in the Yellow Pages under "Woodworking" or "Furniture" for craftspeople offering custom construction. Those are your local professionals.

Local Woodworking Stores

As I said in the previous section, woodworking stores are magnets for, guess what, woodworkers (funny how that works). I'm often amazed at the people I meet and the depth of conversations I have every time I go look for a new tool or some wood. It seems woodworkers love to talk (maybe it's all that time alone in the shop). If you want to feed your inspiration, go to your local woodworking store for a chance to meet other woodworkers. Most stores also offer classes on any number of topics.

Woodworking Shows/Conventions

One company (called The Woodworking Shows) organizes woodworking conventions that offer workshops, demonstrations, and, best of all, tools for you to drool over. These conventions are offered throughout the country and are a great way to learn from some of the world's best teachers and craftspeople. Contact information for The Woodworking Shows is as follows: 1950 Sawtelle Blvd, Suite 280, Los Angeles, CA 90025; Phone 800-826-8257; Web site www.thewoodworkingshows.com.

Also, check out craft fairs in your area. This is another great way to meet other woodworkers and to learn more about the craft (my neighbor discovered a new finishing technique by talking with a guy who was selling his work at one of these fairs).

Index

FOR DUMMIES

The easy way to get more done and have more fun

RSONAL FINANCE

0-7645-5231-7

0-7645-2431-3

0-7645-5331-3

Also available:

Estate Planning For Dummies
(0-7645-5501-4)
401(k)s For Dummies
(0-7645-5468-9)
Frugal Living For Dummies
(0-7645-5403-4)
Microsoft Money "X" For
Dummies
(0-7645-1689-2)
Mutual Funds For Dummies
(0-7645-5329-1)

Personal Bankruptcy For
Dummies
(0-7645-5498-0)
Quicken "X" For Dummies
(0-7645-1666-3)
Stock Investing For Dummies
(0-7645-5411-5)
Taxes For Dummies 2003
(0-7645-5475-1)

SINESS & CAREERS

0-7645-5314-3

0-7645-5307-0

0-7645-5471-9

Also available:

Business Plans Kit For
Dummies
(0-7645-5365-8)
Consulting For Dummies
(0-7645-5034-9)
Cool Careers For Dummies
(0-7645-5345-3)
Human Resources Kit For
Dummies
(0-7645-5131-0)
Managing For Dummies
(1-5688-4858-7)

QuickBooks All-in-One Desk
Reference For Dummies
(0-7645-1963-8)
Selling For Dummies
(0-7645-5363-1)
Small Business Kit For
Dummies
(0-7645-5093-4)
Starting an eBay Business For
Dummies
(0-7645-1547-0)

ALTH, SPORTS & FITNESS

0-7645-5167-1

0-7645-5146-9

0-7645-5154-X

Also available:

Controlling Cholesterol For
Dummies
(0-7645-5440-9)
Dieting For Dummies
(0-7645-5126-4)
High Blood Pressure For
Dummies
(0-7645-5424-7)
Martial Arts For Dummies
(0-7645-5358-5)
Menopause For Dummies
(0-7645-5458-1)

Nutrition For Dummies
(0-7645-5180-9)
Power Yoga For Dummies
(0-7645-5342-9)
Thyroid For Dummies
(0-7645-5385-2)
Weight Training For Dummies
(0-7645-5168-X)
Yoga For Dummies
(0-7645-5117-5)

ilable wherever books are sold.
to www.dummies.com or call 1-877-762-2974 to order direct.

FOR DUMMIES®

A world of resources to help you grow

HOME, GARDEN & HOBBIES

Feng Shui
0-7645-5295-3

Gardening
0-7645-5130-2

Guitar
0-7645-5106-X

Also available:

Auto Repair For Dummies
(0-7645-5089-6)

Chess For Dummies
(0-7645-5003-9)

Home Maintenance For
Dummies
(0-7645-5215-5)

Organizing For Dummies
(0-7645-5300-3)

Piano For Dummies
(0-7645-5105-1)

Poker For Dummies
(0-7645-5232-5)

Quilting For Dummies
(0-7645-5118-3)

Rock Guitar For Dummies
(0-7645-5356-9)

Roses For Dummies
(0-7645-5202-3)

Sewing For Dummies
(0-7645-5137-X)

FOOD & WINE

Cooking
0-7645-5250-3

Cookies
0-7645-5390-9

Wine
0-7645-5114-0

Also available:

Bartending For Dummies
(0-7645-5051-9)

Chinese Cooking For
Dummies
(0-7645-5247-3)

Christmas Cooking For
Dummies
(0-7645-5407-7)

Diabetes Cookbook For
Dummies
(0-7645-5230-9)

Grilling For Dummies
(0-7645-5076-4)

Low-Fat Cooking For
Dummies
(0-7645-5035-7)

Slow Cookers For Dummies
(0-7645-5240-6)

TRAVEL

Italy
0-7645-5453-0

Hawaii
0-7645-5438-7

Las Vegas
0-7645-5448-4

Also available:

America's National Parks For
Dummies
(0-7645-6204-5)

Caribbean For Dummies
(0-7645-5445-X)

Cruise Vacations For
Dummies 2003
(0-7645-5459-X)

Europe For Dummies
(0-7645-5456-5)

Ireland For Dummies
(0-7645-6199-5)

France For Dummies
(0-7645-6292-4)

London For Dummies
(0-7645-5416-6)

Mexico's Beach Resorts For
Dummies
(0-7645-6262-2)

Paris For Dummies
(0-7645-5494-8)

RV Vacations For Dummies
(0-7645-5443-3)

Walt Disney World & Orlando
For Dummies
(0-7645-5444-1)

Available wherever books are sold. Go to www.dummies.com or call 1-877-762-2974 to order direct.

FOR DUMMIES®

Plain-English solutions for everyday challenges

MPUTER BASICS

0-7645-0838-5   **0-7645-1663-9**   **0-7645-1548-9**

Also available:

PCs All-in-One Desk
Reference For Dummies
(0-7645-0791-5)

Pocket PC For Dummies
(0-7645-1640-X)

Treo and Visor For Dummies
(0-7645-1673-6)

Troubleshooting Your PC For
Dummies
(0-7645-1669-8)

Upgrading & Fixing PCs For
Dummies
(0-7645-1665-5)

Windows XP For Dummies
(0-7645-0893-8)

Windows XP For Dummies
Quick Reference
(0-7645-0897-0)

SINESS SOFTWARE

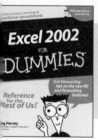  

0-7645-0822-9   **0-7645-0839-3**   **0-7645-0819-9**

Also available:

Excel Data Analysis For
Dummies
(0-7645-1661-2)

Excel 2002 All-in-One Desk
Reference For Dummies
(0-7645-1794-5)

Excel 2002 For Dummies
Quick Reference
(0-7645-0829-6)

GoldMine "X" For Dummies
(0-7645-0845-8)

Microsoft CRM For Dummies
(0-7645-1698-1)

Microsoft Project 2002 For
Dummies
(0-7645-1628-0)

Office XP For Dummies
(0-7645-0830-X)

Outlook 2002 For Dummies
(0-7645-0828-8)

Get smart! Visit www.dummies.com

- **Find listings of even more *For Dummies* titles**
- **Browse online articles**
- **Sign up for Dummies eTips™**
- **Check out *For Dummies* fitness videos and other products**
- **Order from our online bookstore**

Available wherever books are sold. Go to www.dummies.com or call 1-877-762-2974 to order direct.

FOR DUMMIES®

Helping you expand your horizons and realize your potential

INTERNET

0-7645-0894-6

The Internet FOR DUMMIES

The Internet ALL-IN-ONE DESK REFERENCE FOR DUMMIES

0-7645-1659-0

eBay FOR DUMMIES

0-7645-1642-6

Also available:

America Online 7.0 For Dummies
(0-7645-1624-8)

Genealogy Online For Dummies
(0-7645-0807-5)

The Internet All-in-One Desk Reference For Dummies
(0-7645-1659-0)

Internet Explorer 6 For Dummies
(0-7645-1344-3)

The Internet For Dummies Quick Reference
(0-7645-1645-0)

Internet Privacy For Dummies
(0-7645-0846-6)

Researching Online For Dummies
(0-7645-0546-7)

Starting an Online Business For Dummies
(0-7645-1655-8)

DIGITAL MEDIA

Digital Photography FOR DUMMIES

0-7645-1664-7

Photoshop Elements 2 FOR DUMMIES

0-7645-1675-2

Digital Video FOR DUMMIES

0-7645-0806-7

Also available:

CD and DVD Recording For Dummies
(0-7645-1627-2)

Digital Photography All-in-One Desk Reference For Dummies
(0-7645-1800-3)

Digital Photography For Dummies Quick Reference
(0-7645-0750-8)

Home Recording for Musicians For Dummies
(0-7645-1634-5)

MP3 For Dummies
(0-7645-0858-X)

Paint Shop Pro "X" For Dummies
(0-7645-2440-2)

Photo Retouching & Restoration For Dummies
(0-7645-1662-0)

Scanners For Dummies
(0-7645-0783-4)

GRAPHICS

PowerPoint 2002 FOR DUMMIES

0-7645-0817-2

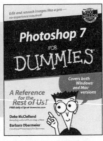

Photoshop 7 FOR DUMMIES

0-7645-1651-5

Macromedia Flash MX FOR DUMMIES

0-7645-0895-4

Also available:

Adobe Acrobat 5 PDF For Dummies
(0-7645-1652-3)

Fireworks 4 For Dummies
(0-7645-0804-0)

Illustrator 10 For Dummies
(0-7645-3636-2)

QuarkXPress 5 For Dummies
(0-7645-0643-9)

Visio 2000 For Dummies
(0-7645-0635-8)

Available wherever books are sold. Go to www.dummies.com or call 1-877-762-2974 to order direct.

FOR DUMMIES®

The advice and explanations you need to succeed

LF-HELP, SPIRITUALITY & RELIGION

Sex For Dummies
0-7645-5302-X

Parenting For Dummies
0-7645-5418-2

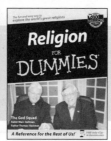

Religion For Dummies
0-7645-5264-3

Also available:

The Bible For Dummies
(0-7645-5296-1)

Buddhism For Dummies
(0-7645-5359-3)

Christian Prayer For Dummies
(0-7645-5500-6)

Dating For Dummies
(0-7645-5072-1)

Judaism For Dummies
(0-7645-5299-6)

Potty Training For Dummies
(0-7645-5417-4)

Pregnancy For Dummies
(0-7645-5074-8)

Rekindling Romance For Dummies
(0-7645-5303-8)

Spirituality For Dummies
(0-7645-5298-8)

Weddings For Dummies
(0-7645-5055-1)

TS

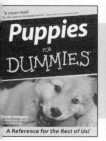

Puppies For Dummies
0-7645-5255-4

Dog Training For Dummies
0-7645-5286-4

Cats For Dummies
0-7645-5275-9

Also available:

Labrador Retrievers For Dummies
(0-7645-5281-3)

Aquariums For Dummies
(0-7645-5156-6)

Birds For Dummies
(0-7645-5139-6)

Dogs For Dummies
(0-7645-5274-0)

Ferrets For Dummies
(0-7645-5259-7)

German Shepherds For Dummies
(0-7645-5280-5)

Golden Retrievers For Dummies
(0-7645-5267-8)

Horses For Dummies
(0-7645-5138-8)

Jack Russell Terriers For Dummies
(0-7645-5268-6)

Puppies Raising & Training Diary For Dummies
(0-7645-0876-8)

UCATION & TEST PREPARATION

Spanish For Dummies
0-7645-5194-9

Algebra For Dummies
0-7645-5325-9

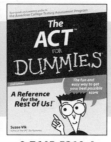

The ACT For Dummies
0-7645-5210-4

Also available:

Chemistry For Dummies
(0-7645-5430-1)

English Grammar For Dummies
(0-7645-5322-4)

French For Dummies
(0-7645-5193-0)

The GMAT For Dummies
(0-7645-5251-1)

Inglés Para Dummies
(0-7645-5427-1)

Italian For Dummies
(0-7645-5196-5)

Research Papers For Dummies
(0-7645-5426-3)

The SAT I For Dummies
(0-7645-5472-7)

U.S. History For Dummies
(0-7645-5249-X)

World History For Dummies
(0-7645-5242-2)

Available wherever books are sold. Go to www.dummies.com or call 1-877-762-2974 to order direct.

FOR DUMMIES®

We take the mystery out of complicated subjects

WEB DEVELOPMENT

0-7645-1643-4

0-7645-0723-0

0-7645-1630-2

Also available:

ASP.NET For Dummies
(0-7645-0866-0)

Building a Web Site For Dummies
(0-7645-0720-6)

ColdFusion "MX" For Dummies (0-7645-1672-8)

Creating Web Pages All-in-One Desk Reference For Dummies
(0-7645-1542-X)

FrontPage 2002 For Dummi
(0-7645-0821-0)

HTML 4 For Dummies Quick Reference
(0-7645-0721-4)

Macromedia Studio "MX" All-in-One Desk Reference For Dummies
(0-7645-1799-6)

Web Design For Dummies
(0-7645-0823-7)

PROGRAMMING & DATABASES

0-7645-0746-X

0-7645-1657-4

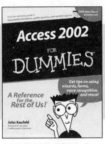

0-7645-0818-0

Also available:

Beginning Programming For Dummies
(0-7645-0835-0)

Crystal Reports "X" For Dummies
(0-7645-1641-8)

Java & XML For Dummies
(0-7645-1658-2)

Java 2 For Dummies
(0-7645-0765-6)

JavaScript For Dummies
(0-7645-0633-1)

Oracle9i For Dummies
(0-7645-0880-6)

Perl For Dummies
(0-7645-0776-1)

PHP and MySQL For Dummies
(0-7645-1650-7)

SQL For Dummies
(0-7645-0737-0)

VisualBasic .NET For Dummies
(0-7645-0867-9)

Visual Studio .NET All-in-On Desk Reference For Dummi
(0-7645-1626-4)

LINUX, NETWORKING & CERTIFICATION

0-7645-1545-4

0-7645-0772-9

0-7645-0812-1

Also available:

CCNP All-in-One Certification For Dummies
(0-7645-1648-5)

Cisco Networking For Dummies
(0-7645-1668-X)

CISSP For Dummies
(0-7645-1670-1)

CIW Foundations For Dummies with CD-ROM
(0-7645-1635-3)

Firewalls For Dummies
(0-7645-0884-9)

Home Networking For Dummies
(0-7645-0857-1)

Red Hat Linux All-in-One Desk Reference For Dummi
(0-7645-2442-9)

TCP/IP For Dummies
(0-7645-1760-0)

UNIX For Dummies
(0-7645-0419-3)

Available wherever books are sold.
Go to www.dummies.com or call 1-877-762-2974 to order direct.